Ezra Pound & William Carlos Williams

Ezra Pound &
William Carlos Williams

The University of Pennsylvania
Conference Papers

Daniel Hoffman, Editor

University of Pennsylvania Press

Philadelphia · 1983

FRONTISPIECE. EZRA POUND and WILLIAM CARLOS WILLIAMS.
Rutherford, New Jersey, June 1958

Library of Congress Cataloging in Publication Data

Main entry under title:

Ezra Pound & William Carlos Williams: the University
of Pennsylvania conference papers.

    "On April 25, 1981, a . . . Pound-Williams Conference
was sponsored by the Writing Program, Department of
English"—Pref.
    1. American poetry—20th century—History and
criticism—Addresses, essays, lectures. 2. Pound, Ezra,
1885–1972—Addresses, essays, lectures. 3. Williams,
William Carlos, 1883–1963—Addresses, essays, lectures.
4. Poets, American—20th century—Biography—Addresses,
essays, lectures. I. Hoffman, Daniel, 1923-   .
II. Pound-Williams Conference (1981: University of
Pennsylvania) III. University of Pennsylvania. Dept.
of English. Writing Program. IV. Title: Ezra Pound
and William Carlos Williams.
PZ323.5.E97 1983   811'.52'09   83-10617
ISBN 0-8122-7892-5

Printed in the United States of America

DESIGN BY CARL E. GROSS

Contents

III. William Carlos Williams

IV. Poets in Their Letters

Preface

What historian of literature would have had the wit to choose, as the venue for so Promethean an act as the re-making of American poetry in the twentieth century, the campus of a stodgy and genteel old university? Or, as the actors in such an emblematic blaze of rebellion, two young fellows active in college theatricals and on the fencing squad? Whatever concatenation of circumstances, personal and cultural, was required for such a departure from the doldrums of verses from Arcady as decorated the respectable magazines of the 1890s and 1900s, those circumstances found each other on the campus of the University of Pennsylvania, where, in the Spring of 1906, Ezra Pound received the degree of Master of Arts and William Carlos Williams was awarded the doctor of medicine.

Seventy-five years later, this anniversary was taken as an opportunity both to celebrate the invention, in a dormitory on the Old Quad, of modernism in twentieth-century poetry, and to honor the two alumni who so acutely anticipated the great changes in method and in style the new century would require. Under the sponsorship of The Writing Program, Department of English, a day-long Pound-Williams Conference was held in the Rare Book Room of the Van Pelt Library on 25 April 1981. It seemed appropriate to invite Hugh Kenner, the chief expositor of the poetry of Ezra Pound, author of *The Pound Era* and many other works elucidating modernist literature, to open the proceedings with his lecture, "Poets at the Blackboard." Wendy Stallard Flory, Assistant Professor in the University of Pennsylvania English Department, spoke on "The Pound Problem." In the afternoon Denise Levertov, the most accomplished poet to have had the benefit of William Carlos Williams' example, gave a close reading of one of his poems; and the long-time friend and publisher

of both poets, James Laughlin, read excerpts from their
correspondence with him and spoke of his own experience as a young
poet taking instruction in Rapallo from the faculty of one at Pound's
"Ezuversity."

This modest program stirred far greater interest than its organizer
had foreseen. Featured before the event in the *New York Times* with
interviews of all the participants, it attracted some 120 attenders from
two dozen institutions as far afield as Maine and Oregon. The
proceedings, taped by the Philadelphia public radio station, WHYY-
FM, were edited to an hour-long program and have since been
released to National Public Radio. A more permanent version of the
conference seemed called for. Augmenting the four conference papers
with studies of our two alumni poets by scholars trained in the reading
of modern poetry at the University of Pennsylvania would further
attest to the hospitality on this campus to contemporary writing—an
attitude quite different from what Pound and Williams experienced
here three-quarters of a century ago. Among the contributors to this
volume, Ronald Bush is a graduate of this university's College of Arts
and Sciences; Michael F. Harper came to Pennsylvania from England
as a Thouron Fellow, taking both his undergraduate and doctoral
degrees. Paul Christensen and Theodora R. Graham received their
doctorates from the university. Emily Mitchell Wallace is a former
member of the Department of English. Neda M. Westlake holds a Ph.D.
in American Civilization from Pennsylvania. To my regret, two other
distinguished scholars from this university were not free to join us
in this celebratory project: Dean Joel Conarroe, then Executive Director
of the Modern Language Association and Professor of English at the
University of Pennsylvania, and author of *William Carlos Williams'
Paterson;* and Stuart Y. McDougal, chairman of the Department of
Comparative Literature at the University of Michigan, whose book,
Pound and the Troubadour Tradition, was his dissertation at
Pennsylvania.

I asked each contributor to prepare an essay on the subject of his
choice. By a serendipity I had not foreseen, the resulting ten papers
formed a pattern which conscious design could scarcely have
bettered. Hugh Kenner gives an intuitive and convincing interpretation
of the probable effects of their education at Pennsylvania upon the
sensibilities, styles, and forms the two poets would later develop. We
are left to reflect how often does a fixed curriculum or a hidebound
instructional philosophy move its recipients by indirections toward
expressions incomprehensible to, and censured by, their staid mentors.
Kenner finds, in the scribblings left at day's end on a classroom

blackboard, the possible sources and models for the content and structure of the *Cantos,* and in the disciplines of clinical observation and taxonomic description the training most useful to the kinds of poems Dr. Williams would write. To complement this essay, Emily Mitchell Wallace, whose early articles have long been primary sources of our knowledge of the poets' college days, has now deepened and extended her research into this period of their lives, re-creating their excitement and the ferment of their development at the university.

xi

The remaining essays comprise, for each poet, a close reading of a single poem, a consideration of his aesthetic premises, and a biographical study. These are followed by James Laughlin's reminiscences and his sharing of his letters from Pound and Williams.

Of course there is an irony, which we savor, in holding our conference in just such a library as Dr. Williams advises, in *Paterson,* Book III, to be set afire, for the Rare Book Collection now contains all of Williams' and Pound's published works, many of their letters, and some of their manuscripts and memorabilia. (Williams' books are his own copies, given to the University of Pennsylvania after his death by Mrs. Williams, no doubt in acknowledgment of the university's having presented her husband with an honorary degree in 1952). Our volume concludes with a *catalogue raisonée* of these Pound and Williams holdings, prepared by the Rare Book Curator, Neda M. Westlake and the University Archivist, Francis James Dallett.

If, as Williams purges the language of the encrustations of its past, our holdings might stay him from burning down Van Pelt, it cannot be denied that were any library back in 1906 a cabinet of philological curiosities it must have been this one—or rather its predecessor in the Furness Building across the campus. In those days, the Pennsylvania English Department was renowned for its work in linguistic and historical scholarship; the Variorum Shakespeare had been undertaken here, and Professor Felix Schelling, the chairman with whom Pound had a correspondence extending many years after his graduation, was a prominent Shakespearean scholar. His colleagues industriously compiled bibliographies and studies investigating the historical and biographical circumstances in which the great and not-so-great works of English literature had been written. But no one on that faculty was ready to accept, much less understand, the new kind of poetry that Pound and Williams felt in their nerves and marrow to be necessary, were their art to tell the truth.

Consequently the University of Pennsylvania has had rather a bad press among critics and historians of the movement Pound and Williams helped to found.

From our perspective the Pennsylvania faculty of 1902–6 seems blinded by gentility to what was thrust before its eyes. Yet contemporary experience may confirm that historical scholars of the Renaissance are not by definition among those most attuned to the need for innovations in contemporary poetic style. Professor Schelling could understandably be impatient with the unbiddable student in the back row who refused to accept the academic disciplines of the department; the historical and philological approaches to English literature that Pound felt so stultifying were in fact innovations that Schelling only some fifteen years earlier had succeeded in organizing into a university department accredited to give graduate degrees. Besides, Schelling doubtless saw himself personally as well as professionally identified with culture in ways that Pound seemed determined to undermine, for Schelling's family as well as himself embodied the institutional acceptance of European traditions. His father had founded the St. Louis Conservatory of Music; his brother Ernest was an acclaimed composer and conductor. To be a Prometheus requires a Titan against whom to rebel; Pound may well have been lucky in his antagonist.

Such a rebellion is as ambivalent as that against one's father, and it is touching that for years after leaving Penn Pound kept seeking his old teacher's approval and acceptance. This was predictably unforthcoming to the ex-student who could never suppress his urge to *épater les bourgeois*, to "wound respectability, sentiment and decency"; gestures forgivable if "buoyed up with wit," but in Pound's work "not always so buoyed," as Schelling wrote, reviewing *Poems* (1922) in a Philadelphia newspaper. Pound's need for Schelling's approval is emblematic of his uneasy relationship with the academy. While kicking and screaming against his professors' lack of critical interest in what they taught, Pound, as Hugh Kenner shows, was nonetheless well introduced by them to the literature of the classical world and medieval romance in which his imagination participated for the rest of his life in ways of which they could not have dreamed.

Despite his and Williams' being approached over the years by many scholars, including several contributors to the present volume, for information about their own work, neither poet changed his notion of the American university as a philistine museum. Once they left the campus, they never came back. Pound did not wait for the academy to catch up with him; he founded his own academy in which he was professor of everything to a student body of acolytes who made the pilgrimage to Rapallo. If the University of Pennsylvania was in Pound's and Williams' day an unwilling and unwitting mother of the muses, it can be said that should they, or their shades, turn up nowadays they would find that not only has the English Department been teaching their work (and that of their contemporaries and successor poets) for many years, but poets themselves are no longer regarded here as idlers and pariahs. The kind of support for young writers which Pound unavailingly urged Schelling to institute is now offered them at Pennsylvania.

Why is it that Pound, whose style aimed at immediate and unequivocal significations, should still generate controversial readings? Take *Homage to Sextus Propertius:* Is this an effort at translation, a cadenza on themes by the Roman poet, or an original poem in which Pound assumes the persona of Propertius as a mask? Now, sixty years after its publication, Ronald Bush, considering its alternative interpretations, must ask, "What *is* the subject that so absorbed Pound that he forgot his existence for the sake of giving it life?" The freedom Pound took with Propertius' text, the ways he interpolated allusions to his own time and circumstances into his adaptation, the intensifications of feeling evoked by the rhythms and structure of this poem are all measures of Pound's originality. Bush finds the "controlling motif and . . . deepest emotional unity" in the *Homage* to be "an affirmation of the life force, figured in images of life interwoven by natural energy." This poem "proclaims the power of imagination rooted in desire to marry self and world, and to redeem the self from a fragmented and ghostly existence." Adopting the persona of Propertius, Pound "displays the spiritual lineaments of Orpheus, the divinity who descended into death and returned, who was dismembered and yet continued to sing, and who singing established harmony in the cosmos."

Few poets in our time have had such artistic courage and ambition, have dared to attempt such heroic reconciliations through poetry, or have felt the necessity of making such broad repudiations of traditional modes of thought. In his essay, "The Revolution of the Word," Michael Harper re-examines the bases and methods of Pound's Imagism and of his reliance on the linguistic theories of Fenollosa. Pound, like Fenollosa, assumed that experience is directly known without the intermediation of language; that scientific induction, from "concretely known particulars," is the method of poetry; and that this method could be used "to generate an ethics and an economics that could redeem society from its errors." It is the mistakenness of these beliefs, Harper maintains, that is the key to much that is baffling about Pound's work and his program. These beliefs "explain why the *Cantos* are the way they are—Images juxtaposed with neither narrative nor commentary to connect them, since their significance . . . is supposedly there on the page if you will only LOOK at it." His reliance on this epistemology with its assumption that language has no part in creating experience, only in recording it, "explains Pound's dogmatism and both the dedication and the violence with which he entered the political arena; for if the poem was the scientific induction he believed it to be, its conclusions were a solid foundation for action." Pound's commitment to a flawed epistemology thus leads, Harper suggests, to "the anti-Semitism, the scurrilous rhetoric, the Rome Broadcasts, Mussolini and Pisa."

All who admire Pound's work are necessarily perplexed by what Wendy Flory has termed "the Pound Problem." It would be beyond our deserts were our geniuses all to leave us not only the bequests of their writings but the flawless examples of their personal character. Shakespeare seems such a one, possibly because we know so little of his life; but then, what makes Shakespeare Shakespeare is the vision of possibilities embodied in the characters he created, and the ways he has made it inescapable that we judge them. The Pound problem begins—as Eliot put it—with his imagining Hell as for other people. In this, and in his choice of victims, he is not unique; we accept the genius of Voltaire and of Shelley, the stature of Eliot and of Henry Adams, though each held anti-Semitic views and wrote them into some of his works. With Pound the problem is exacerbated by the violence of his diatribes, the moral crudeness of his unexamined opinions. In a man whose tolerance for literary rubbish was absolute zero, uncritical acceptance of such canards as the alleged "Protocols of the Elders of Zion" seems surprising. We must ask why he is able, indeed eager, to accept the accusations that the Jews comprised a worldwide network of money-manipulators and munitions-mongers responsible for the death of culture in the Western World.

Wendy Flory attempts to place the poet's obliquity in appropriate contexts. She takes pains to disentangle several strands of anti-Semitic feeling which differ in source, provenience, and intensity. Tracing the prevalence of cultural stereotypes in the community in which Pound grew up, she distinguishes between its negative attitude to Jews (among its other targets of social and business discrimination) and the much more vicious manifestations of anti-Semitism in Germany later in the century. Pound has been wrongly castigated as endorsing Hitler's policies, whereas in fact he had little interest in Hitler or in Germany; Mussolini was the axis leader he endorsed, and Mussolini's Italy was less harsh toward its Jews. Flory reminds us that Il Duce had many admirers in this country before the attack on Ethiopia revealed the brutality and moral squalor of the Fascist state—but not to Pound, who continued to believe that Mussolini was a gifted, noble leader whom he might convert to the economic program of social credit which alone could prevent another world war. It was because Pound could not bring himself to recognize that his faith in and hopes for Il Duce were baseless, Flory maintains, that he needed a scapegoat to protect himself from the truth he would not face.

Harper's delineation of Pound's epistemology proposes one possible cause for Pound's anti-Semitism. Flory's examination of his background and his capacity for self-delusion offers others. These essays, as well as recent explorations of the subject elsewhere, should help make possible an understanding of the grave flaws in the human sympathies and thought of this poet whose work is motivated by high ideals. I would like to suggest several other considerations which may merit further investigation.

Three factors in Pound's personality coalesced to make inescapable this fixation, as well as his seemingly unquestioned faith in Mussolini as a wise and just prince. One is Pound's attraction to power, another his delusions about his own role as a savior of the world, and the third is his misconception of the processes of historical change.

Pound's heroes are on the one hand the bringers of order—Confucius, Li Po—and on the other violent, rebellious, and charismatic men like Sigismundo Malatesta, Bertran de Born, El Cid. We may infer Pound's fascination with power and his relish in its exercise from the vigor and intensity of his entrepreneurial activities on behalf of the writers and artists in whose work he believed. Mussolini must have seemed to him—as to many another—a forceful, charismatic, widely-learned bringer of peace and stability to the fragmented country which had been the seat of Western culture. Dennis Mack Smith's biography *Mussolini* (1982) shows how tawdry was the truth behind this facade. But Pound never peered behind it. For it was his tragic misfortune to assume that if only Il Duce, or Senator Borah, would listen to *him* and enact social credit in Italy or the United States, he, Ezra Pound, would stop war from happening.

It is a tragic paradox that Pound, whose command and reconstruction of the literatures of the European and Oriental past is among the chief embodiments in our time of the literary consciousness of history, should have been so woefully self-misled about the sources, processes, and complexities of historical change. Pound no doubt extrapolated from his own experience in changing literary sensibility by promulgating the fiats of a new movement (whether Imagism, Vorticism, or the more complex prolegomena of his critical writing generally). This readily led him to confuse his ability to enlist a few talented friends in cleansing the Augean stables of poetry with the gathering of forces by which governments and economic systems are overthrown or transformed. In ways that must be retraced and analyzed with care, Pound drifted, or was carried along by the flood of his feelings, from convictions that civilization itself was endangered because the arts had been perverted to his attempts to correct the conditions responsible for this artistic and moral decay. In the Romantic tradition of Shelley, Ruskin, and Morris, Pound undertook the reformation of the life from which art is nourished. So far, a noble purpose. But in the process he somehow proved vulnerable to the cruel baiting of anti-Semitism, the conspiratorial theory which places all blame for the world's ills on a source outside the self and denies the humanity of other people.

There is an unhappy congruence between Pound's notion of how he could manipulate history by persuading a few key leaders to adopt social credit and his diagnosis that what had betrayed Western civilization was the cabal of a few financiers and munitions-mongers, most of whom were Jews. There was of course a virulent popular press in many countries maintaining the same false explanations for the sufferings of the twentieth century. Such are the paranoid fantasies of frightened, desperate, and dangerous men who lust for simplistic answers to complex questions. The role of intellect in the understanding of complexity is abandoned or perverted by such unequivocal placing of blame. If the scapegoat bears the blame, his denouncer is rendered blameless.

For complex historical reasons Christendom for centuries carried this supposition of the guilt of others. The medieval Church's ban on usury had left it to Jews to lend money to finance the Christians' wars—which is not of course the same thing as fomenting those wars. In Pound's day allegations of a supranational web of Jewish warmongers were in the air, a foul popular supposition which Pound tragically seized upon to allay his own inner confusions. Another factor possibly affecting Pound's views may derive from the distinctions between Hebraism and Hellenism suggested by Matthew Arnold in *Culture and Anarchy.* Pound's exalting of Hellenistic impulses may exacerbate his readiness to vilify the contemporary representatives of repressive Mosaic law.

Underlying all such speculations is the question of Pound's sanity, on which there can probably be no informed agreement. I do not suggest that only insane persons hold the antisocial views found in

Pound's broadcasts and occasionally in the *Cantos*, but it is likely that
were Pound's pathology fully comprehended, his predisposition to
the ideas described above could be better understood. The diagnosis
of Pound as insane by Dr. Winfred Overholser, chief physician at St.
Elizabeths, has been vigorously attacked by Dr. E. Fuller Torrey
(*Psychiatry Today*, November 1981). The principal target of this
investigation is not Pound, however, but Overholser, who allegedly
falsified Pound's records. Some of Torrey's evidence seems based
on the verbal testimony of subordinate physicians, now deceased.
Literary critics are unequipped to deal in forensic psychiatry, and a
layman cannot presume to settle the matter. But one can surely identify
features of Pound's personality which, whether or not conformable
to a legal definition of insanity, demonstrate extreme egotism, inordinate
detachment from reality, paranoia, all leading to his uncritical
acceptance of anti-Semitism, his folly in making broadcasts for Italian
state radio in wartime, and his consequent sufferings.

William Carlos Williams was, like Pound, an inveterate theorist
of his own innovative poetic processes. One result of his vigorous
self-definitions has been that unwary readers have tended to reduce
the range and effect of his poetry to the formulas he set forth to justify
and defend his innovations. Of all of his pronouncements none has
more frequently been misapplied in this way than the line, repeated in
Paterson, "No ideas but in things." Denise Levertov reminds us that
for Williams, "the imagination does not reject its own sensory origins
but illuminates them, and connects them with intellectual and intuitive
experience," thus opening to the poem—and to the reader—the ideas
that are in things. She demonstrates this openness to experience,
including its intellectual implications, by analysis of a significant and
ambitious poem of Williams' which has somehow not attracted much
comment. "A Morning Imagination of Russia," written in 1927, just ten
years after the Russian Revolution, dramatizes the response to that
cataclysmic experience of an imagined intellectual, now a member of
a rural soviet. "He recognizes that a great price has been paid, and
will perhaps be further exacted. But what has been gained is precisely
what he had desired: touch itself . . . without which all is dull,
hopeless, ashen." Williams' fable requires a revolution for the intellectual
to be in touch with his society; this may be read not only as expressing
the hopes of the American avant-garde for the Russian experiment,
but also as a paradigm of his own struggles to revolutionize American
poetry in the 1920s.

Paul Christensen takes up Williams' revolutionary poetics a decade later, when, finding himself limited by the static requirements of Objectivism, Williams felt the danger that "the poem enclosed too little too well." Instead, "A deeper, truer measure would have to include the whole poet in its formal symmetry, in which his ragings and desires, his dreams, his fantasies, would be bound into the form of the poem in a way that gave both freedom and participation in the design." What liberated Williams in his search for such a measure was the influence upon him of the exiled European intelligentsia, "German Gestalt psychologists . . . , European physicists, biologists, mathematicians, social scientists (the Frankfurt School in particular), Marxists, the Bauhaus architects . . . a culture of revolutionaries who had fought their various state authorities and had been punished for their daring visions . . . challenged American artists to express themselves with equal freedom and convictions. Here was the 'other' stream of thought that was merging with American culture to create a new zeitgeist at mid-century." In the ferment of this revolutionary milieu Williams felt the need and found the means to merge the influences of European surrealism with the rhythms of American jazz; from the dialectic of native and international influences he synthesized his variable measure, his triadic structure so open to experience and meaning. Where in 1927 he had applied his own achieved style to revolutionary materials, now during and after the war years he absorbed revolutionary energies into his style, applied, in *Paterson,* to the American experience his life was rooted in.

Paterson thus reflects a revolutionary aesthetic, one which greatly extended the possibilities for what the poem may include. One controversial extension is Williams' use of almost unedited and unaltered letters to himself by other persons. Most notable of these is a series of impassioned and self-searching letters from the poet Marcia Nardi, whose correspondence appears over the signature "Cress" in Williams' poem. Until now there has been speculation but little information about either the relationship between them or Williams' intentions in using Nardi's correspondence in such a prominent way in his most ambitious work. Theodora Graham has traced the personal and artistic strands of this rather strained relationship between an older and a younger poet in an essay which tells us much about the ways that Williams conceived of and constructed *Paterson.*

It is fitting that our tribute to Pound and Williams should conclude with James Laughlin's reminiscences and his sharing of letters from the two poets he befriended and published for over forty years. Laughlin, Director of New Directions Publishing Company, tells how as a young poet he dropped out of Harvard to attend Pound's "Ezuversity" in Rapallo, and, at Pound's urging, on his return to this country began to publish the master and his friend Bill Williams. Pound's correspondence is informal, given to idiosyncratic spellings and sudden lapses into dialect, interspersing serious discussions with light jingles, haranguing "Jas." to publish this, propagandize that, follow up a casual contact with Queen Wilhelmina of the Netherlands with a copy of Pound on Confucius, and so on—an unending and disjunctive series of admonitions, outbursts, jokes, and statements of principle from an affectionate guru. "Williams," Laughlin observes, "was very different"; one had "a more placid relationship" with him. "He almost never found fault." Where Pound's letters leap from one subject to another, Williams makes extended comments, giving coherent exposition of his views on publishing, on the qualities of his friend Pound, and on his dismay at the influence of T. S. Eliot on American poetry.

xix

These "gists and piths" reveal the personal presence of both poets. Their letters also make inescapable the inference that both were blessed in their publisher, who stuck by them when their work was read only by a tiny coterie of the faithful. Nor were they unaware of their good fortune—on receiving word that Laughlin would publish one of his novels, Williams addressed his friend as "Dear God"!

While their letters in the university collections are not, with one exception, major sources, all contribute new details to the biographical background of both poets. The largest run of correspondence is the set of seventy-six letters, dated between 1907 and 1959, to Mary Moore, the dedicatee of Pound's *Personae* ("if she wants it"), an early love who remained his friend. Pound's intermittent contacts with the University of Pennsylvania are reflected in his letters to Felix Schelling, Roy F. Nichols, the University of Pennsylvania Press, and Robert E. Spiller; Williams' in his to E. Sculley Bradley and John C. Miller. Other letters deal with a range of literary topics: Pound writes to May Sinclair, James T. Farrell, Henry Bamford Parkes and Arnold Gingrich; and Williams corresponds with Burton Roscoe and Waldo Frank. All of these letters are summarized in Neda Westlake's inventory. Material in the University Archives provides additional views of the poets while in college—including several of the photographs accompanying Emily Wallace's essay in the present volume.

Among the letters and manuscripts given the Library by Mrs. Williams was a small snapshot showing William Carlos Williams, seated, looking gravely at the camera, while behind him, unbuttoned shirt cavalierly thrown over his shoulders, stands Ezra Pound, grizzled and indomitable. This is a contact print of a photograph by Richard Avedon, who was present when, after his release from St. Elizabeths in 1958, Pound on his way to take ship for his last exile in Italy stopped off in Rutherford to visit Bill and Flossie Williams. It was the last time they saw each other. That photograph of their last reunion, along with others of the poets as collegians costumed for roles in plays and in fencing attire, is reproduced in this book, as part of our tribute to them.

DANIEL HOFFMAN

Part One

Poets at Pennsylvania

1. Poets at the Blackboard

Hugh Kenner

The now of this discourse is April 25, 1981; its here in an upper room at the University of Pennsylvania Library, where a group was convened to observe the seventy-fifth anniversary of the graduation of Ezra Loomis Pound, M.A., '06, and William Carlos Williams, M.D., '06. The following reconstruction of what I said makes no effort to conceal the particularities of the event.

Russell Baker has remarked on the proclivity of Americans for combining a good time with something improving; he instanced people who went to the seashore and sang hymns. Today's program, however improving, cannot offer, save to special tastes, an explicit good time; otherwise it would start with the showing of a motion picture which unfortunately has not been produced. *With Bill and Ez at College* would be a marvelous silent film.

The mind's eye can screen many bits: the medium long shot, for instance, in which Williams is standing with a billiard cue in his right hand, its butt resting upon the floor: when suddenly the fat lady beside him is knocked flat by a bolt of lightning. Yes, that happened.

And we might build a long sequence out of Williams' efforts to attend an outdoor performance of *As You Like It*. The opening close-up is cued by his own statement that he was wearing a derby hat. The face he wore under the hat he describes as "a round smooth face," though photographs show something blander and blanker. A bland blank face: the classic Keatonian face for such a hat. We are next to imagine Bill Williams, topped by that hat, climbing the ten-foot fence between the cemetery and the Botanical Gardens. "I climbed," runs his narrative, "straightened myself and jumped inside." Reenacting this for screening, we need to recall that anybody jumping ten feet in such a hat has one hand on top of the hat. He had next to get from the place where he had landed around to the greenhouse embankment where the play would be. Of course, the heavies promptly threw him out.

The director must now idealize the plot. Such deeds in movies are attempted in threes, whereas life here afforded merely twos. Our hero ought to have tried again, been thrown out again, and succeeded on the third try. Anticlimactically, he succeeded on the second. This he did by a simple merge with the crowd that was having its tickets taken at the turnstile. It was after Bill Williams had gotten inside that the number of tickets and the number of people was noticed to differ by one. They yelled after the invader, but couldn't find him.

None of that was undertaken to rescue the heroine: simply to crash *As You Like It.* Imagine any Penn undergraduate going to such ludicrous trouble for that purpose at this end of the twentieth century! Bill Williams was determined to see *As You Like It* because he meant to see any play that came by. Nothing better characterizes American undergraduate culture at the turn of the century than its combination of what Guy Davenport calls "impossible idealism" with an utter and simple passion for theatergoing.

Drama was not even thought of as "culture." Williams, who is our chief witness in such matters because Pound wrote very little about student days, recalled that you could see any play you liked for a quarter. That was what it cost to be at the very top in the back of the theater, the vantage point from which he saw plays aplenty. He kept climbing up there because, he says, he wanted to *write* plays: moreover, plays in verse. The attraction of *As You Like It* is apparent, a pretty good verse-man having set his hand to it.

Every eminent writer of that generation seems not only to have been a habitual playgoer, but, in his schooldays, to have appeared in a play. Joyce played a schoolteacher in *Vice Versa* at Belvedere, T.S. Eliot a Lord in *Fanny and the Servant Problem* at Harvard (where the second footman was played by e. e. cummings). Pound's and Williams' adventures in greasepaint we shall come to. They all went on to write plays. Joyce has left us one play, each of the others more.

Ezra Pound's way of writing plays was to transpose them from foreign languages, but *Kakitsubata* and *The Women of Trachis* are nevertheless *his* plays. And his preparation for translating Sophokles' *Trachiniae* in the 1950s included appearing in the fifteen-man chorus of a production of Euripides' *Iphigenia* at the University of Pennsylvania five decades before.

When we think about that production today what most arrests us is the plausibility of Williams' recollection that the teen-age actors spoke entirely in Greek. The *lexis* and *melos* moreover entailed a long-range collaboration between Euripides and Professor Hugh Archibald Clarke of the Penn faculty, the disappearance of the Euripidean music having obliged Prof. Clarke to undertake a conjectural restoration. And of this Greek play we may note with wonder that while it was being rehearsed, the college paper gave progress reports at two week intervals over perhaps six months, treating *Iphigenia* as one of the great events of the Philadelphia season. It would even "have a great influence upon the general university world of the East." "Impossible idealism," indeed!

5

How many performances there were I do not know, though public demand was presumably less than insatiable; but on 28 April 1903 an audience which included William Carlos Williams was gathered at the Academy of Music for a Greek play whose *Choros* of Captive Women included 18-year-old Ezra Pound. Williams was watching Ezra more than anyone else, though he would also remember how the Messenger brought down the house by delivering his lines "with startling intensity." Ezra was unforgettable, "dressed in a Grecian robe, as I remember it, a toga-like ensemble topped by a great blond wig at which he tore as he waved his arms about and heaved his massive breasts in ecstasies of extreme emotion." That was what Williams wrote several decades later. At the time the college paper had been more restrained. It said that the dances of the chorus were gone through "with care and some grace," and went on to mention the appreciation of the audience. And there was no doubt someone somewhere to point out that Euripides himself directed an all-male chorus, women on stage being unthinkable till Roman times.

On another first night it was Williams who trod the Penn boards, in something called *Mr. Hamlet of Denmark.* This was not written by William Shakespeare, it was written by someone who had looked at something of William Shakespeare's, and it appears to have been a musical comedy. William Carlos Williams played Polonius. From between a huge white beard and a huge white mane of hair his bland blank face peered forth. *Mr. Hamlet* was more popular than the *Iphigenia* had been. It played a week in Philadelphia; it played in Atlantic City, N.J., in Wilmington, Del., in Baltimore, Md., even in Washington, D.C. Medical studies in those days could seemingly sustain much interruption.

As poetic comparatists, we cannot but observe the justice of the casting: Pound immersed in an effort to simulate a classical occasion, Williams in—well, the classical analogy will have to be the New

Comedy: Menander to Pound's Euripides. Subsequent work of the two of them, and especially subsequent dramatic work, is epitomized by this particular contrast.

Such stories are quaint, as though someone had contrived them to sustain the analogy of silent film. The cast photographs—you can see them in Noel Stock's *Ezra Pound's Pennsylvania*—are quainter, and tempt acquiescence in Pound's and Williams' later half-dismissal of the University as a genteel museum. One thing, though, that decades have not turned wholly quaint is the Penn curriculum, particularly as it looks on a piece of paper, the way an incoming freshman first sees it. By the time Ezra Pound had completed the freshman registration process what he had signed up for included the following:

—English Composition;
—Public Speaking;
—Algebra;
—German Grammar;
—American Colonial History;
—The Principles of Government in the United States; and
—Latin. And people have called the *Cantos* heterogeneous.

There is no place you could find such a list save in the curriculum of an American university; I mean that as a sober historical statement. In America you do not "read" a subject the way they do in England, nor undergo formal lectures the way they do in Germany. No, you *take courses* in a sort of checkerboard pattern controlled by the clock, much as in high school. You have been attending to Principles of Government in the United States; a clock strikes; another clock strikes; you are attending to Latin. Such discontinuities were introduced at Harvard by a relative of T. S. Eliot's, President Eliot of Harvard, he of the five-foot shelf, a man by whom T. S. E. seems to have been a little embarrassed: the black sheep, as it were, of the family. President Eliot had destroyed the old rationale of the Harvard curriculum by introducing a smorgasbord of electives, of which T. S. was quick however to avail himself, as was Ezra Pound of the equivalent freedoms at Penn. (Algebra and German Grammar, what are *those* doing side by side?)

A kind of functional mapping is feasible between such curricula and the poetry Pound and Eliot wrote: curricula and poetry in which no transition need be justified, in which everything has been somehow lifted to a plane removed from the plane of historical process, everything is of equal importance, and everything is laid out in an order seemingly arbitrary within which the mind may trace webs.

Classrooms enclose a kind of contemporaneity into which every subject is brought, with always some skeptic at hand to ground talk in the real. A class may comprise every shade in the spectrum, from ultra-intensity to infra-Philistia, and though the class Philistine sometimes falls asleep and sometimes makes irreverent remarks, the one who does these things may not always be the class Philistine. Sextus P. Pound and Apeneck Sweeney Eliot could regard the classics with a somewhat less than perfectly Victorian decorum they'd acquired not from their teachers but from classrooms.

> *The primitive ages sang Venus,*
> *the last sings of a tumult . . .*

"Tumult" is somehow the wrong word for the hallowed intensity with which something classical is supposed to come through. It is exactly the right word for Pound's purposes, and the sort of word, oddly enough, that an inattentive student might come up with on being suddenly challenged by the professor. (The Latin is *tumultus*.) "Tumult" not only looks like but in fact *is* a Latin word. It just doesn't look like what "poetry" looked like at Penn.

Pound's professor in the Penn Latin class remembered him at the back of the room, characteristically at the back of the room where he could evade the scrutiny that bombards the front rows. He was also reported by someone—Williams passes this on—as exhibiting a certain aloofness, which he underscored by taking out and winding with deliberation "an immense tin watch." Something was going on in his mind, all the same, because he kept attending class. In his 80s, Peter Whigham has testified, he could read unfamiliar Latin verse at sight. (Unlike how many of his classmates? It does not do to discount the fellow at the back of the room.)

To return to that wonderful list.

—*English Composition*. That was his lifelong subject. At the Ezuversity in Rapallo you majored, James Laughlin will confirm, in English Composition.

—*Public Speaking:* the voice, the role, the persona. Homer, Odysseus, Sigismundo, Kung, the knack of becoming any of them.

—*Algebra:* recall the famous cadenza of 1914 (reprinted in Ch. XI of his *Gaudier-Brzeska*) which relates Dante's four levels of understanding to four levels of mathematical abstraction, moving upward to analytic geometry. That was only one heritage of Pound's study of algebra at Penn. The way algebra satisfied his aesthetic sense will have sponsored his lust to make arcane manipulation of symbols (see the *Thrones*

Cantos) yield satisfaction and symmetry. He used to say that he passed his last mathematics exam by simply knowing how the solution should look. No mathematician will reprove a statement like that.

—*German Grammar.* German grammar was never an obsession of Pound's, but substitute Chinese and you get the idea. There had to be at any time in his mind some language of which he was interested in the inner workings.

8

—*American Colonial History.* Familiar, isn't it?

—*Principles of Government in the United States:* equally familiar, including their decline all the way to Franklin Roosevelt. And

—*Latin.* . . . "Rome," he would say, explaining his Italian allegiance, "is where they speak Latin." The wellspring of the Spirit of Romance, it drew him lifelong no less bewitchingly than the Fountain drew Ponce.

If that seems a scenario for large stretches of the *Cantos*, it is nevertheless a Penn first-year curriculum, the one Ezra Pound happened to take. And in the time-exempt rituals of the *Cantos*, where all is always now, we may see (scourged by the urgency of Ideas into Action) the classroom rite in which all moves toward one great goal, an exam just two weeks away.

Pound remembered Professor Reithmuller on Whitman, in an exotic immigrant's accent:

> "Fvy! in Tdaenmarck efen dh' beasantz gnow him"
> (meaning Whitman, exotic, still suspect
> four miles from Camden)

He remembered the girl who used to come puffing into German class and "ended in a Baptist learnery / Somewhere near the Rio Grande." But most of all, we may guess, he remembered the curricular rite the *Cantos* reconstruct, everything synchronic, everything interrelated without apology. As the poem extends itself by block after block of knowledge—Renaissance Despots, The Rise and Fall of Venice, The History of China, Roman and Moslem Numismatics, Byzantine Edicts, Comparative Chinese and Greek Philology—we may remark on its likeness to an extended elective curriculum and reflect that there is more to college than the freshman year.

On the other hand Williams said flatly, "I never went to college," defying all effort to link his poetic cosmos to a classroom. He meant that he never took what we now call a pre-med course. The Horace Mann school had sufficed. Consequently, Williams never took a college-level course in any language or literature: in that as in so many ways Pound's and Eliot's polar opposite.

Some years ago SUNY-Buffalo commissioned a trial design for its new campus from Gordon Bunshaft, who proposed that they house the entire university in a single huge building, one of the trim glass elevated boxes of his predilection. A model of this immaculacy was prepared; and SUNY's responsible persons, staring bemused at the model, found themselves asking what on earth it would be like with students in it. A sardonic voice one day crystallized their misgivings: "The students will have to be *sprayed*."

Such a metaphor governs many pre-med requirements, calculated to spray the incult before they gain entrance to white-coated austerities. And noting that Bill Williams had not Ezra's knack for the minutiae of book learning, we may judge it a very good thing that he was not forced through a sequence of courses designed to civilize him. Every reader of the *Autobiography* remembers the ruinous obsession with Keats that misused his energies for many years. Survey courses might merely have transferred the obsession to someone like Swinburne.

As it was, the writing Williams did in Penn courses consisted mostly of Case Histories, a not uninteresting discipline. The case history is dense, it is cryptic, it is crisp, and it is factual. That is not a bad way to be writing day in, day out if God is determined to drive Keats from your mind.

And Williams fondly recalled another antidote: "the wonders of pathology, histology and anatomy." When Pound used to assail his friend's lack of education, "I'd reply that a course in comparative anatomy wouldn't at all harm him if it came to that."

Most of Williams' work, as it happens, can be gathered under those two rubrics: the Case History (see "To Elsie"), the Comparative Anatomy. Many a Williams poem asks to be compared to some other poem that is more like classroom poetry. Compared with this other poem, the Williams poem discloses a system of structural mappings despite its refusal to use the same words: much as a bat, on dissection, proves to be not an anomaly among birds, but a regular vertebrate mammal. Consider a sequence of his best-known lines:

> . . . *under the surge of the blue*
> *mottled clouds driven from the*
> *northeast—a cold wind. Beyond, the*
> *waste of broad, muddy fields*
> *brown with dried weeds, standing and fallen*
>
> *patches of standing water*
> *the scattering of tall trees*
>
> *All along the road the reddish*

> *purplish, forked, upstanding, twiggy*
> *stuff of bushes and small trees*
> *with dead, brown leaves under them*
> *leafless vines—*
> *Lifeless in appearance, sluggish*
> *dazed spring approaches—*

A later mention of "the stark dignity of/entrance" marks one of Williams'
rare recourses to etymology, nudging our recognition that "stark"
means "naked." Who is it that enters so? The comparative anatomist
may discern the return of Persephone, even cite such a locus as
Milton's

> *. . . Not that faire field*
> *Of* Enna, *where* Proserpin *gathring flours*
> *Her self a fairer Floure by gloomie* Dis
> *Was gatherd, which cost* Ceres *all that pain*
> *To seek her through the world. . . .*

No indeed, not that faire field: only

> *. . . the reddish*
> *purplish, forked, upstanding, twiggy*
> *stuff of bushes and small trees*

—something as remote from a fair Italianate field as only a Jersey poet
can imagine. Yet the glimpse of dazed Persephone perdures.

Time and again in this way Williams compels his aggressively
local diction to recapitulate such inherited themes, reminiscent of the
skeletal and neural and muscular themes recapitulated everywhere
among the phylae of mammals. Cherish the ape's shaggy coat; and what
it covers is like what Dirce's fair skin covers.

Clearly, at Penn Pound and Williams were enormously receptive,
if not always to what the authorities thought they ought to be receiving.
Genius never wastes time, because it will always find a use for what
it is putting its time to. One thing we might think the two of them
ought to have been doing was going to hear distinguished literary men
when talks by these were arranged, but as far as can be ascertained
their score at this kind of self-improvement was goose egg. Yeats came
and read in 1903. Williams explicitly did not go to hear Yeats. He
thought Pound heard him, but misremembered; Pound was then at
Hamilton. Henry James came by later. No one of any subsequent
importance seems to have heard Henry James: certainly not Pound,
and certainly not Williams. It is not clear, on reflection, that either

of them was what Williams needed: not at any rate Yeats, who in 1903 was immersed in *The Shadowy Waters,* that disastrous obsession of his late-early years. Lines like

> *I have never been golden-armed Iollan*
> and
> *O O O O for golden-armed Iollan*

would not have done W. C. W. a particle of good. Their possible effect on Pound is another question, but it is probably as well that the Pound-Yeats acquaintance began after Yeats had gotten that particular set of noises out of his system.

So what was acting on their minds at Penn? To our list so far—curricular structures, plays, new acquaintances (most signally one another)—we may add one more item, which may be emblematized by the blackboards.

The National Endowment could (and does) do worse than pay someone to wander form college to college, simply photographing—by preference, late in the day—as many blackboards as possible. In 100 years, the collection would be priceless.

Several hours into the academic day, the blackboard is confronting students with a dense overlay of symbols left over from previous classes. When their instructor in the heat of exposition is moved to chalk up something of his own, no more than his precursors is he likely to wipe the whole expanse clean, not wanting to turn his back to the class for too long (a principle of rhetoric, not of safety). Erasing just a little, he makes his additions slantwise. And as the palimpsest builds up day-long—diagrams, short lists, circles with three points marked on them, bits of math, supply-and-demand curves, bits of Aramaic—all superimposed, all bespeaking the day's intellectual activity in that room—you feel yourself in the presence, as Beckett put it, of something you could study all your life and not understand. The blackboard with its synchronic overlay, its tough and hieroglyphic fragments of a congeries of subjects (nothing obvious goes on the blackboard; what is obvious can merely be stated)—the blackboard is our civilization's Great Smaragdine Tablet (which said "Things below are copies," and was itself one of the things below). Absence of explicit and consecutive sense, teasing intimations of domains of order that others comprehend, that I could comprehend had I world enough and time, these are elements of its daily rhetoric, as it marshals, at random, enigmatic signs.

Minds exposed to the blackboard's daily irradiations can come to prize enigmatic signs for their own sake. There are ideograms and

hieroglyphics in the *Cantos;* an early poem by Williams runs the letters
S O D A down its page within a twinkling border of asterisks;
documents are pinned to the pages of *Paterson;* these deeds bespeak
connoisseurship of the enigmatic, emblematic sign, the one that was
left on the blackboard by somebody else. ("SODA," yes, is an *electric*
sign; but what iconographic fervors attend its emblazonment?
Provided with light bulbs, would Babylon's skies have cried "SODA"?
So much depends on such questions.) In such connoisseurship we
may discern a willingness to cede part of the poem to others, the way
I cede much of the blackbord in my class to the day's earlier instructors.
To cede expertise so, to acknowledge in hermetic signs the authority
of other minds, their deeds and domains, is to inhabit the twentieth
century: also to have encountered the found object, something
somebody other than you has understood and shaped, like the letters
in *Paterson.*

Putting letters into a poem was not a new notion—Browning
did it in *The Ring and the Book*—but formerly the poet worded the letters
himself, as he worded everything else that bore his signature. Nor
was putting learning into a poem new. But Milton or Donne would not
exhibit any learning they had not themselves wholly mastered. The
Pound of *Cathay* was content if Fenollosa and Mori and Ariga
understood Chinese on his behalf. What has been jeered at as egregious
parading of knowledge he didn't have (the cited symptoms include
errors in spelling Greek, though many of those were committed by
typesetters) is better seen as an awareness that other people know much
that is worth acknowledging. By putting a Greek word on your page
you indicate the blessed existence somewhere of a professor who can
explain it. God be praised, one need not carry the whole of civilization
in one's head. "Civ/n, not a one-man job," Pound wrote to Louis
Dudek.

So to the extent that specialized learning belongs in large part to
other people, its tokens can be treated as found objects, arcane,
numinous, penetrable. They will lead the curious somewhere else;
they will lead the curious off the blackboard, in fact *out* of my poem,
which is O.K.; it is my American didactic impulse that directs the
curious out of my poem, just as my Whitmanic inclusiveness
acknowledges large areas of expertise elsewhere which I can
acknowledge but not hope to command.

Discussing a poetic, we circle toward the definition of a university
system as understood by Americans: a system in which other people
are learning things you are not, and you look daily at blackboard
traces left by professors whose subjects you are never likely to study,

nor need you. The break that defined modernist poetics was preceded
by a tacit break with the educational theories of the Renaissance,
when they claimed to understand just what combination of learnings
would constitute an educated man. Though "core curricula" swish
their lissom veils, that claim is no longer seriously made; it was not made
at Penn, nor at Eliot's Harvard; it is not made so far as I know at any
American university today save the ones whose gimmick is the Great
Books Program, out of which no distinguished writer is likely to come.
The worst thing that can happen to a twentieth-century writer is to
be persuaded that somebody else can tell him what he ought to know.
(Pound was always telling people that? Yes, he was; but telling them
what they needed to know about *writing*, a specialty. It is licit to map
specialties.)

13

It is unsurprising that Pound and Williams should have left Penn
feeling they had been taught trivially, much of the time, by people
they could respect only intermittently. That was a natural consequence
of not becoming some teacher's apprentice, instead taking a clutch
of courses taught by specialists who frequently know little save their
speciality and may even be (said Williams) sometimes bastards.

Seeing what they became, though, they were well taught. It is
hard to specify anything they should have been taught instead.
Especially, it is doubtful that creative writing courses would have been
a good idea. God help Williams if he'd been flypapered by such a
course. And if Pound had been enrolled in one, God help the instructor.

2. Youthful Days and Costly Hours

Emily Mitchell Wallace

Part I, adapted from my article in The Pennsylvania Gazette *(1973), focuses mainly on the response of Williams and Pound to their studies at the University of Pennsylvania and their friendship with one another and a third poet, Hilda Doolittle (H.D.). Part II takes its cue from Hugh Kenner's talk, published in this volume, of movies and blackboards.*

I. PENN'S POET FRIENDS

As gentlemen and scholars at the University of Pennsylvania, they played billiards and tennis and fenced and acted in college theatrical productions and went to church and to football games and parties, and they agonized over girls and sex (in a theoretical, turn-of-the-century way), and they had already been to Europe at least once, and they were in good health and good looking as well, one of "dark Spanish beauty" ("I looked at my face in the glass and cursed my 'beauty,' my eyes, my hair curling brown"), the other dramatic looking with a leonine head, tawny hair ("peroxide blond," his classmates teased him), green eyes, and from time to time noticeable accoutrements like a gold-headed cane or a broad brimmed hat with a swooping feather ("a lanky whey-faced youth," he described his mirror image at sixteen, perhaps explaining his need for flamboyant attire).

They were not, however, typical of the young college heroes in Arthur Hobson Quinn's *Pennsylvania Stories* (1899) or Owen Wister's *Philosophy 4, A Story of Harvard University* (1907). The beautiful one was an exotic transplant, the son of first generation immigrants from the West Indies, his father an Englishman who commuted from New Jersey to business interests in South America, his mother of French and Basque heritage on the maternal side, and of Spanish and perhaps Dutch and Jewish ancestry on her father's side. The leonine one was "the Idaho kid," who left the frontier as a baby when his father was appointed assistant assayer at the United States Mint in Philadelphia, and who distrusted the "thin" New England blood he had inherited from ancestors who disembarked in Boston in 1631 from the ship *Lyon*.

15

Neither young man belonged to a fraternity. They did not drink. Their names were not in the Social Register. They had no excess of money. But their interest in poetry was excessive, even hubristic, by the standards of both Philadelphia and the University in that they thought of themselves in relation to the greatest poets (Homer, Ovid, Dante, Chaucer, Shakespeare, Keats) instead of in relation to the contemporary, gracious, genteel tradition. They wrote many poems during their respective four years at the University, but not one was published in *Red and Blue* or *The Punch Bowl*. Nor did they belong to Philomathean or Zelosophic, the literary societies.

Ezra Weston Loomis Pound, '05 C, '06 G, entered the College in 1901 at the age of fifteen (he would be sixteen on October 30) with the "intention of studying comparative values in literature (poetry) and began doing so unbeknown to the faculty." He had told his parents, "I want to write before I die the greatest poems that have ever been written."

William Carlos Williams, '06 M, '52 H, came to the medical school in 1902 straight from three years at Horace Mann, as was allowed in those days (until 1908, when two years of college were added to the entrance requirements). He had just passed his nineteenth birthday on September 17. In letters to his brother Edgar, an architecture student at M.I.T., he wrote about his artistic ambitions, "My interests are bigger than success." "We must . . . do things that will last forever."

The study of medicine was suggested to Williams by his mother, whose only brother Carlos Hoheb had earned a medical degree in Paris and become a distinguished surgeon in the Caribbean. Williams acceded to his mother's wish because he wanted no compromises in his own choice of a vocation: "No one was ever going to be in a position to tell me what to write, and you can say that again. No one, and I meant no one (for money) was ever (never) going to tell me how or what I was going to write." But he liked the study of medicine and confessed to his brother, "I love to dream that I'm going to be a great

16

Ezra Weston
Loomis Pound, 1885–1972
(From *The Hamiltonian*,
1905).

doctor, the best in the world." After graduation and internship in New York City and postgraduate medical study in Leipzig, he returned to his home town of Rutherford, New Jersey, and concentrated on the art of medicine and the medicine of art, for the two were as intricately connected in his mind as in the old Greek myths.

Pound expected to support his writing by teaching, but his international conception of literature was considered a "pose" by the professors of English at Penn. One of them said Pound was a "weed" in a "grove of giant growth." (Williams escaped their notice for many years.) With support of this kind from his alma mater, it is hardly surprising that Pound was not a success in the academic marketplace. Nevertheless, he remained a teacher, and the students who came to the peripatetic "Ezuversity" included Yeats, Eliot, H. D., Joyce, Frost, Hemingway, Cummings, Marianne Moore, James Laughlin, Zukofsky, Robert Lowell, Allen Ginsberg, and countless others. In brief

WILLIAM
CARLOS WILLIAMS, 1883–1963
(From *The 'Scope*, 1906).

summary of their many statements of gratitude and admiration and
affection, Pound performed with genius and without pay all the
functions of a university professor of literature: brilliant lectures,
correction of compositions, encouragement and criticism, letters of
recommendation, help in getting published, and whatever else each
individual needed, whether it was money, food, shelter, books, clothes,
music, reviews, secretarial help, a walk, a swim, tennis, a joke.
Hemingway says in *A Moveable Feast*, "I always thought of him as a
sort of saint." Pound accomplished for a time in twentieth-century
literature precisely what John Henry Newman says in "The Idea of a
University" that "a seat of universal learning should accomplish":
he established a climate in which writers, "rivals of each other," learned
"to respect, to consult, to aid each other." This Pound achieved, out
of meager financial resources, with *hilaritas* and hard work and
without compromising his vision of the "Sophoclean perfection." As

scholar and translator, he reclaimed for English whole areas of literature that had been desert. And his poems, like Williams' poems the creations of an inventor and a master, teach us essential lessons, such as "nothing counts save the quality of the affection."

Williams remembered being "homesick" and "timid" during his first days at the University. He had moved into a small single room on the second floor of Phillips Brooks Dormitory. Next door in 301, a slightly larger room with a fireplace and a grand piano, lived a sophomore music major from Ohio, Morrison Robb Van Cleve, called Van. Billy took out his fiddle and responded to the piano, and immediately Van knocked on his door. As apology for his "awful" violin playing (in fact, he played at an alumni dinner in 1904), Billy said he was really interested in writing and painting. Van replied, according to Williams, "My golly, just the thing! In my class there's a very extraordinary fellow whom you'd like very much to meet. His name is Ezra Pound." In another account of the historic first meeting, a story Williams liked to tell because "before meeting Pound is like B.C. and A.D.," Van "with no more ado . . . went into a neighboring building and came back with him in tow."

The nearby building would have been the dormitory on the east of Memorial Tower Arch, now called Morgan, then called House P because it was too new to have a name. Ezra's room was number 14, on the ground floor in the area of the present reception room and mail room, which seems an appropriate transformation of the former habitation of one of the century's best letter writers.

In any event, "Old Ez staggered up the stairs. I don't remember that though. I don't remember the first meeting at all. But it just took one look and I knew he was it." Here was a fellow creature with the blood royal of the artist. Williams was immediately protective of his new friend. "Ezra" in Hebrew means *help,* and that is what Pound got from Williams and what he gave. Willie wrote to his mother, introducing Pound as "a fine fellow," and adding:

He is really a brilliant talker and thinker, but delights in making himself just exactly what he is not: a laughing boor. His friends must be all patience in order to find him out and even then you must not let him know it, for he will immediately put on some artificial mood and be really unbearable.

This did not dismay Williams, for the secret life of persons and things fascinated him. "It was always important to me," he said, "to go through the somatic part of medicine into the physic part, which is . . . art all the way through." Pound valued this aspect of Williams' genius and later wondered whether Williams as a writer wasn't "at

Memorial Tower—Main Entrance to the Dormitories (Photograph by George Nitzsche, 1906).

his best retaining interest in the uncommunicable or the hidden roots of the consciousness of the people he meets, but confining his statement to presentation of their objective manifests."

Ezra's "optimism" and "cast-iron faith" appealed to Billy: "If he ever does get blue nobody knows it, so he is just the man for me." And even after years of arguments and disagreement, Williams could say that Pound had "an inexhaustible patience, an infinite depth of human imagination and sympathy." For example, Williams had protested in 1920 against being called an American author, and Pound replied in a letter:

Still, what the hell else are you? I mean apart from being a citizen, a good fellow (in your better moments), a grouch, a slightly hypersensitized animal, etc.?? Wot bloody kind of author are you save Amurkun (same as me)?

and then, turning to the other view, to allow Williams the best of both worlds:

(You thank your blooming gawd you've got enough Spanish blood to muddy up your mind, and prevent the current American ideation from going through it like a blighted collander.)

20 With one another, then, the young "grouch" and the young "optimist" were unusually patient, and their friendship was a decisive factor in their efforts to define themselves as poets.

The first two years Pound attended Penn, his grades were unremarkable, with only one "Distinguished," in solid geometry. He was a member of the chess club, learned to fence, played lacrosse, and taught himself enough Greek to be accepted for the Chorus of *Iphigenia among the Taurians*. Pound transferred to Hamilton College for his last two undergraduate years. Williams thought it was because Ezra's father was not happy with his son's progress. Other suggestions have been made, but the most obvious and logical reason for the transfer was simply that Pound could not take the courses he wanted to take.

However innovative Penn may have prided itself on being at the turn of the century, the college had absolutely no way to accommodate a young person who wanted to learn as much as he could about poetry in as many languages as possible. To enter the college, Pound had to pass examinations in two languages chosen from the following pairs: Greek-Latin, Latin-German, Latin-French, French-German. Pound offered Latin and German. The course requirements for the first two years were similar for every student with no room for elective languages. In the third year, the restrictive stipulation was, "No language group can be chosen in the Junior year unless the languages contained in it have been included in the work of the two lower years." This meant Pound could study no languages for credit other than the Latin and German he had offered for entrance. If there had been a way to add another language, Pound would have found it, for he says he "fought every regulation and every professor" who tried to make him conform to the restrictions.

At Hamilton College Pound was able to take twenty-one units of French, nine of Italian, nine of Spanish, and one of Provençal, all under the formidable William Pierce Shepard, who gave Pound additional hours of individual instruction. Another graduate of Hamilton described Shepard as "a man of prodigious learning. . . . If Pound had gone to the finest university he could not have had a better tutor than Shepard." Pound in turn helped Shepard's other students prep for exams. Pound was allowed to take the sophomore and junior French courses simultaneously and at graduation was awarded a French prize. He also flourished under "Schnitz [H.C.G.] Brandt, who was pleased," Pound later said, "that I did NOT want to be bothered with German prose and skipeed me to the poetry courses," for which he received eight credits. The *Cantos*, Pound said, "started in a talk with 'Bib,' " Joseph Darling Ibbotson, Professor of English Literature, Anglo-Saxon, and Hebrew, from whom Pound received nine credits. The 1905 *Hamiltonian* says that Ezra was " 'Bib's' pride." Both Shepard and Ibbotson became lifelong friends of their former student and visited him as often as possible in Europe.

On October 3, 1905, Pound was admitted as a "Regular Student" at the University in the Graduate School Department of Philosophy. He enrolled for every course offered by the Department of Romanics: Old Spanish, Spanish Drama, Spanish Literature, Old French, Provençal, Italian (Petrarch), plus three credits of Special Work (the courses were each only one credit), all taught by Professor Hugo Albert Rennert. Pound's other teacher that year was Walton Brooks McDaniel, whose Latin Pro-seminary, which counted three credits, Pound was delighted to take because of pleasant memories of four undergraduate courses with McDaniel.* On the occasion of his 100th birthday in 1971, Mr. McDaniel recalled for the *Harvard Alumni Bulletin* that he had been "challenged by Pound's exuberance and brilliance."

In every way the year 1905–1906 appears to have been successful for Pound. He had the companionship of Billy, who had grown up in a household where Spanish and French were daily languages, and of Hilda Doolittle, a freshman at Bryn Mawr College. On January 9, 1906, Pound was "accepted by the Executive Committee as a candidate for the degree A.M." After the written examinations for Rennert and McDaniel, he sailed for Madrid on a spring Saturday (either April 28 or May 5) for research in libraries. Pound therefore missed the 1906 commencement, but Dean Child recorded in Pound's *Record Book:* "June 13th, 1906. To Whom It May Concern: This is to certify that Ezra Weston Pound received the degree of Master of Arts at Commencement, 1906."

An entry in Pound's *Record Book* dated September 29, 1906, says: "Mr. Ezra Weston Pound was accepted by the Executive Committee as a candidate for the degree Ph.D. when appointed [Harrison] Fellow

---

*A more complete list of Pound's readings for Romanics and Latin is given in the "Notes" at the end of this chapter.

22

Reading Room of the University Library, c. 1899.

Graduate Seminar Room, University Library (Photograph courtesy of University Archives).

for 1906–1907." Pound again enrolled for every course taught by Professor Rennert (except Portuguese, which he may have studied the previous year as part of his Special Work): Poets, Dante, *Poema de Fernan Gonzalez*, Spanish Drama, *Chanson de Roland*, Provençal. He also registered for French Phonetics taught by the department's new assistant professor, J.P.W. Crawford, Ph.D. '06.

Having exhausted the offerings of Romanics, Pound turned to the English Department. In 1906–1907, only seven graduate courses of one term each were offered: Felix Schelling's two courses covering English drama from the beginning to Dryden, Clarence Griffin Child's Chaucer, Josiah Penniman's English Literary Criticism, Cornelius Weygandt's Contemporary Poetry, Arthur Hobson Quinn's Theory and History of English Versification, and a seminar in Current Criticism taught by the department. Pound enrolled for all of these but Quinn's English Versification. Both Quinn's course, second term, and Penniman's course, first term, conflicted in time with Crawford's course. Probably Crawford changed the time of French phonetics, and Pound chose not to take Quinn's course because he had advanced far beyond the professor's understanding of the subject.

The second year of graduate work promised to be as successful as the first. Felix Schelling, Chairman of the English Department, seems to have been Pound's graduate advisor (or so the letter of January 1907 in Paige's edition of Pound's letters indicates). The proposed dissertation on Lope de Vega should have pleased Rennert, who had written a biography of the dramatist. French phonetics would have been child's play for the poet's ear and eye. As for Chaucer, Pound's studies with Ibbotson would have prepared him superbly, and he particularly liked the Chaucer professor, Dean Child, who was, he told Schelling in 1916, "an ideal companion for the young barbarian," and to Professor Robert E. Spiller he wrote in 1946: "Child was ? is the man with real love of letters & true flair." The 1906 college yearbook reports: "The breezy Child who talks in chunks for all the world like Alfred Jingle's fragmentary conversation, provided a continuous vaudeville. English Literature was vigorously slapsticked by this versatile pedagogical end-man, who told fresh and entertaining jokes and at the same time offered inspiration for the best in art and letters." Weygandt's Contemporary Poetry was evidently the "odd sort of post-graduate course" that Pound remembered as the one where he "first heard of [Lionel] Johnson. . . . One was drunk with 'Celticism,' and with Dowson's 'Cynara,' and with one of two poems of Symons." Pound had prepared for Current Criticism by contributing three scholarly essays to Philadelphia *Book News Monthly* in September and October of 1906, his first publications in prose. Pound was not, however, prepared for Josiah Penniman, an authority on Dennis, Rymer, and Collier, and Dean of the College Faculty. He "flunked" Penniman's course.

Pound's written comments about the failed course sound merely factual and regretful, and are neither a hasty judgment nor a public one. One in "How to Read" (1929): "Those professors who regarded their 'subject' as a drill manual rose most rapidly to positions of executive responsibility (one case is now a provost)." Penniman became Provost in 1923 and remained, as described in the statutes, "the senior educational officer of the University" until 1939. In a separate paragraph after the above, Pound remarks, "One was asked to remember what some critic (deceased) had said, scarcely to consider whether his views were still valid, or ever had been very intelligent." In an unpublished autobiographical note written in 1930, Pound is more specific: "In 1907 I achieved the distinction of being the only student flunked in J.P.'s course in the history of literary criticism. So far as I know I was the only student who was making any attempt to understand the subject of literary criticism and the only student with

Commencement Procession: Faculty assembling in front of College Hall.

Commencement Procession: Students on Broad Street approaching the Academy of Music, where the awarding of degrees took place in 1906.

any interest in the subject." That Pound tried to understand the subject, and succeeded, became a matter of record outside the University. T. S. Eliot judged Pound's own literary criticism to be "the *least dispensable* body of critical writing in our time."

Pound's *Record Book* shows only Professor Rennert's signatures for the year 1906–1907 ("This book must be submitted to every instructor at the end of the year.") It is unlikely that Pound failed all the other courses or any of them. Rather, he seems to have recognized the critical contretemps with Penniman as a sign of determined opposition to the kind of academic career he had imagined for himself. He was right. The Harrison Fellowship he had intended to use to complete his thesis was not renewed, which would have been customary. It was a Hamilton professor, "Bib" Ibbotson, who helped him obtain a job for the following year. The University had withdrawn its support of him, permanently as it turned out.

26

JOSIAH HARMAR PENNIMAN, 1868–1941.
Professor of English. Dean of Faculty, 1897–1909; Vice-provost, 1911–1920; Acting Provost, 1920–1923; Provost, 1923–1939 (Photograph from *The Record of the Class of Nineteen Hundred and Six*).

In March 1920 Homer Pound, whom his son affectionately described as "the naivest man who ever possessed sound sense," called on Dr. Schelling to ask whether a Ph.D. or an honorary degree might be given to his son. In 1920 Ezra was preparing to leave London and was considering all possibilities, even the study of medicine. He did not have enough money for medical school. He did not have a job. His father tried to help by reopening the case of the purloined Ph.D. It was not an unreasonable request. If Pound failed no course other than Penniman's, he had a total of twenty-four hours of credit, the required number for the Ph.D. *The Spirit of Romance* (1910) meets the special requirements of a doctoral dissertation. Among Pound's many contributions to literature and scholarship by 1919 were sixteen other books and hundreds of essays. Furthermore, Dr. Schelling—Class Poet of 1881; LL.B., 1883; A.M. (English), 1885—might have been expected to be sympathetic. Franklin and Marshall College had given him a Ph.D. in 1898 although he had not attended the college. The University had given him two honorary degrees, an Litt.D. in 1903 and an LL.D. in 1909.

27

After the meeting with Homer Pound, Professor Schelling dutifully wrote to at least two persons informing them of the request and offering his opinion. To Professor Rennert, Schelling wrote on March 19, 1920: "I had a call from Mr. Pound, the father of Ezra, yesterday, who, inspired by a letter from his son, came out to ask whether we could not give the Ph.D., which he has not earned, to his son now. Young Mr. Pound has a certain repute in the new poetry, which I have reason to believe is very considerable, but I do not remember him as anything but an idle student. . . ." To Wharton Barker, a prominent trustee (and candidate for President of the United States in 1900 on the Populist Party ticket), Schelling wrote on March 30, 1920: "I may say concerning Mr. Pound that I have met him once or twice in London since he left us. I remember him as a remarkably idle student, absolutely evading all work to such an extent that I recall saying to him, 'Mr. Pound, you are either a humbug or a genius.' . . . The question of an honorary degree for Mr. Pound upon the basis of his eccentric and often very clever verse is quite another matter and one which I hardly feel that I am competent to raise."

"Lord, what would they say / Should their Catullus walk that way!" Yeats exclaims in "The Scholars." A remarkably idle student? Evading all work? I hardly feel that I am competent? In 1917 (8 January) Pound had received a letter from Schelling that unknowingly answered Yeats's question (and which Pound probably showed to Yeats because the Irish poet had first published "The Scholars" in an

28

anthology edited by Pound in 1915). Schelling's letter, in response
to Pound's suggestion (17 November 1916) that the University give a
fellowship for creative ability, not for himself but for others, said: "The
University is not here for the unusual man."

That is Pound's accurate summary of Schelling's response, and
it is certainly a more plausible explanation of the University's hostility
toward Pound than the 1920 statements that he had been an idle
student. What Felix Schelling more fully wrote to Ezra Pound in 1917
is quoted by Schelling himself in an essay he wrote for *The General
Magazine and Historical Chronicle* (January 1938):

I have often wished that I might have the personal power to send two types
of men away from the university. One is the extraordinary man, the one in a
thousand, who usually takes himself away as you did. The others are the
stragglers who loaf along at the end of the procession. They, too, are better
out of it. College, after all, is for mediocrity and as we are overweighted with
mediocrity in the world, there is justification for it.

(H.D. summed it up differently, in an autobiographical novel written in 1927 and published in 1981: "As Nellie says, 'West Philadelphia sustains our mediocrities.' ") Schelling in 1938, in retirement after forty-five years as head of the English Department, quotes his earlier self in order to wonder whether his attitude had been "wholly wise." His essay concludes that, after all, "There is something to be said for Mr. Pound's proposition involving the encouragement, even in academic circles, for the creative spirit," for it might benefit that person "who would fain be, if he could, not merely a doctor, not only a banker, not alone a pettifogger in the law or in anything else, but a cultivated man as well, one of those among us who may yet be of the saving remnant in this most material world, one of the few who may still have visions and dream dreams."

29

The last year of Pound's graduate work, Williams was fully occupied in a grueling internship at the old French Hospital in New York, unable even to attend Pound's twenty-first birthday celebration. His presence during the year would have been a steadying influence on Ol' Ez's precocity. Williams had avoided academic difficulties, but his advice to his sons when they entered college indicates that he comprehended Pound's academic problem. In a letter to his eldest son, Williams cautions that college is a place where you must "work willingly along with the forces that be—at least while you are still a student. Later on," Williams promises, "you can be the wildest revolutionary in any field you choose and I for one will back you to the end of my resources."

Don't think I don't realize that college is an extremely limited field of effort. . . . It is a stronghold of privilege, of dyed in the wool conservatism, even of bought and paid for conservatism, but all you have to do is *realize* that, then work for what you can get out of it. Sure, there are bastards among your very teachers, but give them the best you have.
(To William Eric Williams, 24 October 1935)

Pound would have appreciated such counsel, but in fact he must have been too noticeable, too "extraordinary," to assume a protective conformity. Pound did try to give his teachers his best and he was no "revolutionary" at this time, except in the scope and intensity of his study. (Guy Davenport quotes him as saying, "We studied until we dropped.") The real conflict was that Pound was committed to excellence and, like Henry Adams, he could never accept the prevailing opinion that the limited resources of the system and the limited energies of the professors had to be directed *solely* toward preparing the great majority of students for a prosaic world or that scholarly research had to be conducted along lines already carefully laid out. "Being more live than they, more full of flames and voices" (Canto VII), Pound believed that "Man reading shd. be man intensely alive. The book shd. be a ball of light in one's hand." He believed that "original research" meant just that. The professors of literature, on the other hand, did not understand that Pound wanted to help them with their burdens; that he wanted to find the best in the past and pass it on, make it new; that he would have been pleased if they had said, "A chap with a mind like THAT! the fellow is one of us. One of US." The professors, on behalf of the comfortable status quo, must have reached some tacit agreement that this fellow—this young Diogenes (and Dionysus) with a radiant book in his hand—must remain an outsider, and to protect themselves from his disruptive light, some of them attacked, as Williams observed:

I watched Ezra Pound go through college. I was in the Medical School without academic degree, studying physics, chemistry, anatomy, physiology, pathology. I watched Ezra—by direct effect—suffering the thrusts of his professors. That was the difference between us.
(*The Little Review,* May 1929)

Williams found his medical studies exhilarating and demanding, as his letters to his brother Edgar attest. Pennsylvania's is the oldest medical school (1765) in the nation and at the time of Williams' attendance ranked at or near the top in providing a practical education for the general practitioner, with study in a speciality to be pursued after obtaining the M.D. degree. The schedules for the medical students show class or laboratory from nine to five during the week and from nine to at least noon on most Saturdays. Rigorously organized on the case system, with individual instruction and supervised hospital duty after a certain point, the course of study challenged Williams to do his best, and his grades shot up from the undistinguished record he had made at Horace Mann. During the first year, when he was taking the combined dental and medical course, he may have been sixth in his class: "In my freshman year of college although I was youngest in the class of one hundred and twenty-six I was rated sixth at the finish of the year. Next year I would be first! My interest vanished at that point." Not his interest in the work, but his interest in class rank. The first year credits, when he transferred to the medical course alone, placed him only in the top quarter of the class, and for the other three years, he maintained an average a point or two below the top quarter. His lowest average occurred, understandably, in 1905, the year he traveled with the fencing team and the Mask and Wig play *Mr. Hamlet of Denmark.*

The only sign of possible rebellion by Williams in medical school is one grade much lower than any of his other grades, for a course called Materica Medica and Pharmacy. The textbook required was Mann on Prescription Writing, and one aspect of the course is described somewhat like a college writing course: ". . . supposititious cases are taken and the student required to write a prescription suiting the case, which is criticized, and the prescription returned to the student so that he may see wherein are the mistakes." Anyone who has examined the WCW collections at Buffalo or Yale knows that Williams' prescription pads might contain anything from a poem or part of a novel or play to a letter to a friend. Faced in class with a blank prescription and a "supposititious case," Williams may not have kept the possibilities firmly in check. However, he made grades of 90 or above in General Chemistry, Physiology, Physical Diagnosis, Obstetrics, Ophthalmology, Operative Surgery, and Hygiene.

One of his professors he singled out for praise:

In medical school proper, apart from the wonders of embryology, histology and anatomy, my one enthusiasm was for Professor Spiller in neurology. I loved the man with his big round head and the prominent temporal arteries like twin snakes upon his temples. Had I felt myself stable enough, nothing would have pleased me more than to have gone in then and there for neurology. Treatment at that time was almost nil. Diagnosis was Spiller's forte.

(When Williams spoke at the University in 1952, he wrote afterwards: "I can't get over meeting and talking with my old favorite Dr. Spiller's son [Robert E. Spiller, Professor of American Literature]. . . . The whole past became alive again.") William Gibson Spiller, says George Corner's history of the medical school, "delivered lucid analytic lectures on neurologic diagnosis, gracing that most involved subject with frequent quotations from Shakespeare." It is safe to say that Williams' criticisms of education were not caused by his own experiences in medical school but by his observations of what had happened to others differently situated, especially his friend Ezra Pound.

In and out of class the number of activities Williams engaged in suggest self-discipline and self-assurance and belie the picture he later presented of himself as "a crazy, timid kid . . . mooney, irritable . . . finicky." *The 'Scope* of 1906, of which he was art editor, called him one of the "most versatile" students of '06. His interest in writing and painting he shared not only with Ezra and Hilda and his brother Edgar but also with another close and lasting friend, Charles Demuth, whom he saw daily at meals at Mrs. Adelaide K. Chain's boarding

Surgical Clinic of Dr. J. William White (From *The 'Scope*, 1906).

Close-up of seat "64" left of the clock, occupied by William Carlos Williams.

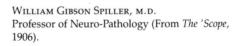

William Gibson Spiller, M.D.
Professor of Neuro-Pathology (From *The 'Scope*, 1906).

house at 3615 Locust Street. Demuth, an art student first at Drexel
and then at the Pennsylvania Academy of the Fine Arts, enjoyed walking
about the streets of West Philadelphia with Carlos (as Charley always
called Billy).*

On the campus then were fragrant, cloistered walkways, vast
expanses of lawn, dedicated trees (along Hamilton Walk twenty-eight
trees each wore a brass tablet with the name of an eminent
Pennsylvanian), and the nearby Schuylkill River was so clean that it
was piped "in its original state" to the University for drinking water
(according to *The Public Ledger*) until a typhoid epidemic at Cornell
in 1903 caused enough worry that a filtering system was installed. In
the Botanic Gardens the botanists nurtured plants of every kind from
common milkweeds, great mulleins, and skunk cabbages to rare
orchids, a monkey puzzle tree, a flowering Judas tree, a nepenthe
plant. For his last three years of medical school, Billy's dormitory room
(318 Joseph Leidy) looked out over Hamilton Walk to the gardens,
a vista he much preferred to his first year's view from 303 Brooks of
the grassy Triangle where Class Day ceremonies and alumni drinking
parties were held and where students sat around on warm evenings
singing of Lydia Pinkham's Vegetable Compound reputed to cure
all female ills. Ol' Ez became rather closely acquainted with the lovely
lotus and lily pond in the gardens when he was thrown into it for
intruding, a mere sophomore, on a senior class ceremony and again
when he wore red and blue socks to class. "It is recorded that he
cursed his classmates in seven languages and returned the next day
wearing the offending socks." The classmates nicknamed him "Lilly"
Pound, according to *The Record of the Class of Nineteen Hundred and Five*:
"Junior year. . . . great changes happened. 'Lilly' Pound could not
bear our teasing any longer and had left us naughty boys."

Williams and Pound were both long distance walkers, and they
liked most of all to visit the University's Astronomical Observatory,
situated two miles beyond the city limits in Upper Darby, where Hilda
Doolittle's father was the astronomer in residence. There were also
the still rural surroundings of the Pound family home in Wyncote
and the Williams home in Rutherford, but Upper Darby, easy to reach
by cross-country trolley, was the place of "really lyrical" fields and

33

*A trace of this close friendship survives at the university in Robert Indiana's felt
construction *Number Five*, which hangs in the lobby of the Annenberg Theater. Indiana's
design is derived from Demuth's famous "poster portrait" *I Saw the Figure Five in Gold
(Homage to William Carlos Williams)* in the Metropolitan Museum of Art, New York, the
Alfred Stieglitz Collection.

Lily Pond in the Botanic Gardens (Photograph by George Nitzsche, 1906).

woods and streams, which tempted them to pastoral thoughts that were later transformed into poems. Billy wrote an "Ode on a Skunk Cabbage" for Hilda and was at work on a long Keatsian poem, "poetically descriptive of nature, trees, for the most part, 'forests,' strange forests." Ezra collected twenty-three of his poems, filled with Ovidian trees and nymphs, written from 1905 to 1907, into a small, handmade volume he titled *Hilda's Book.*

One imagines the conversation of the two young men during their long walks as being a little like Coleridge's and Wordsworth's as they tramped around Nether Stowey or Quantock's airy ridge. Pound, like Coleridge two years younger than his friend William, was the dazzling theorist about poetry who dominated the conversation but not the mind of his companion, who was quieter, slower in temperament, glad to listen and to respond occasionally, a "catalytic," said Pound, "in whose presence some sort of modification would take place." Wordsworth wanted poems to use "the language of real life" about the "things of every day," and Coleridge was interested in "these shadows of Imagination" that require a "willing suspension of disbelief." Just so, Billy and Ezra had "a chronic argument going on," according to Williams, "over which was the proper objective for the writer, caviar or bread."

Hamilton Walk from the West (Photograph by George Nitzsche, 1906).

Williams held out for bread, for things of every day, and Pound for caviar, but each learned the other's attitude toward nature and poems and eventually made use of it, Williams especially in *Paterson* where nature is metamorphosed into people, and Pound especially in *The Pisan Cantos* where "When the mind swings by a grass blade / an ant's forefoot shall save you, / the clover leaf smells and tastes as its flower,"

> *and as for the solidity of the white oxen in all this*
> *perhaps only Dr Williams (Bill Carlos)*
> *will understand its importance,*
> *its benediction. He wd/ have put in the cart.*

If the friendship of Williams and Pound now appears to have been destined, inevitable, like the meeting of Wordsworth and Coleridge, one might consider, as Henry Adams does in *The Education*, that "Life offers perhaps only a score of possible companions, and it is mere chance whether they meet as early as school or college, but it is more than a chance that boys brought up together under like conditions have nothing to give each other." Billy and Ezra were lucky on both chances, and their friendship, later severely tested, never

The University's Flower
Astronomical Observatory in
Upper Darby, Pennsylvania
(Photograph by George
Nitzsche, 1906).

lost the perceptive honesty and loyalty of a relationship established
during a crucial period of their lives, the awkward age when each
was struggling for identity, searching for an uncounterfeitable form.
Billy in a very early sonnet described "The Bewilderment of Youth":

> *And all his purpose stands amazed, unknit*
> *By wonder, knowing naught of where or why,*
> *Compassed about with fresh variety*
> *Where'er his chancing eager looks may flit.*

At such a time, in Ezra's succinct words from an early autobiographical
poem,

> *Certain things really do matter*
> *Love and the comfort of friendship.*

Their friendship could not save them from all harm, but it did give
them courage when "they were men of no fortune and with a name to
come" and hearten them for the poet's journey into the unknown.
When Williams died, Pound sent a telegram to Florence Williams that
said, "He bore with me sixty years. I shall never find another poet
friend like him."

II. MOMENTS IN TIME

In 1905 when Henry James visited "the clustered palestra of the University of Pennsylvania" for an hour one January afternoon, Billy Williams may have rushed past the great domed head and observant eyes on his way to fencing practice in the brand-new gymnasium.

It is a possible small scene for the "marvelous silent film" suggested by Hugh Kenner: The slender figure of the twenty-two-year-old lad passes quickly by the imposing presence of the Master, who is escorted by Dr. S. Weir Mitchell, Philadelphia writer and physician. What is the director to do about the missing front tooth? On this visit to Philadelphia, Henry James lost an upper front tooth. "I look like a 'fright,' " he told his brother William, "but I am cynical, indifferent, desperate—I don't mind it." Should the movie show the Master smiling? Can a man be perceived as a "serious artist" with a missing front tooth, or must James look like his portrait painted a few years later by John Singer Sargent?

No doubt the director would choose not to confuse the scene with *accident,* the *essence* being the brief juxtaposition of the hopeful ephebe with the obstinate finality of the genius of the international artist, the middle of the extreme represented by a writer of local reputation. Furthermore, to establish a source of reliable observation of the character of the University in 1905, it is enough to show Henry James "drinking the tone of things."

In the fencing class the young medical student, who has Spanish eyes and cheekbones like the young Picasso, makes a French thrust, as "in Paris in 1898." No, no, no, gestures the fencing coach, Signor Leonardo Terrone, and shows him the Italian way, "which is somewhat different." Signor Terrone's gestures concern the technique of fencing, but Henry James would have seen another of "the clamorous signs of a hungry social growth" that were as visible to him in 1905 "everywhere in the United States" as "chalk marks on the demonstrative American blackboard."

These clamorous signs clashed with Philadelphia, which did not in 1905 "bristle," which was not "vulgar," because it possessed "the charming old pink and drab heritage of the great time." Philadelphia was "settled and confirmed and content," "of all goodly villages, the very goodliest, probably, in the world." Philadelphia "wasn't a place, but a state of consanguinity, which is an absolute final condition. . . . her imagination was at peace." Would not a great and cosmopolitan university, one that had been founded by a man with a sense of "life the most positive, most human and most miscellaneous," rise above

37

38

WILLIAM CARLOS WILLIAMS as Varsity fencer, 1905 (From *The 'Scope*, 1906).

this provincial serenity? The question is not directly posed by James, but he answers it. He denies himself the "luxury" of deciding whether the "aesthetic note" was muffled or shrill," whether the air was "of old Greece" or of some "fine emphasis of modernism." He notes instead that his "palestra hour . . . fell . . . straight into what [he] had conceived of the Philadelphia scheme, the happy family given up, though quite on 'family' lines, to all the immediate beguilements and activities, the art in particular of cultivating, with such gaiety as might be, a brave civic blindness." Pound a dozen years later, having had time to think about his rejection by this environment, linked James's report of his 1905 visit *(The American Scene)* with "The Constitution," both essential reading, Pound said, for the "serious American."

During the first half of 1905 Pound was studying at Hamilton College. He had already taken lessons from Signor Terrone, and he claimed long afterwards he had learned more from the Master of Fence than from any other teacher at Penn. However, as Williams insists that Ol' Ez was not a precocious fencer, a scene of Pound fencing might be uncertain in its effect. Can a man be perceived as a "serious artist" if his fencing technique is imperfect? (Pound teaching Yeats to fence? Could that scene be made plausible?) The director would probably choose a different introduction to Ezra, such as the "Hallowe'en fancy dress party in Philadelphia" in 1901.

A college freshman who had turned sixteen the day before Halloween, Ezra wore a green robe, a souvenir of his visit to Tunis in 1898. (Flashback to Ezra in Tunis in 1898 with his great-aunt-in-law, the rich, wide-bodied one who had danced with President Grant and had shaken hands with President Cleveland.) At the party Hilda Doolittle notices the Tunisian robe, the "Gozzoli bronze-gold hair," "his green eyes," "his curious beauty that made people hate him." She is three weeks into her fifteenth year, tall, willowy, with ash-blonde hair and blue-grey eyes, an "unquestioned" beauty with "a young girl's giggle and shrug." "Intense, so oddly intense," the two "so intense" teenagers dance together.

Moments in time. It is easy to imagine this dancing scene in vibrant color, a multiple sound track of music enveloping the surround, the two young people speaking. But historically it was the turn of the century, every art in a stage of transition, moving pictures in their infancy. Should this movie be a compendium of cinematic development and styles? This scene in black and white with the slightly jerky movement? The boy with golden hair was not a graceful dancer. "One would dance with him for what he might say." Silent captions, then, with the piano player doing his best? *She:* You look like someone in the Riccardi frescoes. *He:* Yes? I've seen them in the Medici Palace. *She:* I mean you have Gozzoli bronze-gold hair. It's in the Famous Painters' Volume. *He:* I make five friends for my hair, for one for myself. *She:* Who are you? *He:* Who are you, Bellissima?

Teenagers speaking such lines? Shakespeare's Romeo and Juliet speak sonnets at their first meeting, also at a masked ball. Another scene remembered by H.D., this one difficult to mime: Ezra reads William Morris to Hilda "in a field under a very Preraphaelite apple tree." Ezra's reading of "Three red roses across the moon" and *"Ah, qu'elle est belle, la Merguerite"* becomes "at the last repetition an Iroquois battle cry."

Wholesome high spirits. An easier scene to do comes from Williams' memory: Together he and Hilda read *Aucassin and Nicolette.* Phrases from the old romance flash on the screen while Billy must act the part of a young man struggling to pretend that Hilda "is just a good guy." It is so obvious that Ezra is "wonderfully in love with her" that Billy does not want to betray him. The eternal triangle beloved of plot makers.

Hilda Doolittle (H.D.),
1886–1961 (Photograph
courtesy of Perdita Schaffner
and New Directions
Publishing Corporation).

These three young people knew a great deal about plots and role playing. Shakespeare's Rosalind: A boy actor plays the part of a girl disguised as a boy who then pretends to act the part of a girl. Hilda gave that role to Billy to perform while she improvised the part of simple Celia. A good exercise for the imaginative, androgynous mind.

Hilda should have been Artemis or a tree at the great May Day ceremonies at Bryn Mawr College in 1906 but instead played the closest part available to a freshman, an archer in Robin Hood's Merry Band. Billy was her guest at the festival rites. Ezra was either sitting for an exam under Professor Rennert or was on his way to Europe for research on his doctoral dissertation. Some time later both Williams and H.D. wondered whether the Marianne Moore who wrote poems had been present on that memorable day. She had. Her photograph shows her "with her red hair piled high and dressed in green brocade" as a Renaissance lady-in-waiting.

Shakespeare's Polonius as reconceived for the Mask and Wig musical comedy, *Mr. Hamlet of Denmark:* An ancient busybody pronounces sententious non sequiturs and politic moralizings at a

MARIANNE CRAIG MOORE, 1887–
1972. Bryn Mawr College May
Day, 1906 (Photograph courtesy
of Rosenbach Museum & Library
and Clive E. Driver, Literary
Executor of the Estate of
Marianne C. Moore).

bizarre international court crowded with singers and dancers. Billy
would have preferred to sing and dance, but it was an honor to be
chosen for a speaking part. He studied his lines and, in the tradition
of the Elizabethan clown, added his own. At the Washington
performance he "brought the house down" by asking King Claudius
if he had enjoyed his "bear hunt in the Ozarks," or, according to
another version, "Has your Majesty been moose hunting?" One
memory has President Theodore Roosevelt in the audience, the other
does not, but what mattered to Billy was that "even the cast broke
into a roar" of laughter. Back in Philadelphia five days after the
Washington triumph, the cast assembled (May 13, 1905) at the club
house on Quince Street to watch stars of bygone days burlesque "all
the weaker points" of the burlesque of Shakespeare. The parody of
the parody was called *A Ham to Let in Denmark, or Almost an Omelette.*
If Billy's studious application to show business yielded lessons beyond
a lasting suspicion of busybodies and an appreciation of the therapeutics
of comedy, it may have been the recognition that Ezra's study of
comparative values in literature could be pursued on many levels.

Cast members with speaking parts in Mask and Wig *Mr. Hamlet of Denmark*, 1905 (From *The Record of the Class of Nineteen Hundred and Five*).

Grill Room, Mask and Wig Club House, 310 Quince Street.

WILLIAM CARLOS WILLIAMS as Polonius in *Mr. Hamlet* (From *The 'Scope*, 1906).

The theatrical experience that seems to have affected the three young poets most powerfully was *Iphigenia among the Taurians*. Ezra rehearsed for months his part of a captive Greek maiden in the Chorus, which sang in Greek while moving in a circular dance—strophe, antistrophe—like "the astronomic dances of the Egyptians . . . from right to left, to express the astronomical motions from east to west, and reversing these movements to represent the motion of the planets." The Chorus sang about the situation enacted before them, which ends with two young men and one young woman—imagine the thoughts of our three poets—sailing away to Greece, leaving the barbarian Taurians forever. "An optimistic kind of play," says Richmond Lattimore, "by a poet who was no confirmed optimist."

43

From the "top balcony" of the Academy of Music, Billy watched E.W.L. Pound, who was on stage throughout the evening, except for a few lines at the beginning. Also in the Chorus was M.R. Van Cleve, who had brought Billy and Ezra together. At the time of the two performances, April 28 and 29, 1903, Ezra had not yet introduced Billy to Hilda, who, as the daughter of Professor Doolittle, presumably watched the play from a better seat than one in the top balcony. Available for the audience was a program containing the entire play in English prose from Flagg's edition in the College Series of Greek Authors, and the story had been repeatedly summarized in the newspapers, one of which called it "a modern plot [that] appeals to men to-day."

Every detail of this first American production of the play in Greek had been carefully considered. The costumes of the Greek characters resembled those on Greek vases studied by Professors William Lamberton and William Bates, and they had been constructed by the best costumer in Philadelphia, who had also made the "ancient Scythian" costumes for the barbarian characters. "The scenery was painted by New York artists" and included a Doric temple of Artemis "with some of its architectural members painted brilliantly with red and blue," as was "the custom of the ancient Greeks" (lest anyone should think that the University colors were displayed inappropriately). "For the purpose of preserving intact the rich variety of metres of Greek poetry, musical phrases with unusual numbers of bars" were composed by Dr. Hugh Archibald Clarke. A "modern orchestra" and the Orpheus and Saturday Night Clubs, both offstage, accompanied the Chorus, "no attempt being made to reproduce ancient music, because of the paucity of material throwing light thereon."

"A more select and cultivated audience never crowded the Academy than that which witnessed these performances." On both nights, the

Ezra Pound as Greek Maiden in Chorus of *Iphigenia among the Taurians,* 1903.

"distinguished persons, who had come from far and near" were a "brilliant" and "appreciative" audience. One reviewer noted that the chorus, which was "spectacular," received "frequent and prolonged applause." Another reviewer opined: "The chorus work is so far in advance of that of the previous Greek play [*The Archarnians,* presented at the University in 1886] that it may be regarded in the light of a distinct innovation."

However, an unusual opportunity was refused. The business manager of the play, George Nitzsche, wanted to record the performance in "a 'professional' moving picture." He persuaded Provost Harrison to provide a modest budget for erecting "a Greek Temple . . . in the open air." Students and cameramen were ready to make the movie when Dr. Lamberton appeared. "When he observed the movie

Chorus and Messenger of *Iphigenia among the Taurians*, 1903. EZRA POUND is the first chorus member on the left (Original photograph by Gilbert & Bacon in University Archives; copied 1970 by George M. Quay, Head of Photographic Department, University Museum).

cameras, he seemed shocked and exclaimed, 'Do you mean to take moving pictures of this beautiful production and have it hawked around "Nickelodeons" in all parts of the country?' " Nitzsche explained that he "had worked hard to convince the movie officials of the possibilities of this remarkable production of Euripides' Greek Classic." The Lubin Company had "rather reluctantly . . . agreed to take the risk," the Provost had approved, and it would be, Nitzsche insisted, "a splendid opportunity . . . of perpetuating a most notable . . . production." Professor Lamberton "simply replied, 'Well, you'll take it over my dead body.' "

So *Iphigenia* in Philadelphia was not contaminated by the vulgar new art of moving pictures. It would have been the first movie with a plot made in America. As it turned out, the movie of the year 1903 was *The Great Train Robbery,* a twelve-minute thriller made in New Jersey by Edwin S. Porter, and now shown continuously at Disney World with a dozen other early American movies. None of them is more suspenseful or sensational than the Greek play, which at the least would have been a curiosity as a silent movie (edited and with English subtitles) and at best perhaps something more. "The thought of what America would be like," later wrote one of the members of the Chorus, "If the Classics had a wide circulation / Troubles my sleep."

Professor Lamberton's brave deflection of the threat of moving pictures followed an earlier rejection. A New York journalist profiling the University in 1909 recalled that "The Muybridge photographs were . . . the starting point of the moving picture business. If the University of Pennsylvania had developed this idea it would have gained scientific fame and popular appreciation" and "be in receipt of an income of several millions a year. I understand, of course, that a university holds to the principle of Agassiz and has 'no time to make money.' Still it has to have money, and is not it as honorable to earn it as to beg it?"

The three young poets responded to *Iphigenia among the Taurians* in their individual ways. Hilda began to teach herself Greek and to write poems "straight as the Greek!" as Pound told Harriet Monroe, editor of *Poetry.* In 1915 H.D.'s translation into verse of "Choruses from Iphigeneia in Aulis" was published in London in *The Egoist.* Throughout the rest of her life, no matter how complex the materials of her poems, despite occult lore and bombs and flames and subconscious oceans where "Fish / move two ways" and "Indecipherable palimpsest scribbled over / with too many contradictory emotions" and other intricate, arcane, murderous, and divine things, she shaped the poems with the laconic straightness learned from her study of Greek.

For "the light of vers libre," Pound in 1913 referred "the earnest upholder of conventional imbecility . . . to the works of Euripides . . . or to almost any notable Greek chorus." The lustral waters of the Taurian *Iphigenia* may have given Pound the title *Lustra* (1916), even though his book offers a more general definition from a Latin dictionary. Although Greek was only one of Pound's many languages, and one he didn't use often and usually only in phrases and epithets, it remained a most special exclamatory language for his poems, the language in which he ecstatically invokes or evokes some aspect of divinity or essence or alludes to some experience of the highest intensity or significance.

Because of curricula restrictions, Greek had to be extracurricular for all three of these poets, and Williams always regretted that he had not studied Greek, although he admitted to James Laughlin in 1945 that he could "spell out . . . the actual words of the originals [Greek lyrics] and come somewhere near understanding them." In his old age Williams translated some Theocritus and Sappho, and, like Pound and H.D., he frequently used ancient Greece as a touchstone for the modern age, but with a different emphasis. When in 1908 Williams saw Isadora Duncan dance a series of scenes from Gluck's *Iphigenie en Aulis*, he wrote his brother that "It fairly made my hair stand on end, Bo, and best of all she is an American one of our own people and I tell you I feel doubly strengthened in my desire and my determination to accomplish my part in our wonderful future." Several of his early poems are openly Greek in spirit or allusion, but the longest one in *The Egoist* (March 1914) is a defiant announcement that he is "The Wanderer" of another country where his lustral water comes from the Passaic, "that filthy river."

Other scenes come to mind, which there is not space to present. As students, their minds filled with old and new romances and ancient myths and dramas, with Shakespeare and modern parodies and paintings by the Old Masters, Billy and Hilda and Ezra played at different roles each time they met and did their best to interpret other ones thrust upon them by circumstances. In their many volumes of the long years to come, traces of their youthful images of one another radiate with metamorphic energy.

Images are not necessarily an argument, but they do make a point instantaneously. Yes, "an intellectual and emotional complex in an instant of time." Yes, "No ideas but in things," or as Wallace Stevens says with an urbane bow to Williams: "Not Ideas about the Thing, but The Thing Itself. . . . It was like / A new knowledge of reality." Also, H.D.'s "People are in things, things are in people." The poets made these formulas after they had grown beyond their "precinematographic conscience." The last phrase is H.D.'s, for it was she who acquired the most practical knowledge of movie scenes, writing essays for *Close-up* about the cinema as art form, learning to use movie cameras to record the changing effects of light, and appearing as the heroine in a film she also helped to script: *Borderline* (1930), starring (fellow Philadelphian) Paul Robeson.

Even though Pound and Williams were not involved in actual movie making, and were much involved with the other visual arts, they learned to use cinematic techniques in their poems. Perhaps their development as poets making *moving* pictures was in advance of the cinematic masters. The poets concentrated on the art of presenting alive and in action the particular thing, the singular moment, the actual emotion, the exact voice, the quintessence of a changing presence, the verifiably precise details of a situation in flux. Their minds—centaur, satyr—leap in their long poems from one moment in spacetime to another, move from close-up to long-distance view and back, show fadeouts and dissolves, sharply juxtaposed visual and verbal contrasts, voices in harmony and cacophony, and metamorphosis at every speed.

So deeply autobiographical as well as cinematic are *Paterson* and the *Cantos* and the other long poems that one is tempted to think of the possibilities of a new art form of critical biography, a movie that would show the stunning visual and verbal achievements of the poems, moment by moment, line by line, and also show when these are equivalencies for or presentations of actual events in the poet's life. For what is a movie screen but a giant blackboard on which the marvels of technology can arrange presences with their voices, signs with their sounds, equations with their emotions—and show them moving into those surprising moments of mysterious energy when a constellation of details fuse suddenly into the image and phrase that gives "that sense of sudden growth, which we experience in the presence of the greatest works of art."

"We," observed H.D., "are set like a problem on a blackboard." On a huge blackboard—a triple screen of course—Noah Faitoute Paterson's "dreams walk about the city." In the other movie how swiftly the face of "a young boy loggy with vine-must," whose "god-sleight" is unrecognized by the men who want to take him off course, could change to the face of the young scholar-poet, and then change back

WILLIAM CARLOS WILLIAMS in his seventies (Photograph courtesy of Rare Books and Manuscripts Collection, Van Pelt Library, University of Pennsylvania).

to the son of Zeus. Although the Jefferson and Adams cantos are not
as cinematic as the other cantos, some riveting scenes lie in the fullness
of the material and in Pound's intention that the voices of Jefferson
and Adams speaking of their own times be heard over the strife of
his own era. If we think of the risks, the costs, the research, the mass
of detail, the process of selection, the effort required to make these
movies, we are merely reminded of the high daring and heroic
persistence of Williams and Pound.

What moments in time would end these movies? One might be
the doctor-poet at his electric typewriter, reduced by physical
infirmity to typing with one finger held steady by the other hand.
He types and retypes lines for the conclusion of Book Five of *Paterson*.
The lines present an image from Greek vases and the pre-tragic satyric
plays, an archaic, timeless image that has kept his heart devout. The
wise, high-stepping satyrs

> *dance to a measure*
> *contrapuntally,*
> *Satyrically, the tragic foot.*

The faces of the performers? Are they masked or do we see,
momentarily, the artists of Williams' imaginative life? (Asclepius
becomes Freud. Socrates' face fades into Allen Ginsberg's, Gertrude
Stein's into Picasso's, Shakespeare's into Joyce's, Dante's into
Pound's. That must be Martha Graham, contemporary mother of
dancers? No, it's J.L.? St. Francis changes into Einstein. The list of
performers would be very long.) Archaic Greeks dancing to the measure
of Williams' twentieth-century mind—everything in flux: Bless the
moment and continue the contrapuntal dance, the dithyramb linking
art and the natural world.

One of the final moments of the other movie could be the suffering,
beautiful old poet in Venice, captured by silence, accepting "Two mice
and a moth my guides." (A risky scene to be literal about, but as Pound
admired both the Chinese sages and Walt Disney, a solution might
be found.) Out of his deep fatigue and contrition, he drafts fragments
for an ending to the *Cantos:*

> *I have tried to write Paradise*
>
> *Do not move*
> *Let the wind speak*
> *that is paradise.*

EZRA POUND on the Ponte dell'Accademia, Venice, January 1968 (Photograph by Vittorugo Contino, Rome, Italy, by permission of Vittorugo Contino).

> *Let the Gods forgive what I*
> *have made*
> *Let those I love try to forgive*
> *what I have made.*

The young poet-scholar had quoted Plato's and Dante's descriptions of Paradise in *The Spirit of Romance*. He had performed prodigious deeds, traveled through hell, disclosed history past and present, learned that "A man's paradise is his good nature" and "caritas leads to serenity," to reach, at journey's end, this stillness, this meditation on love and forgiveness.

52

Notes

Documents, letters, photographs, and other information were provided by the following persons with charm and efficiency: Dr. Neda Westlake, Curator of Rare Books and Manuscripts, Van Pelt Library; Francis James Dallett, University Archivist, and Hamilton Elliott, Assistant University Archivist, University Archives; Dr. Patricia Cannon Willis, Curator of Marianne Moore Collection, Rosenbach Museum and Library; Leo Dolensky, Curator of Manuscripts and Archival Photographs, Bryn Mawr College Library; Karl C. Gay, Curator, and Beverly VanderKooy, The Poetry Collection, State University of New York at Buffalo; Stephen C. Jones, Beinecke Library, Yale University; Peggy Fox, New Directions Publishing Corporation. Professors Joel Conarroe and Peter Conn first located Pound's *Record Book*. William Eric Williams, M.D., helped in obtaining the transcript of his father's medical school grades. George E. Nitzsche's *University of Pennsylvania Illustrated* (Philadelphia: Published for the University, 1906) is the source of many photographs. Gregory M. Harvey, my husband, assisted in all stages of collecting and assembling the photographs.

The four sources at the University of Pound's reading in Romanics are: (1) The *Record Book* issued to Ezra Weston Pound on October 3, 1905, which was to be submitted to each of his instructors at the end of each year. "If the student has completed all work and passed all examinations to the satisfaction of the instructor, the latter will sign his name in the appropriate blank space" and will specify if "any special credit" is to be given for the course. "At the end of each term, the student must leave his book in the Dean's office to receive the countersignature of the Dean and to be transcribed to the official record." "When the student severs his connection with the University, this book will become his personal property." The *Record Book* is now in the University Archives. (2) Pound's *Record Sheet*, the permanent official transcript of grades, until recently in the Graduate Faculty Office, is now in the Archives. (3) *University of Pennsylvania Fasciculus of the Department of Philosophy (Graduate School) 1905– 1906* (Philadelphia: Printed for the University, April 1905); . . . *1906–1907* (June 1906). (4) *Catalogue of the University of Pennsylvania 1905– 1906* (Philadelphia: Printed for the University, December 1905); . . . *1906– 1907* (February 1907).

The *Fasciculus*, printed before registration each year, and the *Catalogue*, printed after registration, differ in the books they list for Pound's first year of graduate work in Romanics. Pound read much more than the required reading and he may have read everything listed; the *Record Book* and *Record Sheet* give the title of the course in the shortest possible form. The courses are listed below in the order and by the title given in the *Record Book* and *Sheet*.

OLD SPANISH
Fasciculus (April 1905): "Gorra, *Lingua e letteratura Spanguola delle origins* (Milano, 1898); Menéndez Pidal, *Gramatica historica Española* (Madrid, 1904)."
Catalogue (December 1905): *"Poema del Cid."* Pidal, as above.

SPANISH DRAMA
Fasciculus (April 1905): "The Spanish Drama and Theatre in the Period of Lope de Vega," no books named.
Catalogue (December 1905): Two separate courses are given: "The Spanish Drama: Tirso de Molina, *Don Gil de las Calzas Verdes;* Lope de Vega, *El Perro del Hortelano;* Moreto, *El Desdén con el Desdén."* "The Spanish Theatre in the Period of Lope de Vega," no books named.

SPANISH LITERATURE
Fasciculus (April 1905): "History of Spanish Literature: *La Littérature Espagnole,* par J. Fitzmaurice-Kelly, trad. de H.D. Davray (Paris, Armand Colin, 1904*)."*
Catalogue (December 1905): not listed.

SPECIAL WORK
This could have included "Ariosto, *L'Orlando Furioso* (ed. Romizi, Milano, 1900)," listed in the *Fasciculus* but not the *Catalogue* for 1905–1906, and "Portuguese: Foulché-Dilbosc [also as Delbosc]: *Abrégé de Grammaire Portugaise.* Selections from Camões, *Os Lusiadas,"* listed as a course the following year, and additional readings in Provençal. The three hours of Special Work, unusual in itself, would have allowed Professor Shepard's protégé to range widely in his reading under Professor Rennert's guidance.

OLD FRENCH
Fasciculus (April 1905*): "Octavian* (ed. Vollmöller)."
Catalogue (December 1905*): "Erec und Enid* (ed. Förster)."

PROVENÇAL
Fasciculus (April 1905): "Old Provençal: *Flamenca* (ed. Paul Meyer)."
Catalogue (December 1905): "Old Provençal: Appel, *Provenzalische Chrestomathie."*

ITALIAN: PETRARCH
Fasciculus (April 1905): not listed.
Catalogue (December 1905): "Petrarch (ed. Rijutino, Milan, 1901)."

For the year 1906–1907 the *Fasciculus* (June 1906) and the *Catalogue* (February 1907) agree, except for French Phonetics, which is listed only in the *Catalogue.* Pound was the only Harrison Fellow in Romanics during 1905–1907, and as the department was small, the courses offered in 1906–1907 must have been chosen with an awareness of his needs.

SICILIAN POETS *(Record Book)*   ITALIAN POETS *(Record Sheet)*
"Early Italian. The Sicilian Poets," no books named.

DANTE
"Italian: Dante, *La Vita Nuova.* Boccacio. Selections from the *Decamerone."*

POEMA DE FERNAN GONZALEZ
"Old Spanish: *Poema de Fernan Gonzalez.*"

SPANISH DRAMA
"The plays of Miguel Sanchez. Lope de Vega, *La Estrella de Sevilla.*"

CHANSON DE ROLAND
"Old French: *La Chanson de Roland* (ed. Stengel)."

PROVENÇAL
"Old Provençal: Selections from Appel, *Provenzalische Chrestomathie.*"

FRENCH PHONETICS
Catalogue only: "Old French Phonology," no books named.

Pound's readings in Latin at the University of Pennsylvania were as follows:

1901–1902
"LATIN 1
Livy, selections from Books I, XXI and XXII. Derivations of words. Syntax, with Latin Prose Composition." Instructor Walton Brooks McDaniel.

"LATIN 2
Horace. *Odes.* Metres and poetic usage." Professor Henry Gibbons.

1902–1903
"LATIN 432
Cicero, *De Senectute* or *De Amicitia;* Letters. Roman History and Antiquities." Gibbons. First Term.

"LATIN 439
Catullus and Tibullus. History of Roman Lyric and Elegiac Poetry." McDaniel. First Term.

"LATIN 434
Horace, *Satires and Epistles.*" McDaniel. Second Term.

"LATIN 441
Propertius and Ovid. History of Roman Lyric and Elegiac Poetry (continued)." McDaniel. Second Term.

"LATIN 443
Vergil and Lucretius. Expressive reading of Latin verse. Uses of Mythology in Literature and Art. History of Roman Epic and Didactic Poetry." Gibbons. Second Term.

1905–1906
LATIN PRO-SEMINARY (Three Courses)
Fasciculus (April 1905): "Introduction to the methods of textual and exegetical criticism. (In 1905–06, a special study of Martial.) Practice in using the philological periodicals,

and the books of reference that are most important to the teacher of Latin, as well as the dissertations and works that especially deal with epigrammatic literature."
Catalogue (December 1905): "Introduction to the methods of textual and exegetical criticism (a special study of Catullus, Martial, or Tacitus). . . . works that especially deal with the author chosen as the basis of the year's work." Assistant Professor McDaniel.

Scene sources for "Moments in Time"

HENRY JAMES AT THE CLUSTERED PALESTRA OF THE UNIVERSITY (1905)
Henry James, *The American Scene* (1907; rpt. Bloomington and London: Indiana University Press, 1968), with introduction, notes, chronology, and itinerary by Leon Edel. In his 1907 Preface Henry James says of his "gathered impressions" that he would "go to the stake for them." The accuracy of them is supported by E. Digby Baltzell, *Puritan Boston and Quaker Philadelphia* (New York: Free Press, Macmillan, 1979), who offers, as James predicted, evidence from statistical tables and charts and various helpful appendices.
Leon Edel, *Henry James, The Master, 1901– 1916* (Philadelphia and New York: Lippincott, 1972), p. 269. During this visit to Philadelphia, James also dined with Dr. J. William White, whose surgical clinic, attended by Williams, is shown in the photographs.
The Letters of Henry James, selected and ed., Percy Lubbock, Vol. II (London: Macmillan and Co., Ltd., 1920), p. 26.
"drinking the tone of things": Ezra Pound, Canto VII.
"serious American": Ezra Pound, "Henry James," *The Little Review* (August 1918), reprinted in *Literary Essays of Ezra Pound*, ed. with introd., T. S. Eliot (London: Faber and Faber; Norfolk, Conn.: New Directions, 1954), p. 327. Pound called *The American Scene* the "triumph of the author's long practice. A creation of America. A book no 'serious American' will neglect. . . . It is not enough to have perused 'The Constitution'. . . ."

FENCING (1905)
The Autobiography of William Carlos Williams (1951; rpt. New York: New Directions, 1967), pp. 40, 56, 65.
Group photograph of Varsity Fencing Team, 1905, including Williams, in *The Record of the Class of Nineteen Hundred and Five*, p. 219; dates and scores of meets of the Intercollegiate Fencing Association, p. 228.
Individual photograph of Williams in fencing uniform, *The 'Scope*, 1906, p. 150.
Folders labeled "Fencing," University Archives.
"The History of Fencing at Pennsylvania," *The Red and Blue* (May 1905), pp. 21–24.
"Physical Education at Pennsylvania," *The Red and Blue* (October 1905), pp. 2–3.
Pound said he had learned more from Signore Terrone than from anyone else at the University: Douglass MacPherson, "Ezra Pound of Wyncote," *Arts in Philadelphia* (May 1940), p. 28.
Pound and Yeats fencing in London: H.D., *End to Torment, A Memoir of Ezra Pound*, ed. M. King and N. H. Pearson (New York: New Directions, 1979), p. 5.

HALLOWEEN FANCY DRESS PARTY (1901)
"From H.D.," *The Cantos of Ezra Pound, Some Testimonies by Ernest Hemingway, Ford Madox Ford, T. S. Eliot, Hugh Walpole, Archibald MacLeish, James Joyce, and Others* (New York: Farrar & Rinehart, 1933), p. 17.

Flashback to Ezra in Tunis with great "Aunt Frank": Ezra Pound, *Indiscretions or, Une Revue De Deux Mondes* (Paris: Three Mountains Press, 1923); reprinted in Pound, *Pavannes and Divagations* (Norfolk, Conn.: New Directions, 1958), pp. 5, 6, 9, 18. Noel Stock, *The Life of Ezra Pound* (New York: Pantheon, 1970), pp. 10–11.

Pound's "curious beauty": H.D., *HERmione* (New York: New Directions, 1981), p. 65.

Hilda Doolittle's "unquestioned" beauty and "a young girl's giggle and shrug": Williams, *Autobiography*, p. 68.

"intense, so oddly intense": description by Pound's mother of the two teenagers as remembered by H.D., *HERmione*, p. 105.

"One would dance with him for what he might say": H.D., *End to Torment*, p. 3.

"Famous Painters' Volume": *HERmione*, p. 69.

"I make five friends for my hair": *End to Torment*, p. 3.

"Bellissima": *HERmione*, pp. 42, 64.

EZRA AND HILDA READING WILLIAM MORRIS

"From H.D.," *The Cantos of Ezra Pound, Some Testimonies*, p. 18.

BILLY AND HILDA READING *AUCASSIN AND NICOLETTE* (1906)

Aucassin and Nicolette, trans. Andrew Lang, on list for "Private Reading," Semester II, 1905–1906, for "Lectures on Literature" section of required freshman and sophomore English, Bryn Mawr College. List printed in *Marianne Moore Newsletter* (Spring 1981), pp. 15–16. Miss Moore and Miss Doolittle were members of the Bryn Mawr freshman class in 1905–1906. Miss Doolittle dropped out of Bryn Mawr during the fall semester of 1906 and did not return.

Williams, *Autobiography*, p. 52; Hilda "just a good guy," and Ezra "wonderfully in love," p. 68.

Compare H.D.'s memory of Pound and *Aucassin and Nicolette*, *HERmione*, p. 61.

BILLY AND HILDA AS ROSALIND AND CELIA (1905)

Letter to Edgar I. Williams, 12 April 1905, *The Selected Letters of William Carlos Williams*, ed. John C. Thirlwall (New York: McDowell, Obolensky, 1957), p. 9.

Compare H.D.'s memory of Pound and the Forest of Arden, *HERmione*, pp. 64–67.

BILLY IN MASK AND WIG *MR. HAMLET OF DENMARK* (1905)

Williams, *Autobiography*, p. 52.

Reed Whittemore, *William Carlos Williams, Poet from Jersey* (Boston: Houghton Mifflin, 1975), p. 41.

The Pennsylvanian, April 18, 1905, pp. 1–2.

The Red and Blue (May 1905), pp. 5–6, 17–20.

The Pennsylvania Punch Bowl, issue in honor of Mask and Wig (May 1905), pp. 4–7.

The Pennsylvanian, May 15, 1905, p. 1.

Individual photographs of stars of *Mr. Hamlet*, including Williams, *The Pennsylvanian*, April 15, 1905, p. 1. Two group photographs of cast of *Mr. Hamlet*, including Williams dressed as Polonius, *The Record of the Class of Nineteen Hundred and Five*, pp. 156–157. Individual photograph of Williams as Polonius, *The 'Scope*, 1906, p. 155. Group photograph of members of Mask and Wig, including Williams (picture evidently taken in 1906), *The Record of the Class of Nineteen Hundred and Seven*, p. 296.

BRYN MAWR COLLEGE MAY DAY (1906)

Williams, unpublished letter to Edgar I. Williams, May 6, 1906 (Poetry Collection, Buffalo); *Autobiography*, p. 52.

Folders of photographs, Bryn Mawr College Library: pictures of the Great Procession,

the May Poles and dancers, the various plays and other costumed groups, and the
spectators, who included gentlemen in silk top hats and ladies with parasols.

Pound's absence: Williams told his brother, Thursday, April 26, 1906, "Pound has been
given a fellowship so he sails for Madrid this Saturday to study some old books
there and get a line on the Spanish language. He's a bright cuss" (unpublished letter,
Buffalo). Pound's *Record Sheet* gives "April 30–May 1" as the dates for Pound's written
examinations with Rennert. Williams could have meant not April 28 but Saturday,
May 5, as Pound's departure date. More likely, the *Record Sheet* gives the official
dates of the examinations, but Pound had taken them earlier. Unable to attend the
celebration of spring, the scholar may have compensated by researching May Day.
See Pound's comments in *The Spirit of Romance* (1910) that "the feast of Venus Genetrix
. . . survived as May Day" (p. 18) and "Provençal song is never wholly disjunct
from pagan rites of May Day" (p. 90).

57

Patricia Willis, "Marianne Moore on May Day, 1906," with photograph, *Marianne Moore
Newsletter* (Spring 1981), p. 21.

GREEK PLAY (1903)

*TRANSLATION OF THE IPHIGENIA AMONG THE TAURIANS OF EURIPIDES AS PERFORMED AT THE ACADEMY
OF MUSIC IN PHILADELPHIA APRIL 28TH AND 29TH, 1903* . . . , program, with list of "Characters
of the Drama" and names of actors, given to the audience. Van Pelt Library.

"Music for Choruses of *Iphigenia among the Taurians* by H. A. Clarke, Mus.D.," University
Archives. The words sung by the Choruses are transliterated from Greek into our
alphabet.

The Pennsylvanian, May 27, 1902, p. 1

The Pennsylvanian, October 16, 1902, p. 2.

Old Penn Weekly Review, April 25, 1903, pp. 1–2, with Prize Poster for Greek Play, which
is in Greek at the top, in English at the bottom, with a stylized drawing of Iphigenia,
Orestes, and Pylades in the center.

The Pennsylvanian, April 28, 1903, p. 1, with group photograph of cast and chorus dressed
in suits and ties.

The Pennsylvanian, April 29, 1903, p. 1

The Pennsylvanian, April 30, 1903, p. 1

Old Penn Weekly Review, May 2, 1903, pp. 1–2, with photograph of Chorus in costume.

The Pennsylvania Punch Bowl, IV, 8 (May 1903), p. 4.

Richmond Lattimore, *Story Patterns in Greek Tragedy* (Ann Arbor: University of Michigan
Press, 1964), p. 59.

Euripides, *Iphigenia in Tauris*, trans. Richmond Lattimore (New York and London: Oxford
University Press, 1973).

One of the Scythian Guards was Eugene Stock McCartney (A.B. '06, Ph.D. '11), who
was still alive in 1946, a professor of Latin at the University of Michigan, according to
the University Archives; he therefore cannot be the subject of Pound's elegy "For
E. McC. That Was My Counter-blade under Leonardo Terrone" (1908), as is generally
supposed. With the assistance of Hamilton Elliott, I searched all available lists and
records of students, but we were unable to identify Pound's "counter-blade," who
indeed seems "Gone as a gust of breath."

One of the Herdsmen was Robert Lamberton, who saved Hilda Doolittle from drowning
in the ocean at a party he gave at the New Jersey shore in June 1906; this was the
same party at which Williams was almost struck by lightning (Williams, *Autobiography*,
pp. 69–70). Bob Lamberton, son of the professor of Greek who directed the *Iphigenia*,

Vol. XIX.—No. 152   PHILADELPHIA, TUESDAY, APRIL 28, 1903.

CAST AND CHORUS OF THE GREEK PLAY.

58

Cast and Chorus, *Iphigenia among the Taurians* (Photograph by Philadelphia *Evening Bulletin* and reprinted in the *Pennsylvanian*). EZRA POUND is in back row, second from left.

became Mayor of Philadelphia in 1940 and died the following year of amyotrophic lateral sclerosis, the rare nerve disease that afflicted Lou Gehrig. From St. Elizabeths Pound sent out queries concerning all his friends, including questions to Williams about Van Cleve and Lamberton.

IPHIGENIA IN PHILADELPHIA ALMOST BECOMES THE FIRST MOVIE WITH A PLOT

George E. Nitzsche, "Philadelphia: Birthplace of Moving Pictures," *Germantowne Crier*, 2, 1 (March 1950), pp. 12–14, 25–57.

John D. Mahoney, "Dr. Hugh A. Clarke, Musician," *The General Magazine and Historical Chronicle* (April 1941), pp. 357–358.

"If the Classics had a wide circulation": Ezra Pound, "Cantico del sole."

Eadweard Muybridge pictures: Edwin E. Slosson, "University of Pennsylvania," *The Independent*, New York, November 4, 1909, p. 1024. Reprinted in Slosson, *Great American Universities* (New York: Macmillan, 1910), p. 368.

H.D. AND MOVIES

"precinematographic conscience": *HERmione*, p. 60.

Hilda Doolittle to Viola Baxter Jordan, June 15, 1930 (unpublished letter, Yale).

H.D., *Tribute to Freud* (New York: Pantheon, 1956; Oxford: Carcanet Press, 1971; Boston: Godine, 1974).

Bryher, *The Heart to Artemis* (London: Collins, 1963), pp. 247–275.

Francis Wolle, *A Moravian Heritage* (Boulder, Colo.: Empire, 1972), p. 59.

Eric W. White, *Images of H.D.* (London: Enitharmon Press, 1976), p. 16.

The Globe-Times, Bethlehem, Pa., September 18, 1981, pp. D1, D6.

"We are set like a problem on a blackboard": *HERmione*, p. 83.

Part Two

Ezra Pound

3. Gathering the Limbs of Orpheus: The Subject of Pound's Homage to Sextus Propertius

Ronald Bush

I cannot leave
My honied thought
For the priest's cant,
Or statesman's rant.

If I refuse
My study for their politique,
Which at the best is trick,
The angry Muse
Puts confusion in my brain.
   —Ralph Waldo Emerson, "Ode
   Inscribed to W. H. Channing"

Of all sexual aberrations perhaps
the most curious is chastity.
   —Remy de Gourmont, The Natural
   Philosophy of Love

Neither expensive pyramids scraping the stars in their route.
Nor houses modelled upon that of Jove in East Elis,
Nor the monumental effigies of Mausolus,
           are a complete elucidation of death.

Homage to Sextus Propertius. A mistake. In 1921 Thomas Hardy advised Pound the poem should be called "Propertius Soliloquizes." And Pound agreed: "I ought—precisely—to have written 'Propertius soliloquizes'—turning the reader's attention to the reality of Propertius— but no—what I do is to borrow a term—aesthetic—a term of aesthetic *attitude* from a french musician, Debussy. . . . There are plenty of excuses—and no justification. . . . I imitate Browning. At a tender age London critics scare me out [of] frank and transparent imitation— even 'Propertius Soliloquizes' would sound too much like one of R.B.'s titles. . . . I ought to have concentrated on the subject—(I did so long as I forgot my existence for the sake of the lines)—and I tack on a title relating to the treatment. . . ."[1]

Perhaps Pound was thinking of Harriet Monroe, who on reading the suite for publication in *Poetry* had so little notion of its subject that she printed only its "left foot, knee, thigh and right ear."[2] Whatever the reasons for his second thoughts, he sat on Hardy's advice for seven years, and then it was too late. In 1928, Eliot wrote that "if the uninstructed reader [of the *Homage*] is not a classical scholar, he will make nothing of it," implying that the translation, not the subject, mattered.[3] Eliot's remarks began a tradition still alive in 1979, when Michael Alexander, in an otherwise exemplary reading, concluded that the *Homage* finally strikes us as "unfinished" because it is too "dependent on the Latin."[4] As for Pound, in 1945 he could still remember *Propertius* and Hardy's advice about it with the same wistful nostalgia for a promise nearly achieved that he extended to the great adventures of his life:

> *so that leaving America I brought with me $80*
> *and England a letter of Thomas Hardy's*
> *and Italy one eucalyptus pip*
> *from the salita that goes up from Rapallo*
> (Canto LXXX)

But let us assume, just for the moment, that time *can* be blocked out with the rubber and that the unfortunate title of the *Homage*, with all it implies, can be curtained off. Let us even, when it suits us, feel free to assume that its speaker is no more than one of Pound's fictions. (Did Pound not appropriate the Latin by the bias of his selections and the shading of his translation?) Approaching the wraith of "Propertius Soliloquizes," the question arises: "What *is* the subject that so absorbed Pound that he forgot his existence for the sake of giving it life?"

Fifty years after the poem's composition, its first full-length expositor asked himself a similar question and sought enlightenment in an aside. The *Homage*, Pound wrote, "presents certain emotions as vital to me in 1917, faced with the infinite and ineffable imbecility of the British Empire, as they were to Propertius some centuries earlier, when faced with the infinite and ineffable imbecility of the

Roman Empire."[5] In response, J. P. Sullivan suggested that the *Homage* calls up "the atmosphere of those [World War I] days, when the military stupidity of generals was equalled only by the militant stupidity of jingoists" to make a case for the social value of poetry. According to Sullivan, a classical scholar, Pound makes the case by silhouetting his work against Propertius': "Propertius' private themes [were] . . . love, passion and his mistress Cynthia. . . . Here he differs from Pound [whose] prime concern is art and artistic freedom."[6]

Nor was Sullivan entirely wrong. A poem that begins "Shades of Callimachus, Coan ghosts of Philetas / It is in your grove I would walk" does not shirk the subject of poetry, and one that speaks of "Tibet full of policemen" betrays more than a whiff of the age of Lloyd George. But in Pound's poem, Propertius soliloquizes about more than that. His eulogies for poetry, for one thing, are as much about love as verse and are ultimately about the energies that power both. And his complaints against imbecility indict more than war propaganda or Empire; their deepest protest is against the death-like state of modern existence, and they dwell at some length on the cold fact of death that lies past metaphor.[7] From his opening words Propertius moves among "shades" and "ghosts" and discovers, to borrow a phrase Pound uses elsewhere, that it is not enough to be alive; one must also be "full of flames and voices" (Canto VII).

To appreciate what the *Homage* affirms, though, one must first recognize Propertius' awareness of the darkness that surrounds him— an awareness that is as intense as it is understated. As Hardy perceived, the suite operates most vividly as a dramatic monologue. (Pound once called it one of his "major personae."[8]) Its life is in what Joyce, speaking of one of his own self-portraits, termed "the curve of an emotion,"[9] and the emotion in question has as much to do with death as with life. Consider the first section of the poem, in which Propertius speaks of Roman poetry and "the distentions of Empire." In the interstices of his address, where conscious concern shades into subconscious anxiety, his preoccupations are quite different. Defending his work, Propertius quips, "I shall have, doubtless, a boom after my funeral," and his preoccupation with funerals returns twice more before the section ends:

> *And I also among the later nephews of this city*
> > *shall have my dog's day,*
> *With no stone upon my contemptible sepulchre;*

> *Happy who are mentioned in my pamphlets,*

the songs shall be a fine tomb-stone over their beauty.
But against this?
Neither expensive pyramids scraping the stars in their route,
Nor houses modelled upon that of Jove in East Elis,
Nor the monumental effigies of Mausolus,
are a complete elucidation of death.

64 We find, in fact, that by the conclusion of the *Homage*'s opening movement, Propertius' imagination of death all but overwhelms his other concerns, revealing something about the ache that stung him into speech. ("To me," Pound wrote, "the short so-called dramatic lyric— at any rate the sort of thing I do—is the poetic part of a drama the rest of which (to me the prose part) is left to the reader's imagination. . . . I catch the character I happen to be interested in at the moment he interests me, usually a moment of song, self-analysis, or sudden understanding or revelation."[10])

Flame burns, rain sinks into the cracks
And they all go to rack ruin beneath the thud of the years.
Stands genius a deathless adornment,
a name not to be worn out with the years.

Nor does this tension between Propertius' anxious glance into the future and his defiant assertion of the power of genius diminish as the poem proceeds. Perversely, explaining how Pound refashioned his model, one reader tells us a great deal about what never changed. In the words of Mark Turner, although Pound de-emphasized the theme of death to give priority to his anti-Imperial satire, in the original Propertius "death gives love a boundary and an intensity, just as the wars of the Empire give death immediacy."[11] But Pound—precisely— does not de-emphasize the theme of death. It is apparent from his manuscripts, now at Yale, that the theme always held a prominent place in Pound's plans.[12] In this expository first section and throughout the finished *Homage*, Propertius' awareness of darkness recurs with remarkable insistence, appearing in the corners of his laughter and on the edges of his loveplay. (The emphases of a twentieth-century dramatic lyric are marked not by the pronouncements of a speaker but by his hesitations. To con the *Homage* without making that adjustment is to get everything backwards.) So in section III, an invitation from Cynthia leads Propertius to anticipate muggers on the road to her house, and the way he mocks his premonitions only makes them harder to dismiss. At first ironically and then with palpable seriousness he entertains the old saw that lovers are immune from harm, and—at poignant length—he decides against the common wisdom. Once again his utterance concludes with a presentment of the grave:

> *What if undertakers follow my track,*
> > *such a death is worth dying.*
> *She would bring frankincense and wreaths to my tomb,*
> > *She would sit like an ornament on my pyre.*
>
> *Gods' aid, let not my bones lie in a public location*
> *With crowds too assiduous in their crossing of it;*
> *For thus are tombs of lovers most desecrated.*
>
> *May a woody and sequestered place cover me with its foliage*
> *Or may I inter beneath the hummock*
> > *of some as yet uncatalogued sand;*
> *At any rate I shall not have my epitaph in a high road.*

Cynthia, it seems, will have to do without him for the night. But Propertius' worries are not over. In the logic of the *Homage,* efforts to avoid death only make the idea of living free of it harder to sustain. Having persuaded himself that it is better to live without love than to die for it, Propertius discovers confusions in his categories. In section IV, life without love is, unexpectedly, "discomfort," and Cynthia's projection of a future without her calls up an image that is at first grotesquely funny and then haunting. She imagines Propertius, once out of her protection, wooed by a nameless "other woman" who uses black magic to draw him toward the earth.[13] Latent in her words, a suggestion of how easily death infiltrates the unamplified life drives Propertius back to poetry and provokes the opening resolve of section V: "Now if ever it is time to cleanse Helicon." Poetry makes Propertius feel alive, but poetry is not enough. So, in the second division of the section, Propertius calls upon love as well as poetry to release him from the disquieting obligation of the mask of tragedy. He does not wish to associate himself with the unfortunate Achilles or with Ixion, whom Pound would later acknowledge as a totem of his own destructive tendencies.[14] And for a moment it looks as if he will avoid it. Propertius (thank you) would do

> *Without an inferno, without Achilles attended of gods,*
> *Without Ixion, and without the sons of Menoetius and the Argo and without*
> *Jove's grave and the Titans.*

Alas, the shades will not be denied. What was latent in section V becomes manifest in the justly celebrated sections VI and VII. At the emotional center of the poem death seems inescapable, poetry has been apparently forgotten, and Propertius summons his love to save him. At first the outcome of the struggle seems foregone, and he is overcome with melancholy:

> *For it is a custom:*
> *This care for past men,*
> *Since Adonis was gored in Idalia, and the Cytharean*
> *Ran crying with out-spread hair*

Then, miraculously, love triumphs, with what triumph life allows:

> *Nor can I shift my pains to other,*
> *Hers will I be dead,*
> *If she confer such nights upon me,*
> *long is my life, long in years,*
> *If she give me many,*
> *God am I for the time.*

Sections VIII and IX, less celebrated but equally moving, treat the same struggle with the kind of wit that in 1921 prompted Eliot to compare Propertius to Marvell: an "alliance of levity and seriousness by which the seriousness is intensified."[15] By the last lines of the suite there is no question but that Propertius, writing of Cynthia, "taking his stand" with Varro and Catullus, Calvus and Gallus, takes his stand against death. As Pound would put it in the "Envoi" of *Hugh Selwyn Mauberley* (that "translation of the *Homage* . . . for such as couldn't understand the latter"[16]),

> *Tell her that sheds*
> *Such treasure in the air,*
> *Recking naught else but that her graces give*
> *Life to the moment,*
> *I would bid them live*
> *As roses might, in magic amber laid,*
> *Red overwrought with orange and all made*
> *One substance and one colour*
> *Braving time.*

Life versus death, then. But not quite. For those who can hear it, an echo of Pater in the "Envoi" complicates Pound's assertion. In Pound's work, even in a pastiche like the "Envoi" or a translation like the *Homage*, matters of life and death have a peculiarly modern resonance. In the citation just given, Pound would give "life to the moment" as Pater would remind us that art proposes to give "the highest quality to your moments as they pass, and simply for those moments' sake." And for similar reasons:

our failure is to form habits: for, after all, habit is relative to a stereotyped world, and meantime it is only the roughness of the eye that makes any two persons, things, situations, seem alike. While all melts under our feet, we may well grasp at any exquisite passion, or any contribution to knowledge that seems by a lifted horizon to set the spirit free for a moment. . . . Not to discriminate every moment some passionate attitude in those about us, and in the very brilliancy of their gifts some tragic dividing of forces on their ways, is, on this short day of frost and sun, to sleep before evening. . . .
    One of the most beautiful passages in the writings of Rousseau is that in the sixth book of the *Confessions*, where he describes the awakening in him of the literary sense. An undefinable taint of death had clung always about him, and now in early manhood he believed himself smitten by mortal disease. He asked himself how he might make as much as possible of the interval that remained; and he was not biased by anything in his previous life when he decided that it must be by intellectual excitement, which he found just then in the clear, fresh writings of Voltaire. Well! we are all *condamnés*, as Victor Hugo says: we are all under sentence of death but with a sort of indefinite reprieve—*les hommes sont tous condamnés à mort avec des sursis indéfinis:* we have an interval, and then our place knows us no more. Some spend this interval in listlessness, some in high passions, the wisest, at least among "the children of the world," in art and song. For our one chance lies in expanding that interval, in getting as many pulsations as possible into the given time. Great passions may give us this quickened sense of life, ecstacy and sorrow of love, the various forms of enthusiastic activity, disinterested or otherwise, which come naturally to many of us. Only be sure it is passion—that it does yield you this fruit of quickened multiplied consciousness. Of this wisdom, the poetic passion, the desire of beauty, the love of art for art's sake has most.[17]

Death, that is to say, in a time of skepticism has a double aspect: death and the death-in-life of an existence so confined by habit and stereotype that the seeds of passion have nowhere to germinate. And, to judge by *Mauberley* and *Homage to Sextus Propertius*, for Pound the latter is as chilling as the former. In the *Homage*, certainly, Propertius is haunted by death-in-life, obviously in the prospect of living without Cynthia, less obviously in his vision of the diminished world around him. In the verse paragraph where he first thinks of his "contemptible sepulchre," for example, he assays dwellings outside the necropolis and pronounces them no less ghoulish. These other houses of death are situated in the suburbs and modelled upon the clichés of popular taste. Like an arranged marriage, they oppress the spirit instead of setting it free. In another of Pound's poems they will spur the poet to frame his "Commission":

67

Go, my songs, to the lonely and the unsatisfied,
Go also to the nerve-wracked, go to the enslaved-by-convention,
. . . .
Speak against unconscious oppression,
Speak against the tyranny of the unimaginative,
Speak against bonds.
Go to the bourgeoise who is dying of her ennuis,
Go to the women in suburbs.

68

In the *Homage*, the lifelessness of such houses is exposed in a blast of rhetoric drawn from the pseudo-speech of the advertising writer, the hack journalist, and the pedant:

Though my house is not propped up by Taenarian columns from Laconia
*   (associated with Neptune and Cerberus),*
Though it is not stretched upon gilded beams:
My orchards do not lie level and wide
*   as the forests of Phaecia,*
*   the luxurious and Ionian,*
Nor are my caverns stuffed stiff with a Marcian vintage,
My cellar does not date from Numa Pompilius,
Nor bristle with wine jars,
Nor is it equipped with a frigidaire patent;

As almost everyone who has written about the poem has commented, moreover, Propertius' self-conscious rhetoric is as significant as what it mocks. An intuition of how linguistic patterns permit convention its ultimate slavery animates Propertius' irony and provides the scenario for the second poem of the suite. At first Propertius reluctantly accedes to what the age demands, and vows:

Alba, your kings, and the realm your folk
*   have constructed with such industry*
Shall be yawned out on my lyre—with such industry.

But his heart isn't in it. Almost before the words are out of his mouth, his self alive, speaking with the voice of Apollo, admonishes him,

*   "You idiot! What are you doing with that water:*
"Who has ordered a book about heroes?
*   "You need, Propertius, not think*
"About acquiring that sort of a reputation.
*   "Soft fields must be worn by small wheels,*
. . . .
"No keel will sink with your genius
*   "Let another oar churn the water,*
"Another wheel, the arena: mid-crowd is as bad as mid-sea."

But the point is not simply that poetry in the chains of convention is a contradiction in terms. Propertius' resistance stems from something deeper than literary scruple. It grows out of revulsion against betraying not art, but life. He realizes here that were he to substitute "industry" for inspiration and succumb to the literary prescriptions of the Imperial marketplace he would lose what Pater says is our "one chance" in a stereotyped world and condemn himself to a life of stifled impulse. What Apollo reminds him is that to live such a life is to forfeit one's being. To be "mid-sea" is to drift without the rudder of a will; to be "mid-crowd" is to drift without a self. The images recall Pound's earlier account of abulia, "Portrait d'une Femme":

> *Your mind and you are our Sargasso Sea,*
> *London has swept about you this score years*
> *And bright ships left you this or that in fee:*
> *Ideas, old gossip, oddments of all things,*
> *Strange spars of knowledge and dimmed wares of price.*
>
> *In the slow float of different light and deep,*
> *No! there is nothing! In the whole and all,*
> *Nothing that's quite your own.*
>   *Yet this is you.*

Surrendering one's power to imagine the world, in other words, not only reduces one's impulses but loosens the grip of one's identity. As Pound wrote in the 1940s, "Without strong tastes, one does not love, nor, therefore, exist."[18] And it is the spectre of attenuated identity that most disturbs Propertius' soliloquy. Beneath his rebellion against consumerist mentality and literary convention, Pound's Propertius has a horror of becoming a ghost of himself, a horror that gives the depths of his monologue their special sombreness. To point to the most prominent instance, in section VI of the *Homage*, where Propertius' awareness of mortality is strongest, he does not fear annihilation so much as annihilation of self. The famous lines about Marius and Jugurtha do not, after all, stand by themselves but are gathered up and redirected by the image of a menace which death only screens—the formless emptiness of the living dead:

> *Upon the one raft, victor and conquered together,*
> *Marius and Jugurtha together,*
>   one tangle of shadows.

In what follows, Propertius, deprived of Cynthia, goes on to imagine his own funeral, this time in considerable detail. And in the epitaph, he sees on his tombstone he gives us a vision of the emotional absolutes of his life:

> *"He who is now vacant dust*
> *"Was once the slave of one* passion"

So intensely does Propertius feel deprived of being, in fact, that for the moment it seems even love cannot redeem him. Although the next section will reverse the mood, section VI ends:

> *In vain, you call back the shade,*
> *In vain, Cynthia. Vain call to unanswering shadow,*
> *Small talk comes from small bones.*

If, as Michael Alexander has suggested, "Pound's emotions are those of the exile" and his characteristic tone the "elegiac,"[19] here his emotional signature receives its quintessential expression. And here, I suggest, we find the keynote of Pound's defiance of the "imbecility" of modern life. Propertius will not follow Virgil into the shade, even if it be "Phrygian pine shade" (XII). To accept acquired forms of feeling is to empty oneself. And so Propertius' penultimate remarks, addressed to a friend who has slept with Cynthia and yet writes of Troy, are steeped in as much terror as disdain: a terror of becoming shreds and patches, not "after we cross the infernal ripples," but here and now:

> *And you write of Achelöus, who contended with Hercules,*
> *You write of Adrastus' horses and the funeral rites of Achenor,*
> *And you will not leave off imitating Aeschylus.*
> *Though you make a hash of Antimachus,*
> *You think you are going to do Homer.*
> *And still a girl scorns the gods,*
> *Of all these young women,*
> *not one has enquired the cause of the world,*
> *Nor the modus of lunar eclipses*
> *Nor whether there be any patch left of us*
> *After we cross the infernal ripples,*
> *nor if the thunder fall from predestination;*
> *Nor anything else of importance.*

The suite's last clear image before its peroration is an emblem of what man becomes without passion, disgorged with contempt born out of dread. Propertius, foreshadowing Canto VII's evocation of "Dry casques of departed locusts / speaking a shell of speech," calls up the creature his public requires, and shudders:

For the nobleness of the populace brooks nothing below its own altitude.
One must have resonance, resonance and sonority
. . . like a goose.

II

The *Homage;* then, delivers what it promises: a "complete elucidation
of death." But it elucidates death in more senses than one. Exploring
his deepest anxieties, Propertius also alleviates them by affirming
a force more powerful than mortality. Pater, as I have suggested, helps
us to put a name on that force. But even more helpful than Pater are
Nietzsche and Remy de Gourmont.

In 1911 Pound listened to Nietzsche's virtues sung by A. R. Orage
and W. B. Yeats,[20] and wrote in "Redondillas, or Something of that
Sort":

> *I sing of natural forces*
> *I sing of refinements*
>
> *I believe in some parts of Nietzsche*
> *I prefer to read him in sections;*[21]

Needless to say, the sections Pound preferred to read were not
the ones that anticipate Derridean skepticism but the ones that recall
the "natural forces" celebrated by his beloved Whitman. In *The Will
to Power,* just translated and still something of a sensation in 1911,
one finds:

The phenomenon "artist" is still the most transparent:—to see through it to
the basic instincts of power, nature, etc.!
. . . .
The feeling of intoxication, in fact corresponding to an increase in strength;
strongest in the mating season: new organs, new accomplishments, colors,
forms; "becoming more beautiful" is a consequence of *enhanced* strength.
Becoming more beautiful as the expression of a *victorious* will, of increased co-
ordination, of a harmonizing of all the strong desires. . . .
    Artists, if they are any good, are (physically as well) strong, full of surplus
energy, powerful animals, sensual; without a certain overheating of the sexual
system a Raphael is unthinkable—
. . . .
love, and even the love of God . . . remains the same in its roots: a fever that
has good reason to transfigure itself . . . one seems to oneself transfigured,
stronger, richer, more perfect, one *is* more perfect. . . . If we subtracted all
traces of this intestinal fever from lyricism in sound and word, what would be
left of lyrical poetry and music?—*L'art pour l'art* perhaps: the virtuoso croaking
of shivering frogs, despairing in their swamp—All the rest was created by
love—[22]

By the end of the decade, Pound's impressions of these passages would be strengthened by his having read the works of a number of Nietzschean popularizers, principally Remy de Gourmont.[23] Having discovered Gourmont in 1912 Pound became something of a disciple and used essays on the Frenchman in 1915 and 1919 to formulate some of the central ideas of his later work.[24] Perhaps his most extended tribute, though, was the translation he made in 1922 of *The Natural Philosophy of Love*. In that book Gourmont traces the arts to their origin in sexual force in a way familiar to students of Nietzsche and Freud:

It is in love that this alliance of all the senses is most intimately exercised. In superior animals, as well as in man, each sense, together or in groups, comes to reinforce the genital sense. . . . Thus one explains . . . dance [and] song.[25]

More usefully than either Nietzsche or Freud, Gourmont—at least as far as Pound was concerned—explained how the imagination mediates between sexuality and the life of art. Like any other artist, the poet allows his senses to be the "unique gateway of everything that enters and lives in the mind."[26] Arising out of the sensuous manifold of experience and energized by what Coleridge called the shaping power of the imagination, poetic vision puts both life and literature in touch with the energies of nature. Without it, nets of linguistic convention abstract us from the source of our being. With it we may truly be said to exist:

To write, as Flaubert and the Goncourts understood it, is to exist, to differentiate oneself.

without that reservoir of images from which the imagination draws new and infinite combinations, there is no style, no artistic creation. It alone allows us not only to paint the various movements of life by means of verbal figures, but to immediately transform into vision every association of words, every second-hand metaphor, even every isolated word—in short, to give life to death.[27]

Of course, one can, as Richard Sieburth allows, make too much of the connection between Gourmont and Pound.[28] Gourmont's account of the sexual roots of poetic vision reinforced an intuition of Pound's that had as much to do with Emerson and Whitman as with any European—an intuition which Pound, on other occasions confirmed in the troubadours, in Dante, and in Fenollosa's essay on the Chinese written character.[29] That said, an observation Pound makes in a postscript to his translation of *The Natural Philosophy of Love* remains our most useful commentary on the attitudes which distinguish what

Hardy called "Propertius Soliloquizes" from the Latin work it resembles:

Perhaps the clue is in Propertius after all:
Ingenium nobis ipsa puella fecit.
There is the whole of the twelfth century love cult, and Dante's metaphysics a little to one side, and Gourmont's Latin Mystique; and for image making both Fenollosa on "The Chinese Written Character," and the paragraphs in [Gourmont's] "La Problème du Style."[30]

"*Ingenium nobis ipsa puella fecit:* my genius is no more than a girl." With that "clue" in mind, and with Gourmont's Nietzschean notes on sexuality and genius to interpret it, the emphases of the *Homage* begin to come clear. One understands, for example, why, in what may properly be called the suite's moment of epiphany, sexual intensity and vision are coupled, and together are linked to the force of natural fertility:

And she then opening my eyelids fallen in sleep,
Her lips upon them; and it was her mouth saying:
    Sluggard!

In how many varied embraces, our changing arms,
Her kisses, how many, lingering on my lips.
"Turn not Venus into a blinded motion,
        Eyes are the guides of love,

Fool who would set a term to love's madness,
For the sun shall drive with black horses,
        earth shall bring wheat from barley,
The flood shall move toward the fountain
        Ere love know moderations,
        The fish shall swim in dry streams.
No, now while it may be, let not the fruit of life cease.

So understood, the *Homage* aligns itself with the *Cantos* along an axis of Romantic primitivism. And yet to approach it by way of the *Cantos* does the poem a real disservice.[31] In the *Cantos*, Pound's vitalist preoccupations frequently overreach themselves; they draw us away from human affairs into extended mythological sequences whose prominence implies a philosophical weight the material will not bear. The *Homage* entertains the same preoccupations but employs them as strains of emotional music, elements of a psychological drama rooted in the here and now. Not the truth of religious insight but a sense of quickening saves Propertius from the rudderless drift that he fears, and the moments of his quickening move us and convince us of the deeps of life in a way that even the breathing stillness of Canto XVII cannot and does not.

Permitted to emerge into the foreground only in instants of strong emotional pressure, an affirmation of the life force, figured in images of life interwoven by natural energy, gives the *Homage* its controlling motif and its deepest emotional unity. In section II, for example, heeding the admonition of Apollo, Propertius opposes the machine-like industry of the court poet to the ways of Venus, whom we see with "roses *twined* in her hands" as she "binds" ivy to Pan's thyrsos. Then in section V, following his ominous apprehension of "entangled shadows" (III), Propertius is moved to praise the endless web of creation and re-creation: Despite the forces of darkness, as long as Cynthia is with him "Whatever she does or says / We shall *spin long yarns* out of nothing."

But the motif sounds most emphatically in section VII, where we hear it both before and after Propertius' vision of the "fruit of life." "While our fates *twine* together," he cries out to Cynthia as they make love to each other, "Let the gods lay chains upon us / so that no day shall unbind them." Thanks to his love and his vision, the fragments of his life have been woven into a charmed wreath, still rooted in the earth, that will withstand the raveling of wind and time. In comparison,

> Dry *wreaths drop their petals,*
> *their stalks are woven* in baskets,

Pound mimes the words of Sextus Propertius, but his accents remind us of Blake and Yeats:

> *Love and harmony combine,*
> *And around our souls entwine,*
> *While thy branches mix with mine,*
> *And our roots together join.*
>
> *Beloved, gaze in thine own heart,*
> *The holy tree is growing there;*
> *From joy the holy branches start,*
> *And all the trembling flowers they bear.*[32]

Finally, then, *Homage to Sextus Propertius* proclaims the power of imagination rooted in desire to marry self and world, and to redeem the self from a fragmented and ghostly existence. The poem confronts fears that life is a "tangle of shadows," but in asserting the joy of fashioning new forms out of desire proposes that a power exists within us to knit up the disconnected shadows of this world into a garland beyond the reach of death. If the *Homage*'s initial movement is a descent toward the "veiled flood of Acheron" (VI), its last six poems are sustained in their unflinching look at death by the culminating promise of Propertius' passion: "God am I for the time" (VII). It is thus entirely appropriate that Pound preface his suite with the epigraph "Orfeo" and that he associate Amphion with Orpheus, who "tamed the wild beasts" (I). In the *Homage*, Propertius redeems himself from the accidents of existence and identifies himself with the redemptive power of the imagination. As he does so, he transcends his historical self and becomes one of the "Masters of the Soul" Pound wrote about in his early poem "Histrion."[33] Remaining Sextus Propertius, he displays the spiritual lineaments of Orpheus, the divinity who descended into death and returned, who was dismembered and yet continued to sing, and who by singing established harmony in the cosmos.[34]

Nor, we must add, is Propertius alone transformed. Just as in the *Homage*, he is rescued from death-in-life by the exercise of the Orphic imagination, so also is Pound, speaking through him. I cannot make the point better than Lilian Feder, though I do not share her animus. Citing a letter from Pound to William Gardner Hale, Feder observes Pound's statment that "there never was any question of translation, let alone literal translation. My job was to bring a dead man to life, to present a living figure." To which Feder adds, "the question this last sentence raises . . . is which dead man, Propertius or Pound?" Professor Feder sees the *Homage* as Pound's attempt to efface his "troublesome identity and his personal desires" in the outlines of classical literature and mythology, and bring a false, idealized image of himself to life.[35] But with the announced goals of modernist poetry in mind, we might accept her perception and reject her implication. If, as writers from Pater and Gourmont to Hulme and I.A. Richards have assured us, modern man is freed from the straitjacket of stock response and connected to reality only by taking Orpheus' journey into the earth, then the operations of the *Homage* are neither idiosyncratic nor invidious. Pound, in resurrecting first Propertius and then himself gives us a paradigm of poetry's power to renovate existence. And if in the process he submerges his "troublesome identity" in something larger than a conditioned self, we should not hastily conclude that he has evaded something essential. T.S. Eliot once wrote that in our everyday lives we are all so "encrusted with parasitic opinion" that we do not know "what we really are and feel, what we really want, and what really excites our interest."[36] Our essential selves may have less to do with what Emerson called the "erring passionate moral mind" than with the impersonal energies of the oversoul. And the essential Ezra Pound may not be the bundle of fragments that once resided on Kensington Church Walk but rather the central man of the *Homage,* who speaks the words of Sextus Propertius but who lives through the rejuvenating power of the Orphic imagination. Or, as Pound put it in his most famous lines, "What thou lovest well remains, / the rest is dross, / What thou lov'st well shall not be reft from thee / . . . though it were in the halls of hell."

Notes

1. Pound to Thomas Hardy, 31 March, 1921. Quoted in Patricia Hutchins, "Ezra Pound and Thomas Hardy," *Southern Review* 4, no. 1 (January 1968), 99.

2. Pound to Harriet Monroe, December 1918. Quoted by K.K. Ruthven, *A Guide to Ezra Pound's Personae* (Berkeley and Los Angeles: University of California Press, 1969), p. 87.

3. T.S. Eliot, Introduction to the *Selected Poems of Ezra Pound* (1928; reprint ed., London: Faber and Faber: 1973), p. 19.

4. Michael Alexander, *The Poetic Achievement of Ezra Pound* (Berkeley and Los Angeles: University of California Press, 1979), pp. 112–113.

5. Pound to the Editor of the *English Journal* 24 (January 1931). Quoted in J.P. Sullivan, *Ezra Pound and Sextus Propertius: A Study in Creative Translation* (London: Faber and Faber, 1964), p. 26.

6. Sullivan, *Ezra Pound and Sextus Propertius,* pp. 26, 29.

7. Two recent studies which acknowledge the importance of death as a theme of the *Homage* are Lilian Feder, *Ancient Myth in Modern Poetry* (Princeton: Princeton University Press, 1971), pp. 90–99; and Vincent E. Miller, "The Serious Wit of Pound's *Homage to Sextus Propertius,*" *Contemporary Literature* 16, no. 4 (Autumn 1975), 452–462.

8. See *Umbra, The Early Poems of Ezra Pound* (London: Elkins Matthews, 1920), p. 128.

9. In the 1904 essay, "A Portrait of the Artist." I quote from its reprinting in James Joyce, *A Portrait of the Artist as a Young Man: Text, Criticism and Notes,* ed. Chester G. Anderson (New York: Viking, 1968), p. 258.

10. Pound to William Carlos Williams, 21 October 1908. In *The Letters of Ezra Pound 1907–1941,* ed. D.D. Paige (New York: Harcourt, Brace and World, 1950), pp. 5–6.

11. Mark Turner, "Propertius through the Looking Glass," *Paideuma* 2 (Fall 1976), 244.

12. Composing a draft of section I, Pound introduced the theme in the eighth line. Then, when he had a clearer vision of the section's proportions, he spotlighted the theme in the concluding lines and allowed it to emerge more casually in Propertius' speech. The typescripts for the *Homage* are included in the Yale collection along with other papers relating to *Quia Pauper Amavi,* the volume in which the *Homage* was originally published. For the most part (the exceptions are sections I, VI, and XI), these typescripts are polished drafts not substantially different from their published counterparts.

13. Pound associated the woman and her spinning rhombus, also alluded to in sections II and IX, with a poem of Theocritus, and made the figure a private touchstone

for the chthonic powers of the earth. Cf. Canto LXXXII, in which he cites a fragment of Theocritus in the darkest moment of the *Pisan Cantos:*

> *How drawn, O GEA TERRA,*
> *what draws as thou drawest*
> *till one sink into thee by an arm's width*
> *embracing thee. Drawest,*
> *truly thou drawest.*
> *Wisdom lies next thee,*
> *simply, past metaphor.*
> *Where I lie let the thyme rise*
> *and basilicum*
> *let the herbs rise in April abundant*
> *By Ferrara was buried naked, fu Nicolo*
> *e di qua di la del Po,*
> *wind:* 'εμὸν τὸν 'ἄνδρα
> [Theocritus: draw home to me my man]

14. Cf. Canto CXIII: "Out of dark, thou, Father Helios, leadest, / but the mind as Ixion, unstill ever turning."

15. "Andrew Marvell," *Selected Essays* (1932; reprint ed., New York: Harcourt Brace and World, 1960), p. 255.

16. *Letters*, p. 239.

17. From Pater's "Conclusion" to *The Renaissance: Studies in Art and Poetry* (1873). I cite from a reprint edited by Louis Kronenberger (New York: The New American Library of World Literature, 1963), pp. 158–9.

18. From "A Visiting Card" (1942). See *Ezra Pound, Selected Prose 1909–1965*, ed. William Cookson (London: Faber and Faber, 1973), p. 298.

19. Alexander, *Poetic Achievement*, p. 47.

20. When Pound met him in 1911, Orage was an enthusiastic Nietzschean. In 1906 he had published *Friedrich Nietzsche: The Dionysian Spirit of the Age*, and he used *The New Age* to disseminate the latest in Nietzschean translation and criticism. See Wallace Martin, *The New Age Under Orage: Chapters in English Cultural History* (New York: Barnes and Noble), 1967. For Nietzsche's impact on Yeats, exerted via John Quinn, see Denis Donoghue, *William Butler Yeats* (New York: Viking, 1971), esp. pp. 52–69. (Donoghue cites repeatedly from *The Will to Power*.)

21. *Collected Early Poems of Ezra Pound*, ed. Michael King (New York: New Directions, 1976), pp. 216–17. The poem was originally intended for publication in *Canzoni* (1911), but was withdrawn from the proofs at the last moment.

22. For convenience I cite from the paperback translation by Walter Kaufmann and R.J. Hollingdale. See Friedrich Nietzsche, *The Will to Power* (New York: Vintage, 1968), pp. 419, 420–21, 426–27.

23. Compare, for example, the second excerpt from *The Will to Power* with the fragment of Gourmont's *The Natural Philosophy of Love* cited below.

24. See Richard Sieburth, *Instigations: Ezra Pound and Remy de Gourmont* (Cambridge: Harvard University Press, 1978).

25. *The Natural Philosophy of Love*, trans. Ezra Pound (1922; New York: Macmillan Co., 1972), pp. 146–47.

26. From *Le Problème du style* (1902). Cited by Sieburth, *Instigations*, p. 62.

27. From "La Culture des Idées" (1899) in *Selected Writings of Remy de Gourmont*, trans. and ed. Glenn S. Burne (Ann Arbor: The University of Michigan Press, 1966), p. 92; and *Le Problème du style*, cited by Sieburth, *Instigations*, p. 63.

28. Sieburth, p. 27.

29. For a discussion of Fenollosa's Emersonian roots, see Hugh Kenner, *The Pound Era* (Berkeley and Los Angeles: University of California Press, 1971), pp. 157–58.

30. *The Natural Philosophy of Love*, p. 158.

31. See, for example, Miller (who anticipates my discussion of the *Homage* and Gourmont), "The Serious Wit," pp. 458–59.

32. From Blake's *Poetical Sketches* and Yeats' "The Two Trees" (1893). I quote from the fourth chapter of Frank Kermode's *Romantic Image* (London: Routledge and Kegan Paul, 1957), which provides a great deal of useful background to the Romantic attitudes of the *Homage*.

33. See *Collected Early Poems*, p. 61.

34. For the contours of the Orpheus myth in classical antiquity and in modernist poetic practice, see Walter A. Strauss, *Descent and Return: The Orphic Theme in Modern Literature* (Cambridge: Harvard University Press, 1971).

35. Feder, *Ancient Myth*, p. 93.

36. From "Blake" (1920), in *The Sacred Wood* (1920; reprint ed., New York: Barnes and Noble, 1966), p. 154.

4. The Revolution of the Word

Michael F. Harper

In "The Serious Artist," published in 1913, Pound argues that since ethics are based on the nature of man, "we must know what sort of an animal man is, before we can contrive his maximum happiness, or before we can decide what percentage of that happiness he can have without causing too great a percentage of unhappiness to those about him." This information about the nature of man, his desires and his idea of the highest good, comes to us from the arts, which constitute a science providing "a great percentage of the lasting and unassailable data regarding the nature of man, of immaterial man, of man considered as a thinking and sentient creature."[1] Although Pound did not expound this theory of art as the basis of ethics until 1913, it had been the basis of his practice for some years. The value of poetry for him lay precisely in "referentiality"; since poems reported the poet's experience, poetry as a whole was an archive, and an exploration of the archive provided the data which should serve as the basis of ethics.[2]

The kind of experience which most interested Pound in his first years in London was the ecstasy, the mystic experience: his first poems are an archive of his own transactions with "the gods," not simply "poetic" fancies derived from bookish study of Provence. Pound believed fervently in the world of experience that such poems record:

> I believe in a sort of permanent basis in humanity, that is to say, I believe that Greek myth arose when someone having passed through delightful psychic experience tried to communicate it to others and found it necessary to screen himself from persecution. Speaking aesthetically, the myths are explications of mood: you may stop there, or you may probe deeper. Certain it is that these myths are only intelligible in a vivid and glittering sense to those people to whom they occur. I know, I mean, one man who understands Persephone and Demeter, and one who understands the Laurel, and another who has, I should say, met Artemis. These things are for them *real*.[3]

Myths, works of art, were generated by such experiences and were
reports of them.

Pound's view of art and its function as the basis of ethics involved
heavy responsibilities for the artist reporting his mystic experiences.
The serious poet, of course, had to tell the truth, but this meant more
than good intentions; it involved *technique,* in that the poem should
confine itself to the experience and avoid any *interpretation* not strictly
warranted by the experience. The poet should not go beyond the
evidence. The clearest statement of these principles is to be found in
"Axiomata," published in 1921:

> The theos may affect and may have affected the consciousness of
> individuals, but the consciousness is incapable of knowing why this occurs,
> or even in what manner it occurs, or whether it be the *theos;* though the
> consciousness may experience pleasant and possibly unpleasant sensations,
> or sensations partaking neither of pleasure or its opposite. Hence mysticism.
> If the consciousness receives or has received such effects from the theos, or from
> something not the theos yet which the consciousness has been incapable of
> understanding or classifying either as theos or a-theos, it is incapable of reducing
> these sensations to coherent sequence of cause and effect. The effects remain,
> so far as the consciousness is concerned, in the domain of experience, not
> differing intellectually from the taste of a lemon or the fragrance of violets or
> the aroma of dung-hills, or the feel of a stone or a tree-bark, or any other
> direct perception. As the consciousness observes the results of the senses, it
> observes also the mirage of the senses, or what may be a mirage of the senses,
> or an affect from the theos, the non-comprehensible.[4]

The principle set forth here explains a great deal of Pound's early poetry,
of poems written ten and fifteen years before. Pound believes that
the mystic experience is a "direct perception," that it presents itself to
the poet as sense experience unmediated by language or ideology.
Furthermore, it cannot be "reduced to" cause and effect, cannot be
reliably interpreted or explained. In "Axiomata," Pound goes on to
say that he does not wish to "deny any of the visions or auditions or
sensations of the mystics, Dante's rose or Theresa's walnut"; these
for him are immediate experience and phenomenologically irrefutable.
But he does wish to claim, among other things, that "We have no
proof that this God, Theos, is one, or is many, or is divisible or
indivisible," that "Dogma is bluff based upon ignorance," and that
"Belief is a cramp, a paralysis, an atrophy of the mind in certain
positions." In other words, no inference from the direct mystic
experience to the categorical statements of religious dogma is valid;
any report of the experience which *interprets* it is to be distrusted and
discounted.

The "vagueness" of Pound's very early poems is to be explained in just these terms. Usually these poems are dismissed as " 'prentice-work," as evidence that the young Pound was in the grip of Pre-Raphaelite dreaminess, of "Romantic" cloudiness, and that he was shortly to see the error of his ways and invent Imagisme, the poetry of hard, clean, sharp outlines. I suggest that the vagueness of the early poetry is the result of an ethical imperative, that Pound espouses a certain kind of reticence because he does not want to "interpret" an experience that he believes to be as "pure" and immediate as the taste of a lemon. So in 1909, in a preface to *A Quinzaine for This Yule*, he wrote:

81

Beauty should never be presented explained. It is Marvel and Wonder, and in art we should find first these doors—Marvel and Wonder—and, coming through them, a slow understanding (slow even though it be a succession of lightning understandings and perceptions) as of a figure in mist, that still and ever gives to each one his own right of believing, each after his own creed and fashion.

Always the desire to know and to understand more deeply must precede any reception of beauty. Without holy curiosity and awe none find her, and woe to that artist whose work wears its "heart on its sleeve."[5]

Even at this early stage, technique for Pound is a matter of epistemology and hence of ethics. The poem which presents or reports the ecstasy has the vagueness of a "figure in mist," and the lack of precise definition is a refusal to falsify the experience by assimilating it to the dogma of specific creeds. Thus the reader is allowed his own interpretation, "each after his own creed and fashion." As for interpretations, he was later to claim in "Axiomata" that "A choice of these fancies of the *theos* is a matter of taste." In matters of taste it is dangerous to set up orthodoxies, and in *Guide to Kulchur* many years later he castigated those who did:

Two mystic states can be dissociated: the ecstatic-beneficent-and-benevolent, contemplation of the divine love, the divine splendour with goodwill toward others.

And the bestial, namely the fanatical, the man on fire with God and anxious to stick his snotty nose into other men's business or reprove his neighbor for having a set of tropisms different from the fanatic's, or for having the courage to live more greatly and openly.[6]

Persecution, the burning of heretics, came about because, Pound thought, the mystic or visionary did not distinguish between the experience itself and the traditional, i.e., conventional, formulae of his society for its expression; he made an invalid interference from one to the other and persecuted others who—did he but know it—had had the same experience but used a different vocabulary to talk about it.

In a catechism entitled "Religio or, The Child's Guide to Knowledge" we find:

> Are there names for the Gods?
> The gods have many names. It is by names that they are handled in the tradition.
> Is there harm in using these names?
> There is no harm in thinking of the gods by their names.
> How should one perceive a god, by his name?
>
> It is better to perceive a god by form, or by the sense of knowledge, and after perceiving him thus, to consider his name or to "think what god it may be."[7]

This is from *Pavannes and Divisions* (1918) and implies very strongly Pound's belief in direct experience—perception "by form" or by the even more cryptic "sense of knowledge"—and corresponding distrust of language. It is not good to perceive a god "by his name," or at least the other ways are better; the best that may be said of language is that "there is no harm in thinking of the gods by their names." Pound distrusted conventional symbols and an iconography arbitrary in origin. In 1914 he counseled the poet to avoid symbols and to use images:

> An *image*, in our sense, is real because we know it directly. If it have an age-old traditional meaning this may serve as proof to the professional student of symbology that we have stood in the deathless light or that we have walked in some particular arbour of his traditional paradiso, but that is not our affair. It is our affair to render the *image* as we have perceived or conceived it.[8]

Pound believed that all symbols of this kind were once *images*, which were *known directly* because they were an integral part of an intense experience. They become symbols when they are abstracted from experience and codified, and the poet should abjure their use because as *symbols* they attest to nothing; anyone who can learn the symbolic system can use them, whether or not he has had an experience. Yet as *images* they are genuine signifiers, warrant of the experience they signify. So Dante's rose and Theresa's walnut are, for Pound, images and not symbols. Pound here seems to brush aside the interesting question of how one tells a symbol from an image—"that is not our affair." Yet the problem is always lurking beneath the surface of his criticism and is behind his denunciations of symbols.

Pound was unable to assent to a conventional creed. To Pound it would be unjustifiable to assimilate a mystical experience to a particular religious tradition; but for a poet who *believes*, the problem does not exist in this way. Eliot worked his way back to an acceptance of the Anglo-Catholic faith and thus had a frame of reference providing symbols, terminology, and other orienting devices, all of which then became available to him for poems. A poet with a philosophy has a "language" and Pound to begin with had neither. To say this is not to minimize Eliot's achievement—to deny that the poet who uses the Christian frame of reference must struggle to reinvigorate that system and, in each poem, to raise it from the level of cliché to something dynamic and vital. As Eliot himself said in connection with Dante, "the task of the poet, in making people comprehend the incomprehensible, demands immense resources of language. . . ."[9] But the problem took a different form for each poet. Pound always had an active distrust of conventional systems of thought and was unwilling to attempt to put his own thought in the usual kind of logical order, which he believed would falsify it. To order his thought in this way would be to risk violating the integrity of individual insights and "truths" in the interest of a systematic scheme which, he thought, in no way reflected reality. In "Redondillas" in 1911 he was forcefully explicit: "I sing of the special case, / The truth in the individual," he avowed, declaring that "The chief god in hell is Convention" and warning his readers to "Mistrust the good of an age / That swallows a whole code of ethics." Pound's early poetry is usually thought of as "bookish," but he was convinced that his own direct experience had to provide him with his subject matter, since all else was, if not unknowable, at least unknown: "I know not much save myself, / I know myself pretty completely."[10]

These ethical concerns lay behind Pound's early advocacy of vagueness in poetry. But this proved an unsatisfactory solution to the problem of rendering intense experience as honestly as possible, without making claims for its interpretation. If a vague rendering of an experience solved one ethical problem, it created another equally important one; the less precise the rendering, the easier it was to "fake" a poem without having had the experience which the poem claimed to record. If poetry was written in conventional, regular meter and if it employed a conventional "poetical" diction and standard imagery, anyone who became adept at manipulating these techniques could produce "poems" by the yard and it would be impossible to distinguish the "false" poet from the "true." That Pound considered this important is clear from "The Serious Artist":

83

This brings us to the immorality of bad art. Bad art is inaccurate art. It is art that makes false reports. If a scientist falsifies a report either deliberately or through negligence, we consider him as either a criminal or a bad scientist according to the enormity of his offence, and he is punished or despised accordingly.

What is obvious in the case of the scientist is not so obvious when it comes to the arts, but Pound fervently believed that the two cases are parallel and that the serious artist is one who operates under the same ethical constraints:

> If an artist falsifies his report as to the nature of man, as to his own nature, as to the nature of his ideal of the perfect, as to the nature of his ideal of this, that, or the other, of god, if god exist, of the life force, of the nature of good and evil, if good and evil exist, of the force with which he believes or disbelieves this, that, or the other, of the degree in which he suffers or is made glad; if the artist falsifies his report on these matters or on any other matter in order that he may conform to the taste of his time, to the proprieties of a sovereign, to the conveniences of a preconceived code of ethics, then that artist lies.[11]

Pound objected to much Victorian poetry primarily on ethical grounds. What was wrong with the mode of Victorian poetry in Pound's view was that it was an "artificial" universe of discourse divorced from common speech; this meant that its postures and attitudes were similarly artificial and false, constituting a never-never land of "literary" sentiment instead of accurate reports of "real" experience. The Victorians, he believed, did not for the most part say what they really felt but professed to have felt whatever their Philistine readers would find acceptable:

> The British public liked, has liked, likes and always will like all art, music, poetry, literature, glass engraving, sculpture, etc. in just such measure as it approaches the Tennysonian tone. It likes Shakespear, or at least accepts him in just so far as he is "Tennysonian." It has published the bard of Avon expurgated and even emended. There has never been an edition of "Purified Tennyson."
> "Is it credible that his (Tennyson's) whole mind should be made up of fine sentiments," says Bagehot. Of course it wasn't. It was that lady-like attitude toward the printed page that did it—that something, that ineffable "something," which kept Tennyson out of his works. When he began to write for Viccy's ignorant ear, he immediately ceased to be the "Tennyson so muzzy that he tried to go out through the fireplace," the Tennyson with the broad North accent, the old man with the worst manners in England (except Carlyle's), the Tennyson whom "it kept the whole combined efforts of his family and his publishers to keep respectable." He became the Tate Gallery among poets.[12]

This was written in 1917, but in 1908 Pound had told Williams that "you must remember I don't try to write for the public,"[13] and in *Patria Mia* he attacked the commercial pressures which tried to make the artist tailor his expression to the public taste:

> When a young man in America, having the instincts and interiors of a poet, begins to write, he finds no one to say to him: "Put down exactly what you feel and mean! Say it as briefly as possible and avoid all sham of ornament. . . ."
>
> On the contrary, he receives from editors such missives as this:—'Dear Mr——, Your work, etc., is very interesting, etc., etc., but you will have to pay more attention to conventional form if you want to make a commercial success of it."
>
> . . . .
>
> Of course, art and prosperous magazines are eternally incompatible, for it is the business of the artist to tell the truth whoever mislikes it, and it is the business of the magazine editor to maintain his circulation.[14]

Magazines enforced convention, and conventional meter and diction were a refuge for the false artist, whose verse pretended to report experiences that had never occurred. Pound's determined opposition to this kind of poetry led to his long effort to go beyond his distrust of language and to forge a poetry that would be recognizably isomorphic with experience. Since regular meter could be easily learned and imitated, Pound in 1912 was insisting on *vers libre* not as a relaxation of discipline but as an intensification:

> I believe in an "absolute rhythm," a rhythm, that is, in poetry which corresponds exactly to the emotion or shade of emotion to be expressed. A man's rhythm must be interpretative, it will be, therefore, in the end, his own, uncounterfeiting, uncounterfeitable.[15]

"Uncounterfeiting, uncounterfeitable." This is the key to an understanding of Pound's technical reforms. The "danger" of conventional meter was not simply that it could be used to counterfeit poems but also that it allowed lazy poets to use prefabricated materials, the result being not an accurate report but an approximation:

> As far as the "living art" goes, I should like to break up *cliché,* to disintegrate these magnetized groups that stand between the reader of poetry and the drive of it, to escape from lines composed of two very nearly equal sections, each containing a noun and each noun decorously attended by a carefully selected epithet gleaned, apparently, from Shakespeare, Pope, or Horace. For it is not until poetry lives again "close to the thing" that it will be a vital part of contemporary life. As long as the poet says not what he, at the very crux of a clarified conception, means, but is content to say something ornate and

approximate, just so long will serious people, intently alive, consider poetry as balderdash—a sort of embroidery for dilettantes and women.[16]

Imagism was the crystallization, in the form of a "movement," of the technical measures Pound thought necessary to solve these problems. In 1917, in "a brief recapitulation and retrospect" written to clear up confusion caused by "so much scribbling about a new fashion in poetry," Pound began by reprinting the three famous principles which were the basis of the Imagiste "movement":

1. Direct treatment of the "thing" whether subjective or objective.
2. To use absolutely no word that does not contribute to the presentation.
3. As regarding rhythm: to compose in the sequence of the musical phrase, not in sequence of a metronome.[17]

The first of these rules is somewhat cryptic, since one cannot understand what Pound means by the "thing" without examining the "Doctrine of the Image" presented in the March 1913 issue of *Poetry* that contained the three rules. But the force of the second and third rules is clear: it is to rob the bad poet—"bad" in the sense of "dishonest"—of the means of producing "sham" poems. The second rule forbids the use of a conventional "poetic" diction and would make it impossible to generate "poems" by manipulating a stock vocabulary. The third would rule out the stock metrical schema which the vocabulary could be arranged to fill out.

The evil that Pound is attacking in these two rules is truly evil for one who believes, as Pound did, that poems report experience, that language must follow the contours of a prior reality; the object of his attack is the poem generated by language, the "metrical exercise" that Pound considered the characteristic product of the second-rate versifier. In *ABC of Reading* he says of Gower:

He had a go at metrical exercises in all three of the current tongues: English, French and Latin. Books, used in the wrong way. The hunt for a subject, etc.
He was the perfect type of English secondary writer, condemned recently but for all time by Henri Davray with his:
"Ils cherchent des sentiments pour les accomoder à leur vocabulaire."
They hunt for sentiments to fit into their vocabulary.[18]

To begin with a vocabulary and to allow it to dictate what one says clearly results in poems that cannot be used, as Pound would use them, as "the basis of ethics," since they are not reports on pre-existing reality. It is important to note once again in Pound's thinking the implied gulf between language and experience. Experience is independent of language; experience is direct perception and language is only a means of expressing that experience. The idea that language is involved in *creating* experience, since its structure provides the interpretations that constitute what is popularly and mistakenly supposed to be "immediate" experience—such an idea seems to be precluded by much of Pound's critical writing.

The Imagist rules prescribed that the experience create the poem, and not the other way around, and they were an important step for Pound on his way to the poetic of the *Cantos*. Hugh Kenner, however, sees them as relatively unimportant: "(Imagism's) specifications for technical hygiene . . . which can be followed by any talented person, help you to write what may be a trivial poem."[19] Kenner goes on to locate Imagism's true importance in Pound's Doctrine of the Image, and to assimilate this—surprisingly—to a Symbolist aesthetic in which "poems were producing things that had not preceded them, that were not part of a pre-existing array called 'the subject of the poem,' the array of things one supposes a poem to be 'about,' as a statement about a horse is 'about' some horse whom we understand to have stood or walked or grazed before the statement was thought of."[20] Hence Kenner's analysis of "In a Station of the Metro":

> For Pound's Imagism is energy, is effort. It does not appease itself by reproducing what is seen, but by setting some other seen thing into relation. The mind that found "petals on a wet, black bough" had been active (and for more than a year on that poem, off and on). The "plot" of the poem is that mind's activity, fetching some new thing into the field of consciousness. The action passing through any Imagist poem is a mind's invisible action discovering what will come next that may sustain the presentation—what image, what rhythm, what allusion, what word—to the end that the poem shall be "lord over fact," not the transcript of one encounter but the Gestalt of many, from the Metro traveller's to that of Koré in the underworld.[21]

Kenner's argument is a long and subtle one and should be consulted in full, since I shall doubtless misrepresent it by sparse quotation. One sees clearly enough what Kenner is trying to do—to dissociate Pound's Imagism not only from Amy Lowell's dilution but also from what he calls the mere "pictorialism" of Symons and the post-Symbolists of the 1890s. Yet the terms in which Kenner makes the dissociation are misleading insofar as they imply that Pound embraced the Symbolist formula of "words set free in new structure," that Pound's poems are generated by words:

"In a Station of the Metro" is not formally a sentence; its structure is typographic and metric. Words, similarly, without loss of precision, have ceased to specify in the manner of words that deliver one by one those concepts we call "meanings." "Apparition" reaches two ways, toward ghosts and toward visible revealings. "Petals," the pivotal word, relies for energy on the sharp cut of its syllables, a consonantal vigor recapitulated in the trisyllabic "wet, black bough" (try changing "petals" to "blossoms"). The words so raised by prosody to attention assert themselves as *words,* and make a numinous claim on our attention, from which visual, tactile and mythic associations radiate. Words set free in new structures, that was the Symbolist formula. And as we move through the poem, word by word, we participate as the new structure achieves itself.[22]

88

It is strange that Kenner, once the champion of Pound as a poet who registers realities, should here claim that in Pound's Imagism words are set free from "those concepts we call 'meanings' " in order to "assert themselves as *words,* and make a numinous claim on our attention." Taking his cue from Pound's frequent denunciations of writing that is merely "mimetic" in a derogatory sense, in that it is content to transcribe surface appearances, Kenner wants to acquit Pound of the charge that Imagism is merely pictorialism and to describe Pound's Imagism in the governing terms of *The Pound Era* as dynamic, as the presentation of Vorticist energies. His point about pictorialism is well taken, but the terms of his argument are not convincing. There is no reason to believe that Pound intended his Imagist poems to call attention to themselves as *"words,"* by which Kenner seems to mean "sounds" as opposed to concepts. The critic can of course choose, as Kenner chooses, to pay attention to sound qualities and to talk of "consonantal vigor," but a critic can do this with any poetry whatsoever; it is not an intrinsic and defining mark of Pound's Imagism. In the example Kenner gives, one could accept his invitation to substitute "blossoms" for "petals." Clearly one would have, as a result, a different poem— one would not be able to talk of the "consonantal vigor" of "petals" recapitulated in "wet, black bough"—but one would not have a poem different in *kind.* It would still be possible to pay attention to words as sound and to talk of the "consonantal softness" of "blossoms" contrasting sharply with the "hardness" of "wet, black bough" and hence establishing a contrast between "these faces" and their surroundings. The problem with Kenner's method of reading Pound is not that it doesn't work but that it works too well; it can be applied to any piece of language with predictable results (all strings of words have consonants, and "consonantal vigor" can be found wherever it is sought). The argument about prosody allowing words to make numinous claims is unconvincing because Pound had no interest in autonomous structures of words:

One, or at least the present, writer is mildly bored with the tosh emitted during more than a decade by Mr. Joyce's epigons; blather about the revolution of the word. The renovation of the word may stem out of Stendhal. Flaubert was certainly grandfather to any further renovation of our time . . . Joyce's [renovation was] merely, in the main, sonorous, an attraction of the half-awake consciousness to and by similar sounds.[23]

Pound intended his Doctrine of the Image in a different way, one that is very much in harmony with the second and third of the Imagist commandments and is deeply involved in the first. "An 'Image' is that which presents an intellectual and emotional complex in an instant of time" runs the Doctrine, and the first rule admonishes "direct treatment of the 'thing' whether subjective or objective." In *The Spirit of Romance* in 1910 Pound had declared: "Poetry is a sort of inspired mathematics, which gives us equations, not for abstract figures, triangles, spheres and the like, but equations for human emotions. If one have a mind which inclines to magic rather than science, one will prefer to speak of these equations as spells or incantations; it sounds more arcane, mysterious, recondite."[24] This idea of poetry as an "equation" is what Pound was getting at in his concept of the Image. When it was clear to him that Imagism had been misunderstood, the idea of an equation was the one he returned to in his efforts to clarify the matter; "By the 'image' I mean such an equation; not an equation of mathematics, not something about *a*, *b*, and *c*, having something to do with form, but about *sea, cliffs, night*, having something to do with mood."[25] The poet was to be deprived of all the props from which he might make "insincere" poems. He was forbidden to *assert* that he had had a certain emotion, and he was not permitted to describe it. Instead he had to find a verbal formula—an *equation, image* or *vortex*—which would generate the emotional experience in the reader. This formula was not to be made up simply of visual images, although as in most poetry they would probably be part of it; it would also derive much of its power of signification from rhythm—"a rhythm, that is, in poetry which corresponds exactly to the emotion or shade of emotion to be expressed."

This "equation" had to carry the burden of the "meaning"; the poet was forbidden to be discursive. The Imagist poem was supposed to create in the reader an emotion identical to the emotion which inspired the poet to write the poem, in a manner somewhat akin to Eliot's "objective correlative." But this did not mean that poetry was confined to feelings and had to ignore thought. Just as Eliot believed in a unified sensibility in which a poet could have a "direct sensuous apprehension of thought," so Pound believed that the "equation" or Image generated "an intellectual and emotional complex in an instant of time." An emotion, Pound believed, was inextricably bound up with its concomitant ideas, but the poet was not to make these explicit in discourse; the equation he created for the emotion would itself have definite repercussions in the reader's intellect, and the poet would not have to force his ideas, his "interpretation," down the reader's throat: "The image is not an idea. It is a radiant node or cluster; it is what I can, and must perforce, call a VORTEX, from which, and through which, and into which, ideas are constantly rushing."[26] Pound believed that the ideas which would arise in the reader's mind would therefore be the intrinsic significance of the image and not an extrinsic "interpretation" asserted by the author.

The Image was not what Pound thought of as a symbol, and the Imagist poem was not an allegory: "Imagisme is not symbolism. The symbolists dealt in 'association,' that is, in a sort of allusion, almost of allegory. . . . The symbolist's *symbols* have a fixed value, like numbers in arithmetic, like 1, 2, and 7. The imagiste's images have a variable significance, like the signs a, b, and x in algebra."[27] Pound's objection to what he here presents (or misrepresents) as symbolism is that it does not really solve this problem of sincerity. Having taken away from the dishonest poet the props of conventional meter and diction, Pound is not about to give him another opportunity to counterfeit. Symbols with a fixed value constitute a kind of code, and the false poet merely has to learn the code in order to produce "fake" poems. Pound believed that Images, having no fixed—i.e., conventional—value, cannot be faked in the same fashion as the poem written in a symbolist code. But if Images had no *fixed* value, how could they have those certain and definite meanings which would permit them to be a source of knowledge and the basis of ethics? On the surface it looks as if Kenner's reading of Imagism must be right and that Pound's Images offer themselves up to the "dynamic energies" of the free play of signification. This is indeed the case, but Pound thinks otherwise. He believes that his Images exist outside conventional codes and yet have certain meanings because they are tethered to their origin—because they are for him *natural* and not arbitrary signifiers. Images, he believes, constitute a natural language.

The Image is made by the poet but the "raw material" out of which it is shaped is *given* to him along with the emotional experience and is practically indistinguishable from it. An emotional experience, claims Pound, is not simply a feeling, but is always manifest to the poet in what he calls a "primary form": "Every concept, every emotion, presents itself to the vivid consciousness in some primary form."[28] This primary form may arise from outside the poet or from inside. If from outside, if "objective," as the first Imagist rule calls it, the Image that is the work of art will bear a certain relation to the external object which inspired the emotion, but it will not be what Pound thought of as a simple copy of surface appearances. The artist will seize upon the external object and in his art he will render it as he has seen it, so that his representation will convey its intrinsic significance. So when Gaudier sculpted the head of Pound, the work of art—the sculpture— sprang from Gaudier's perception of the living head but was not an imitation of it: "You understand it will not look like you, it *will* . . . *not* . . . *look* . . . like you. It will be the expression of certain emotions which I get from your character."[29]

This primary form, this Image, may also be what the first rule calls "subjective," may arise from *inside* the poet. This is the case with "In a Station of the Metro":

> *The apparition of these faces in the crowd;*
> *Petals on a wet, black bough.*

Here what Pound *saw* is named in the title and first line; this inspired in him a certain complex emotion, the equation of which, he said, came to him in the form of "little splotches of colour." This "equation" he eventually translated into the words which make up the second line, and the two lines together present the reader with the "intellectual and emotional complex in an instant of time" that was Pound's experience. The Image is something *given* to the poet in its primary form and he must render it as precisely as he can. Hence the first Imagist rule—"Direct treatment of the 'thing' whether subjective or objective." Pound believed that the "thing" *naturally* embodies the poet's emotion because it is an integral part of the original experience. For Pound "the natural object is always the *adequate* symbol"[30] because it is not an arbitrary symbol nor a conventional one; it is not a symbol at all in Pound's sense, but an element of the original experience, as he maintained in the passage I quoted earlier: "An *image*, in our sense, is real because we know it directly."[31]

"In a Station of the Metro," which has become in critical discussions the epitome of Imagist technique, is *atypical*, an exception rather than the rule. Pound did *not* render the image as he had conceived it, for he had conceived it as "little splotches of colour" and the poem is a *translation* of the Image from color into words, splotches into petals. Pound declared quite plainly that "my experience in Paris should have gone into paint"[32] and hints that if his experiences had presented themselves to his imagination as color very often, he would have

91

seriously considered taking up painting: "That evening, in the Rue Raynouard, I realized quite vividly that if I were a painter, or if I had, often, *that kind* of emotion, or even if I had the energy to get paints and brushes and keep at it, I might found a new school of painting that would speak only by arrangements in colour."[33] This explains why the visual element of Pound's Imagism has been overestimated, for this mistaken notion of Imagism has been derived not from Pound's Imagist propaganda but from his experiments in translation from the Chinese, which came a little later. Fenollosa's widow gave to Pound in late 1913 her husband's materials—notebooks containing glosses on Chinese poems, notes on the Noh drama, and his essay on the Chinese written character. Pound's work on this material profoundly influenced his poetry and theory, as Herbert Schneidau and Hugh Kenner have both shown, and the translations he published in *Cathay* in 1915 relied as heavily on visual imagery as he believed the originals did. Eliot noted in 1917:

Inasmuch as "Cathay," the volume of translations from the Chinese, appeared prior to "Lustra," it is sometimes thought that his newer idiom is due to the Chinese influence. This is almost the reverse of the truth. The late Ernest Fenollosa left a quantity of manuscripts, including a great number of rough translations (literally exact) from the Chinese. After certain poems subsequently incorporated in "Lustra" had appeared in "Poetry," Mrs. Fenollosa recognized that in Pound the Chinese manuscripts would find the interpreter whom her husband would have wished; she accordingly forwarded the papers for him to do as he liked with. It is thus due to Mrs. Fenollosa's acumen that we have "Cathay"; it is not as a consequence of "Cathay" that we have "Lustra." This fact must be borne in mind.[34]

In other words, Fenollosa's theories about the importance of the Chinese written character, which depend upon the claim that it is an abbreviated picture and not an arbitrary representation of a sound, had nothing to do with Imagism at first.

II

Fenollosa's essay, "The Chinese Written Character as a Medium for Poetry," has been treated extensively by both Herbert Schneidau and Hugh Kenner. I do not intend to duplicate their work here, but I think it important to argue against a mistaken emphasis in current reinterpretations of what Pound derived from Fenollosa's work. The reasons for the reinterpretation are clear. For a long time Fenollosa's theory of the Chinese written character was seen as the basis of Pound's ideogramic method and hence the inspiration for the organization of the *Cantos;* but the fact that Fenollosa's theory is mistaken has proved an embarassment for Poundians worried lest Fenollosa's errors imply a similarly erroneous foundation for Pound's poem. Herbert Schneidau has argued that what Pound essentially derived from Fenollosa was the idea that verbs are the basis of language.[35] Hugh Kenner agrees, and concludes that the central intuition of Fenollosa and of Pound the Vorticist was that the universe is dynamic, composed not of "things" but of processes, forces, and energies. This intuition, argues Kenner, derives from the Emersonian organicism with which Fenollosa was imbued at Cambridge; moreover, Transcendentalism has affinities not only with the Far East but also "with Whitehead and Darwin and Frazer, and Gestaltists and field physicists, and the synergism of Buckminster Fuller: with the coherent effort of 150 years to rectify Newton's machine. . . ." Hence Fenollosa's "sinological mistakes" did not affect his "right intuitions"; Pound's poem, implies Kenner, is congruent with modern scientific thought.[36] But to play down the ideogramic method leads to other problems, since such a change in emphasis seems to deprive the *Cantos* of its structural principle. Ronald Bush claims that the ideogramic method is a "red herring" and maintains that "no programmatic use of the term 'ideogram' or 'ideograph' appears until 1927," that the method is at best a "structural device" and not the "form of the whole."[37] His alternative theory—that the *Cantos* is modeled upon Dante's *Commedia*—is not convincing, but one can see why he was driven to propose it. He claims that Kenner's description of Pound's procedure amounts only to establishing "patterns of recurrence" and concludes:

93

> By denying the *Cantos* "a line of philosophic development," Kenner denied them exactly that *entelechy* which we take to be the sign of an accomplished work of art.
> Pound's readers are still waiting for a description of the *Cantos'* major form that will assimilate into one whole the poem's structural idiom, its generic characteristics, and its hierarchy of psychological values.[38]

Bush was writing after the publication of *The Pound Era*, but his objection to Kenner's arguments recalls that of George P. Elliott to Kenner's *The Poetry of Ezra Pound* (1951):

> But behind recurrence there is the fundamental question: why the recurrence? Anybody can concoct ten dozen disparate themes, subjects, image-types, rhythms, attitudes, cultural quiddities, and keep popping them up one and another in patterns of varying complication and banality. This is merely technique; anyone who studied Kenner hard enough could do it. If the recurrence and juxtapositions of the *Cantos* are there for their own sake, the

poem is elaborately trivial. Kenner fails to make clear what structurally valuable end these recurrences serve.[39]

These objections are good ones, and they expose a fundamental weakness of Kenner's work on Pound. For the depth of his research and the local brilliance of his arguments have obscured the fact that Kenner has not been able to make of the *Cantos* the kind of sense that Elliott and Bush demand. "The aim of technique," said Pound, "is that it establish . . . the total significance of the whole"; but Kenner has never made clear his concept of the significance of Pound's *Cantos* as a whole, preferring instead to attempt a validation of Pound's techniques as techniques, assimilating them to the theories and operations of a broadly conceived modernism. Yet all Kenner proves is that Pound's poetics can be described in terms associated with various areas of modern scientific thought and that Pound himself— particularly in his Vorticist years—frequently used such terms. That Pound should talk of vortices and energies is hardly surprising—in the age of Edison and Marconi these metaphors were quite literally "in the air." But science took hold of Pound's imagination in a more radical manner than is implied in Kenner's concept of "consonantal vigor": Pound found in science a mode of investigating the world which could be used—not metaphorically but literally, he believed—as the principle of organization of a long poem. The poem would not be "about" a scientific investigation but would itself constitute one; it would be a poem that would "include history." This is the key to the "ideogramic method."

Fenollosa's declaration, "Poetry agrees with science and not with logic,"[40] crystallized much of Pound's own thinking. As we have seen, Pound had striven for a way of writing that would cleave to the contours of experience and constitute true reports. Imagism was the result, but it had left him with what has been called an aesthetic of glimpses, poems that recorded epiphanies. Although Pound believed that these poems were important as the basis of ethics, it was nevertheless true both that lawmakers did not use poetry in this way and also that an Imagist poetic seemed to offer no mode of apprehending a larger vision, of building larger meanings. Through Fenollosa, Pound developed a theory which would solve his problem. Scientific induction—the use of concretely known particulars to arrive at a general statement that would be true because grounded in those particulars—was the way Pound would proceed, conducting his own investigation of the archive of art and chronicle in order to generate an ethics and an economics that could redeem society from its errors. And this would not, he believed, be a metaphorical application of science, but science itself; for Fenollosa was to convince him that the method of science *is* the method of poetry, that good writing and accurate language are themselves scientific. What Fenollosa offered was not a replacement for Imagism but an extension of it; for a scientific induction apparently rests upon particulars that must first be accurately known, and the particulars of Pound's inductive poem were to be those "direct experiences" which the Imagist poet had taught himself to record in his own poems and to recognize in the poems of others.

Pound was seeking a poetic that would achieve larger meanings because the times seemed to him to demand more than discrete, individual truths. The Great War, and the experience of a Europe plunged into chaos, forced upon him a new urgency. He had long detested the governing values of the world he lived in, and the outbreak of war seems to have inspired in him the hope that the conflict would be a cleaning of the Augean stables. In November 1914 he told Harriet Monroe:

> Ricketts has made the one mot of the war, the last flare of the 90's: "What depresses me most is the horrible fact that they can't *all* of them be beaten." It looks only clever and superficial, but one can not tell how true it is. This war is possibly a conflict between two forces almost equally detestable. Atavism and the loathsome spirit of mediocrity cloaked in graft. One does not know; the thing is too involved.[41]

But even at this early stage the hope that bloodletting might heal the patient was not a very firm one. Pound suspected that war was not a *cure* for the diseases of civilization but the major symptom, and he continues:

I wonder if England will spend the next ten years in internal squabble *after* Germany is beaten. It's all very well to see the troops flocking from the four corners of Empire. It is a very fine sight. But, but, but, civilization, after the battle is over and everybody begins to call each other thieves and liars *inside* the Empire. They took ten years after the Boer War to come to. One wonders if the war is only a stop gap. Only a symptom of the real disease.

His fears were confirmed by events, and he was soon convinced that "civilization" would not be improved in any way by the war. In 1915 he told Felix Schelling that "Gaudier-Brzeska has been killed at Neuville St. Vaast, and we have lost the best of the young sculptors and the most promising. The arts will incur no worse loss from the war than this is. One is rather obsessed with it."[42] As the war progressed Pound became more and more convinced that it was "only a symptom of

95

the real disease," and his considered judgment is rendered with controlled savagery in *Mauberley*.

If civilization had broken down, then it had to be rebuilt on sound principles. But what were these principles, and how were they to be discovered? Pound characterized his generation as

a generation of experimenters . . . which was unable to work out a code for action. We believed and disbelieved "everything," or to put it another way we believed in the individual case.

The best of us accepted every conceivable "dogma" as a truth for *a* situation, as the truth for a particular crux, crisis or temperament.

And a few serious survivors of war grew into a tolerance of the "new synthesis," saw finally a need for a "general average" in law.[43]

It was to this need for a "general average" that Pound addressed himself, and he confronted a major problem almost immediately. The business of discovering the true principles on which civilization must be founded is the proper business of the poet, for the truth, he believed, is founded in direct experience, and exploration of experience is the poet's task; politics is too important to be left to politicians. The Imagist poem, the poem that Pound had spent years schooling himself to write, was a means of exploring and rendering intense experience; the Imagist's poetic task was to render that experience accurately and honestly, not to comment and interpret. The relevance of this kind of experience to the political and economic rebuilding of society is not self-evident. Pound wanted to write an epic poem with lyric materials.

Pound's earlier claims in "The Serious Artist" had been merely that poetry in the aggregate supplies the lawmaker with raw data about human aims and desires; it is hard to see how the Imagist poet could provide more than this. One of Mauberley's virtues was that he eschewed the cheap sermonizing that characterized the insincere artist and refused to supply what "The Age Demanded":

> *The glow of porcelain*
> *Brought no reforming sense*
> *To his perception*
> *Of the social inconsequence.*
>
> *Thus, if her colour*
> *Came against his gaze,*
> *Tempered as if*
> *It were through a perfect glaze*
>
> *He made no immediate application*
> *of this to relation of the state*

> *To the individual, the month was more temperate*
> *Because this beauty had been.*

But this virtue was a strictly limited one, like most of Mauberley's
virtues. If he was to be praised for eschewing rhetoric and rejecting
the role of propagandist, his devotion to aesthetic experience led to
the opposite sin of mere hedonism, and he was to be censured for his
inability to forge an art that would have wider significance without
betraying its integrity as art. Pound needed to transcend the limitations
of a Mauberley, and Fenollosa helped him to see how he might do it.

    First of all, in Fenollosa Pound discovered confirmation of his
own distrust of categorical statement, of discursive prose organized
by a logic fundamentally Aristotelian. In "I gather the limbs of Osiris,"
Pound had defined the "expert" as one who "does not, as a rule, sling
generalities; he gives the particular case for what it is worth; the truth
is the individual."[44] And in *Patria Mia* he praised the arts as "a
statement of motor forces" in opposition to discursive reasoning:

Argument begets but argument and reflective reason, if stated only as reflective
reason, begets either a state of argumentativeness or a desire for further
information wherewith to refute the man who opposes your own comforting
prejudice to the effect that you and your sort are right.[45]

Generalities were to be distrusted because terms such as "Christianity"
and "Socialism" are "indefinable," and by "indefinable" Pound clearly
means that they cannot be easily reduced to the particulars of direct
experience, which for him are by definition *known*. Art, because it
presents direct experience, is a statement of phenomenologically
irrefutable truth and therefore superior to reflective reason *unless* it is
bad art, and bad art is bad because it is not such a presentation:

    The force of a work of art is this, namely, that the artist presents his
case, as fully or as minutely as he may choose. You may agree or disagree,
but you cannot refute him. He is not to be drawn into argument or weakened
by quibbling. If his art is bad you can throw him out of court on grounds of
his technique. Whether he be "idealist" or "realist," whether he sing or paint
or carve, visible actualities as they appear, or the invisible dream, bad
technique is "bearing false witness". . . .
    For instance, you can wrangle with any statement about the relationship
of Christianity (one undefinable term) with Socialism (another undefinable
term). But with Sabatte's painting, *"Mort du premier Socialiste,"* you cannot
argue.[46]

Fenollosa both confirmed Pound's distrust of argument and provided
a theory to support that distrust. For him the universe is indeed

process, action; good writing is writing that accurately mimes these processes—writing that is primarily composed of transitive verbs, while bad writing is removed from the reality of process because it follows not the contours of the reality but the logic of the Middle Ages:

> According to this logic, thought deals with abstractions, concepts drawn out of things by a sifting process. These logicians never inquired how the "qualities" which they pulled out of things came to be there. The truth of all their little checkerboard juggling depended upon the natural order by which these powers or properties or qualities were folded in concrete things, yet they despised the "thing" as a mere "particular," or pawn. It was as if botany would reason from the leaf-patterns woven into our table-cloths.[47]

The reasoning of the logician is useless because it depends upon nouns and adjectives which correlate not with reality but with the classes distinguished by his own system of classification—one cannot think certain thoughts because the method "has no way of bringing together any two concepts which do not happen to stand one under the other" in what Fenollosa calls the "pyramid" of classification.[48]

Fenollosa's critique of logical reasoning runs along lines that contemporary criticism would endorse: language is a structure that constitutes reality. Yet Fenollosa does not concede that this is true of *all* such structures, that "reality" is a forever unknowable metaphysical concept which we can never *perceive* but which is always already *interpreted* for us by language. He believes that we can know reality— it is the reality of process and dynamic change—and that language did originally and can again capture it. Fenollosa's romanticism is apparent here. For he believed that primitive man grasped such a reality in language fundamentally metaphorical. "The whole delicate substance of speech is built upon substrata of metaphor," and metaphor itself reflects a reality:

> But the primitive metaphors do not spring from arbitrary *subjective* processes. They are possible only because they follow objective lines of relations in nature herself. Relations are more real and more important than the things they relate . . . Had the world not been full of homologies, sympathies, and identities, thought would have been starved and language chained to the obvious. There would have been no bridge whereby to cross from the minor truth of the seen to the major truth of the unseen.[49]

Furthermore, primitive sentence structure—"Farmer pounds rice"— is also isomorphic with reality, Fenollosa claims: "the form of the Chinese transitive sentence, and of the English (omitting particles), exactly corresponds to this universal form of action in nature."[50]

Pound's ideogramic method is an extension and application of Fenollosa's ideas about verbs and metaphor. The Chinese written character, Fenollosa thought, mimes "abstract" concepts by juxtaposing abbreviated pictures of things in order to make a metaphor—a metaphor which is for Fenollosa "objective" in that what it signifies is the real relationship between the things juxtaposed. Pound conceived a poem that would operate in the same way. "Things"—in this case images, scraps of poems and other documents—could be placed in simple juxtaposition, eschewing the logical connectives of a grammar that Fenollosa had shown to be out of touch with reality; the result would be an ideogram—a signifier indivisible from its signified, since what it would signify would be the *real* relationship between its component parts. The result would be a poetry that was, Pound believed, a *natural* language, signifier and signified being one and the same and not two halves of an arbitrarily constituted sign.

This ideogram would not be—as it has too often been misconstrued—a means of *expression* of a thought or concept already known by the poet (this would make it a tiresome circumlocution, and a lot of resistance to Pound's poetry has been based upon the belief that the ideogramic method is just that). Rather, it is a method of investigation, a scientific induction. Particulars are placed next to other particulars, each one yielding up to the reader its "meaning" as a luminous detail; but then the reader—who is in this case the writer also—perceives the relationships between particulars and has a new thought, a new concept. Since the new concept *is* that newly perceived relationship, the ideogram is the only adequate sign for it—"the proper and perfect symbol is the natural object," as Pound says elsewhere. An attempt to formulate the concept as an argument will always distort and falsify it, and since such an attempt will be abstract, it will not convince, it will lead instead to what Pound thought of as useless argument; hence his reluctance to say what the *Cantos* is about. But the ideogram, Pound believed, had to convince. The meaning the reader would derive from his reading would be the meaning present in the ideogram; one could not derive it unless it were really there.

The clearest statement of the way such a poem is supposed to work appears in *Guide to Kulchur* when Pound quotes a statement by Katue Kitasono on the relationship between images and ideas. It is worth quoting at some length:

Now the most interesting subject to us is the relation between imagery and ideoplasty. Contemporary young poets are all vaguely conscious of, and worry about this . . .
The formation of poetry takes such a course as:

A. language   B. imagery   C. ideoplasty
That which we vaguely call poetical effect means, generally, ideoplasty which grows out of the result of imagery. . . .

What we must do first for imagery is (in this order) collection, arrangement and combination. Thus we get the first line: "a shell, a typewriter and grapes" in which we have an aesthetic feeling. But there is not (in it) any further development. We add the next line and then another aesthetic feeling is born. Thus all the lines are combined and a stanza is finished. This means the completion of imagery of that stanza and then ideoplasty begins.[51]

"Ideoplasty," the generation of ideas and thoughts in the minds of author and reader alike, is the result of the imagery. Imagery is not chosen and arranged in order to generate certain ideas; this selection and arrangement is determined by "aesthetic feeling" only. A poem in which the imagery is created to express previously held ideas is, for Kitasono and Pound, invalid. Kitasono insists that "it cannot be allowed as orthodox of poetry that imagery is performed by ideoplasty," and at this point Pound breaks off his quotation to suggest that the reader "pause for reflection." Kitasono goes on to specify the kind of poem in which imagery is performed by ideoplasty, asserting that "Morality poems, political poems and satirical poems are written, almost without exception, with such an illogical principle."[52]

Obviously Kitasono is differentiating between what some critics, following Aristotle, have preferred to call "mimetic" and "didactic" poetry, and it is clear that Pound recognized in didactic poetry the discursive reasoning of the despised logician. He was also aware that some of his critics treated the early Cantos as if they were a didactic poem, in the technical sense, and in Canto 46 he inserted a cryptic warning to the reader:

> And if you will say that this tale teaches . . .
> a lesson, or that the Reverend Eliot
> has found a more natural language . . . you who think you will
> get through hell in a hurry . . .
>
> (46/231)

On the contrary, the most important aspect of the ideogramic method for Pound—what makes it *science*—is that it makes the writing of a poem such as the *Cantos* an act of discovery yielding knowledge that has not before been thought or known. It can do this, he thought, because it dispenses with grammar, with the logical connectives that circumscribe thought and determine its boundaries. Logical connectives represent acts of classification, or predication, by a speaker-writer, manipulations of concepts within limits permitted by the grammar employed. Grammar forbids certain combinations, but there is no limit to what can be juxtaposed and hence no limit to the meanings that an ideogramic poem can generate. Juxtaposition allows us to think the previously unthinkable, to escape the confines of language by employing it in a new way. New thought will free us, striking the chains of convention that have held us in thrall and permitting us to organize our collective lives in accordance with principles that are true because derived from and through reality, from a scientific exploration rather than a rearrangement of old and baseless concepts. The ambition of the *Cantos* is Promethean.

Thus the "ideogramic method" that Pound derived from Fenollosa is a cluster of related concepts, some of which he had arrived at or had been working towards before the Fenollosa materials came into his hands. First, there is the opposition between scientist and logician, the former defined as dealing with reality and the latter as the prisoner of language. Next is a concept of writing that would permit writer and reader access to reality *through* language. And then comes an equally important concept—a way of writing and reading as scientific induction, permitting the serious artist to develop an aesthetic of glimpses into an epic voyage in search of larger truths, the truths of scientific law. These beliefs inform the *Cantos* from the beginning, but the clearest and most simple statement of Pound's notion of science is to be found in a textbook published in 1933. In *ABC of Reading*, Pound begins by advocating "the method of contemporary biologists, that is careful first-hand examination of the matter, and continual COMPARISON of one 'slide' or specimen with another," claiming that Fenollosa's essay was "the first definite assertion of the applicability of scientific method to literary criticism."[53] It is by the method of direct examination that "modern science has arisen, not on the narrow edge of mediaeval logic suspended in a vacuum." The opposition between science and logic, between reality and language, is ascribed to Fenollosa:

The simplest statement I can make of his (Fenollosa's) meaning is as follows:
In Europe, if you ask a man to define anything, his definition always moves away from the simple things that he knows perfectly well, it recedes into an unknown region, that is a region of remoter and progressively remoter abstraction.
. . . .
In the middle ages when there wasn't any material science, as we now understand it, when human knowledge could not make automobiles run, or electricity carry language through the air, etc., etc., in short, when learning

consisted in little more than splitting up of terminology, there was a good deal of care for terminology. . . . But all your teachers will tell you that science developed more rapidly after Bacon had suggested the direct examination of phenomena, and after Galileo and others had stopped discussing things so much, and had begun really to look at them, and to invent means (like the telescope) of seeing them better.

The most useful living member of the Huxley family has emphasized the fact that the telescope wasn't merely an idea, but that it was very definitely a technical achievement.

By contrast to the method of abstraction, or of defining things in more and still more general terms, Fenollosa emphasizes the method of science, "which is the method of poetry," as distinct from that of "philosophic discussion," and is the way the Chinese go about it in their ideograph or abbreviated picture writing.

Pound then gives a rather simplified explanation of Fenollosa's (mistaken) theory of the Chinese ideograph, emphasizing that "Chinese ideogram does not try to be the picture of a sound, or to be a written sign recalling a sound, but it is still the picture of a thing." And he insists that the Chinese method of devising a sign for an "abstract" concept— putting together, for example, the abbreviated pictures of *rose, iron rust, cherry, flamingo* to signify "red"

is very much the kind of thing a biologist does (in a very much more complicated way) when he gets together a few hundred or thousand slides, and picks out what is necessary for his general statement.

This is certainly a simplistic version of Fenollosa. Pound was writing a school textbook and was probably adapting his explanation to his reader, but that is not grounds for concluding that he was consciously misrepresenting what he believed to be the essence of the ideogramic method. He boldly declares that "The Chinese 'word' or ideogram for red is based on something everyone KNOWS," believing that Chinese writing yielded its significance to direct perception. The sculptor Gaudier-Brzeska, Pound had claimed elsewhere, could "read" some characters simply by looking at them.[54]

Fenollosa's ideas are mistaken, and the errors are important. For it is not a mere matter of "sinological mistakes," as Kenner would have us believe; it is Fenollosa's epistemology that is flawed, and the same epistemology is responsible for the *Cantos.* Pound believed that reality was accessible to "direct" examination, that the significance or essence of any part of that reality was there to be perceived. Language, too, was transparent; the skilled reader could know the intention and character of long-dead writers, and the serious artist—sincere in his intentions and conscientious in his technique—could render his own language transparent to all. These beliefs, and the fact that they are mistaken, explain so much that is at first puzzling about Pound. The beliefs explain why he complained endlessly about writing criticism— "If you want to find out something about painting you go to the National Gallery, or the Salon Carré, or the Brera, or the Prado, and LOOK at the pictures. For every reader of books on art, 1,000 people go to LOOK at the paintings. Thank heaven!"[55] The fact that the beliefs are mistaken—art is not a matter of "direct" or "natural" perception but of a trained and actively interpreting "seeing"—explains why Pound, despite his protestations, wrote more criticism than most other authors. The beliefs explain why the *Cantos* are the way they are— images juxtaposed with neither narrative nor commentary to connect them, since their significance, individual and cumulative, is supposedly there on the page if you will only LOOK at it. The fact that the beliefs are mistaken explains the difficulty of the poem and why no fully convincing and coherent reading of it exists. The beliefs explain Pound's dogmatism and both the dedication and the violence with which he entered the political arena; for if the poem was the *scientific* induction he believed it to be, its conclusions were a solid foundation for action. The fact that the beliefs are mistaken—the poem yielded not knowledge but at best hypotheses that a man less convinced of the invulnerability of his method would have regarded more sceptically— explains the anti-Semitism, the scurrilous rhetoric, the Rome broadcasts, Mussolini, and Pisa.

103

The Pound/Fenollosa epistemology is flawed, but its flaws are neither outrageous nor unusual. For this epistemology is not far removed from the "common sense" theory of knowledge upon which daily life is—and must be—based. Whatever reservations we may have *in theory,* we do and must act as if what we perceive is "really there," as long as our interpretations are corroborated by the interpretations and behavior of others. All knowledge is "theory-impregnated," as Karl Popper puts it, yet we regard as objective reality the world as constituted by the "theories" of the society to which we belong. The source of Pound's errors is not simply the epistemology to which he subscribed nor the concept of science based upon it, but the lengths to which he trusted it. "Common sense" is based upon an epistemology like Pound's, but common sense also dictates reservations and qualifications which Pound, convinced of the soundness of his procedures, ignored. As Karl Popper points out,

With my hands in my pockets, I am quite "certain" that I have five fingers on each of my hands; but if the life of my best friend should depend on the truth of this proposition, I might (and I think I should) take my hands out of my pockets to make "doubly" sure that I have not lost one or the other of my fingers miraculously.[56]

Our common sense "certainty," in other words, depends upon what is at stake. But as the stakes rose and Europe erupted into world war, Pound became not less but more certain, accepting without question "evidence" that required much closer examination. No profound doubt enters the poem until Pisa, when his own situation amid the "wreckage of Europe" changed the poem's tone and its direction, so that it ends not in the firm conclusions which he had set out to find but in drafts, fragments, and silence.

> *I have tried to write Paradise*
> *Do not move*
> *Let the wind speak*
> *that is paradise*

This recognition, and a prayer for forgiveness, are the last page of the *Cantos*, a poem which amounts in the end to a refutation of the hope which gave it birth, to an implicit admission that "we are seekers for truth but we are not its possessors."[57]

Notes

1. *Literary Essays of Ezra Pound*, ed. T. S. Eliot (1954; reprint ed., New York: New Directions, 1980), pp. 41–57. Hereafter cited as *LE*.

2. This essay is excerpted from my work in progress, *Truth and Calliope: The Poetry of Ezra Pound*.

3. "Psychology and Troubadours" (1912), incorporated in *The Spirit of Romance* (1910; new ed., Norfolk, Conn.: New Directions, 1953), p. 92.

4. *Ezra Pound: Selected Prose 1909– 1965* (New York: New Directions, 1973), p. 50. Hereafter cited as *SP*.

5. This preface appeared as a quotation over the pseudonym "Weston St. Llewmys." It is reprinted in *Collected Early Poems of Ezra Pound*, ed. Michael King (New York: New Directions, 1976), p. 58.

6. *Guide to Kulchur* (1938; reprint ed., New York: New Directions, 1968), pp. 89–90. Hereafter cited as *GK*.

7. Reprinted in *Pavannes and Divagations* (New York: New Directions, 1958), p. 97, and in *SP*, p. 48.

8. From "Vorticism," *Fortnightly Review* 96 [n.s.] (1 Sept. 1914), 573. I quote from the article as reprinted in Pound's *Gaudier-Brzeska: A Memoir* (1916; reprint ed., New York: New Directions, 1970), p. 86. Hereafter cited as *GB*.

9. From "A Talk on Dante," a 1950 lecture collected in *Selected Prose*, ed. John Hayward (London: Penguin Books, 1963), p. 96.

10. This poem was deleted from the proofs of *Canzoni* (1911) and later issued as *Redondillas* (New York: New Directions, 1968) in a limited edition. It is now reprinted as "Redondillas, or something of that sort" in *Collected Early Poems of Ezra Pound*, pp. 215–222.

11. *LE*, pp. 43–44.

12. *LE*, p. 276.

13. *The Selected Letters of Ezra Pound: 1907– 1941*, ed. D.D. Paige (1950; new edition, New York: New Directions, 1971), p. 6. Hereafter cited as *Letters*.

14. *Patria Mia*, a revision of articles appearing in the *New Age* in 1912, was intended for publication in book form in 1913 but did not appear until 1950. I quote from *SP*, pp. 112–3.

15. *LE*, p. 9.

16. *SP*, p. 41.

17. *LE*, p. 3.

18. *ABC of Reading* (1934; reprint ed., New York: New Directions, 1960), pp. 101–2.

19. Hugh Kenner, *The Pound Era* (Berkeley and Los Angeles: University of California Press, 1971), p. 186.

20. Ibid., p. 189.

21. Ibid., p. 186.

22. Ibid., pp. 186–7.

23. *SP*, p. 455.

24. *Spirit of Romance*, p. 14.

25. *GB*, p. 92.

26. Ibid.

27. Ibid., p. 84.

28. Ibid., p. 81.

29. Ibid., p. 50.

30. *LE*, p. 5.

31. *GB*, p. 86.

32. Ibid., p. 8.

33. Ibid., p. 87.

34. *Ezra Pound: His Metric and Poetry* (New York: Knopf, 1917), p. 22.

35. See *Ezra Pound: The Image and the Real* (Baton Rouge: Louisiana State University Press, 1969), pp. 56ff, and "Wisdom Past Metaphor: Another View of Pound, Fenollosa, and Objective Verse," *Paideuma* 5, no. 1 (Spring-Summer 1976), 15–29.

36. See "The Persistent East" in Kenner, *Pound Era*, especially pp. 231–2.

37. *The Genesis of Ezra Pound's Cantos* (Princeton, N.J.: Princeton University Press, 1976), p. 10ff.

38. Ibid., p. 16.

39. "Poet of Many Voices," in Walter Sutton, ed., *Ezra Pound: A Collection of Critical Essays* (Englewood Cliffs, N.J.: Prentice-Hall, 1963), p. 161.

40. *The Chinese Written Character as a Medium for Poetry*, ed. Ezra Pound (San Francisco: City Lights, 1969), p. 28. Pound had prepared Fenollosa's essay for publication by early 1915, but did not succeed in getting it into print until 1920, when he incorporated it into *Instigations* (New York: Boni and Liveright).

41. *Letters*, p. 46.

42. Ibid., p. 61.

43. *GK*, p. 291.

44. *SP*, p. 33.

45. Ibid., p. 130.
46. Ibid.
47. *Chinese Written Character*, p. 12.
48. Ibid., p. 27.
49. Ibid., p. 22.
50. Ibid., p. 13.
51. *GK*, pp. 137–8.
52. *GK*, p. 139.
53. This and the following quotations are from *ABC of Reading*, pp. 17–23.
54. See *Chinese Written Character*, pp. 30–31n, and *ABC of Reading*, p. 21.
55. *ABC of Reading*, p. 23.
56. *Objective Knowledge: An Evolutionary Approach* (1972; reprint ed. with corrections, London: Oxford University Press, 1975), p. 79.
57. Ibid., p. 47.

5. The Pound Problem

Wendy Stallard Flory

The central issue of the "Pound Problem" and the hardest and most necessary to understand is, in my opinion, not the charge of treason but the charge of anti-Semitism. One response to this is, of course, outrage and the feeling that the anti-Semitism vitiates everything else that Pound did. A more common recourse is to divide Pound into three more or less separate people—the brilliant poet, the crack-brained economist, and the hate-filled, fascistic anti-Semite. Hilton Kramer made use of this division when he wrote in a recent book review, "For professional Poundians, of course, everything the master produced— whether it was gibberish on economics, foul-mouthed ravings on politics or sound guidance on the esthetics of poetry—is taken for pure gold."[1] But Pound was, after all, one person—not three—and it is evasive to act as if this were not so. Yet the critic who wants to put the three Ezra Pounds back together again is faced with no easy task. To do this means to attempt to understand Pound's motives and intentions more clearly than he at the time understood them himself.

We have been slow to understand exactly what Pound was about for two rather different reasons. On one hand, his motives were complex and his program of action highly idiosyncratic. On the other hand, his anti-Semitism generated an understandable outrage. The outrage is often based, however, on some assumptions that have not been carefully examined: first, that there is a connection between Pound's anti-Semitism and Nazi anti-Semitism, and second, that he was moved by violent hatred. I suspect that, to some degree, we have had an ulterior motive for assuming the worst about Pound and believing him guilty of a form of anti-Semitism so extreme that we could then dissociate ourselves from it. It seems likely that outrage at Pound has partly served as a distraction from two facts about the recent American past that we would like to forget: how much enthusiasm there had been for Mussolini in the United States before 1935 and, much more serious, how extreme and widespread anti-Semitism had been in America from the 1920s to the 1940s.

We will not be able to be precise about Pound's anti-Semitism until we are able to be precise about anti-Semitism in general. Although it is obviously not possible to examine the subject in detail here, it does seem necessary to give a general and abbreviated overview of some of the basic patterns of anti-Semitic thinking.[2] We are often evasive in our thinking on anti-Semitism because of an understandable desire to distance ourselves as far as possible from a phenomenon which, in its most extreme manifestations, has given free reign to the worst kinds of bestiality that human beings are capable of. Most people want to believe that a great gulf separates the active persecutor of Jews from the rest of "normal" humankind, themselves included, and to this end emphasize the abnormality of the "rabid" or "hysterical" anti-Semite, glossing over the variety of "milder" forms of anti-Semitism. The "rabid" anti-Semite would be a person who is driven by a pathological fear of inadequacy which dates from childhood and is independent of circumstances and impervious to reason. If we consign Pound to this category, we can put him "beyond the pale," conveniently obviate the need for any serious discussion of his case and relegate him to the status of an object of hatred, scorn, or pity. Yet when we study the facts of the case, it becomes clear that until the mid-1930s he was considerably less anti-Semitic than was usual at that time in America, in England, and in France. When, after 1935, he started to take some anti-Semitic ideas seriously, this was the direct result of choices made at that time.

In an attempt to gloss over or divert attention from the extent of tacit anti-Semitism in America, we are likely to brand as a rabid anti-Semite anyone who expresses publicly the very anti-Semitic prejudices to which the vast majority of gentiles subscribe privately. If anti-Semitism is taken to mean a viewpoint that holds that negative stereotypes about Jews in general are likely to be true of any Jew as an individual, it would be true to say that anti-Semitism in some form or another has been almost universal among gentiles in Europe and America. When we try to account for this, it quickly becomes clear that even as far-ranging an influence as the Christian Church's historical encouragement of anti-Semitic attitudes is not sufficient to explain the almost infallible readiness of gentiles to give some degree of assent to derogatory stereotypes of the Jews as a group. I believe that there is an explanation for this readiness and that it has nothing whatever to do with Jewish characteristics or attributes. It lies in an impulse to which all human beings are subject to some degree and that could hardly be more tenacious, rooted as it is in an instinctive selfishness.

Anti-Semitism is one of a series of possible manifestations of a fundamental moral weakness of which all human beings are guilty at some time and to some degree and by which every adult who does not make the conscious decision to resist is bound to be trapped. This moral weakness is the temptation to inflate one's sense of self-worth by taking satisfaction from the idea that others are at a disadvantage, unfortunate, or merely different. There is a strong incentive to think of any kind of difference from the norm which one has chosen to subscribe to as automatic inferiority, since this enormously increases the number of people to whom one can feel superior. The desire for this satisfaction that lies behind all kinds of prejudice is endemic and, although immoral, is certainly not abnormal. Very few people are able to attain the degree of maturity which would make them completely indifferent to the appeal of this type of satisfaction, but for many the pleasure of condescension is enough, and they have no inclination to act upon their prejudices.

The stimulus which intensifies prejudice and makes it active rather than passive is always fear. This is in fact a fear of personal inadequacy which refuses to acknowledge itself as such and claims to have discovered in the objects of its prejudice the reasons for its existence. It is possible to identify two common kinds of fear which are likely to intensify prejudice.

The first is a fear of loss of social status and of the respectability, esteem, or power that goes with this. Although this is primarily a specifically personal problem, it is often aggravated by patterns of social change on a large scale. The second and usually the more pervasive and potentially dangerous fear is the one that accompanies personal economic difficulties and that becomes most militant in periods of national economic crisis. The process by which such fears lead to anti-Semitism is the same in both cases. When, as almost always happens, people refuse or are unable to see that the fear springs from a sense of personal inadequacy, the fear is impossible to deal with and there is a strong tendency to attempt to externalize it by inventing some outside source for it. Since nothing short of self-confrontation will allay the anxiety, the charade of blaming some supposed hostile influence cannot offer any possible resolution to the problem and is likely to intensify it. The subconscious awareness of lying to oneself gives rise to further confusion and frustration, and the sense of suppressed guilt at one's self-delusion is added to the original sense of inadequacy and of being trapped by circumstances beyond one's control. The inexorable consequences of self-delusion lock the anti-Semite into reflexive suspicion and hatred and require increasingly emphatic assertions of the guilt of the scapegoat. Hence the strong appeal of anti-Semitic demagogues, since they seem to offer authoritative sanction for the spurious charges and help to relieve the anti-Semitically inclined individual of some or all of the burden of proof.

It is likely that our reactions to individual anti-Semites will partly be influenced by their motives. When the underlying fear is related to financial hardship, they may appear to be primarily guilty of selfishness or cowardice. When the motive is snobbery or the fear of loss of social status, we may be more tempted to charge them with pettiness or meanspiritedness. In the case of Pound, the evidence shows that he was not moved by either of these fears. Nor does he belong in the category of people whose anti-Semitism is an outlet for the personal grudge which comes from a deep-rooted and long-standing fear of inadequacy.

The most recent and also most detailed presentation of the latter view is Daniel Pearlman's essay "Ezra Pound: America's Wandering Jew." Pearlman's premises are that Pound was first and foremost an aesthete who despised the common man, that he had an authoritarian personality and coveted power himself, and that the psychological compulsion behind the anti-Semitism of the radio speeches was a long-standing suppressed envy of people with financial security, stemming in large part from his resentment at the decline of the fortunes of the Pound family.[3]

Pound's grandfather Thaddeus had plenty of energy and determination, but it would be a mistake to think of his career as a high point of success and prosperity in comparison with which the family fortunes of the next generation seemed to be in decline. Of all of Thaddeus's many schemes—some of them well-conceived, some of them impractical—none really "paid off" for him in the long run and his grandson was well aware of this. In *Indiscretions* he draws attention to a particular characteristic of his grandfather—his "ability to regard possibilities rather than facts." This characteristic was so pronounced in his father that Pound described him as "the naivest man who ever possessed sound sense," and although he almost certainly would not have seen it at the time, it was a characteristic that Pound himself had inherited in good measure.

When Pearlman refers to the text of the speeches to make his case, he frequently insists that Pound means the opposite of what he is saying. As I intend to show, I believe that this explanation of

Pound's motives is fundamentally wrong and is based on an inaccurate view of his personality. The suggestion that Pound means the opposite of what he says about the persecution of Jews—or about anything else—is highly suspect. We cannot begin to understand Pound's motives until we realize that he was not in any sense a devious or designing person. He never consciously did things for ulterior motives and was, in fact, candid to a fault. Those who were close to him tell how he never managed to break his habit of saying exactly what was on his mind and, as a result, was constantly hurting people's feelings in ways that he never seemed able to anticipate and guard against. Not that they resented him for this. It was obvious that he spoke without any intention of giving offense—it was "just the way he was." Perhaps because he was so free from duplicity himself he was astonishingly oblivious to it in others. This partly accounts for the way in which he continued to rely on Mussolini's good faith long after he should have seen through the Duce's public professions and propaganda. Pound was a person who could not lie to himself with impunity, so when he did deceive himself about Mussolini's intentions, beginning in 1935 with the invasion of Ethiopia, he would have to pay a very heavy price for it.

To the extent that Pound was anti-Semitic before the mid-1930s, his anti-Semitism was of a nineteenth-century variety far less virulent than that which surfaced in America in the 1920s and 30s after he left the country. It is only when Pound began to lie to himself about the dangers of Mussolini's imperialist ambitions that he began to take seriously and to advocate publicly the idea of an international conspiracy of predominantly Jewish bankers to start wars. His decision to turn to this paranoid theory was a direct result of his refusal to acknowledge his misgivings about the direction that Mussolini's policies had taken. The self-delusion that was the root of the problem was unusual in that it originated in altruism rather than in selfishness and was the result of overconfidence and overoptimism rather than pettiness, meanspiritedness, or sullen fatalism. His was the predicament of the over-sanguine reformer who expects too confidently an imminent solution to major social problems and then, when the evidence begins to invalidate his optimism, tries to close his eyes to it and, when this is no longer possible, lashes out in anger. We see the culmination of this process very clearly in Carlyle's *Latter Day Pamphlets.*

If we are to arrive at any valid conclusions about the nature of Pound's anti-Semitism we must begin by making some important dissociations between Nazi and Italian fascist anti-Semitism, between both of these and anti-Semitism in America, and between American agrarian anti-Semitism of the 1890s and that of the WASP establishment in the 1920s.

Because Pound broadcast over Rome Radio during the war, expressing anti-Semitic sentiments and reiterating his faith in the good intentions of Mussolini, he has usually been assumed to be an anti-Semite of the Nazi variety and has been execrated accordingly. What his accusers have conveniently omitted to mention or chosen to overlook is the important fact that Italy in the 20s and 30s was not only less anti-Semitic than Germany but far less anti-Semitic than the United States. Italy was, in fact, the least anti-Semitic of all the countries of Europe, and until 1938 Mussolini himself in his public pronouncements was actively philo-Semitic. Some American anti-Semites accused Mussolini of as much: an editorial of July 18, 1925, in Henry Ford's *Dearborn Independent* claimed, "When Italy emerged from the chaos of war and discovered that the International Jewish Bankers had hamstrung the country, a strong anti-Semitic feeling threatened to arise, but the Mussolini movement broke forth, and is now the protector of the pro-Jewish program throughout Italy." Meir Michaelis points out that "[a]fter a decade of Fascist rule, Italy was still a model of tolerance as far as treatment of her Jewish minority was concerned. Relations between the authorities and the Jews had never been better."[4]

Until the early 1930s, "Italian anti-Semitism was still only an oddity," and it was not until Mussolini decided to conquer an Empire for Italy that race became an issue for him. Despite his "unfeigned repugnance" at Hitler's theories of race, Mussolini, once he had chosen opportunistically to ally himself with the Führer, realized that this rapprochement would "automatically bring him into conflict with Jews all over the world, despite his tolerant attitude to the Jews of Italy."[5] He produced the "Manifesto of the Race" and from July 1938 on introduced a series of racial laws severely limiting the freedom of Jews in Italy. Dismayed at his reversals in Africa and angry at Hitler's treatment of him, Mussolini lashed out at his generals, the Church, and the Italian middle classes, yet rather than trying to blame the Jews, "his references to his Jewish subjects became increasingly philo-Semitic" and he continued steadfast in his resistance to the murder of Jews. As long as he was in power, no Jews were deported from Italy to the death camps. Despite the best efforts of the SS, Jews were also safe in the Italian-occupied areas of Croatia, France, and Greece, which became havens or escape routes for Jewish refugees from German or Bulgarian zones of occupation, thanks to the inventiveness of the

Italian consular authorities and full cooperation of Italian soldiers of all ranks. It was only after the Duce's overthrow that the Germans were able to begin the deportation of Italian Jews. As Michaelis says, "If the 'Jew-lovers' of Salò [Giovanni Preziosi's term for Mussolini and his Cabinet] had been masters in their own house, no Italian Jew would have perished in the Holocaust."[6]

Pound developed his enthusiasm for Mussolini in the 1920s at a time when the Duce was strongly philo-Semitic and when Italy, unlike America, was virtually without anti-Semitism in any form. Clearly the received opinion that Pound became a slavish follower of the Duce because this would allow free scope for his repressed anti-Semitism is hard to prove.

Pound in Italy considered himself to be first and foremost an expert on fiscal theory. He had been raised in a family with a strong tradition of commitment to social reform. He had formulated his economic ideas in England in the 1910s under the influence of A. R. Orage and Major C. H. Douglas. After he added Silvio Gesell's idea of stamp script, he held tenaciously to his economic theories throughout his residence in Italy. He advocated them with increasingly desperate emphasis as the war approached, broadcast them over Rome Radio, and continued to believe in them for the rest of his life. Mussolini was important to him not because he admired the Duce's ideas but because he thought that Mussolini might be persuaded to put into practice Pound's own ideas. He saw himself not as the Duce's follower but as his economic advisor and the economic advice he gave was intended not simply to help Italy but to save Western culture and civilization—to save America in particular—and to stop wars.

Pound had sound reasons for believing, in 1933, that "the fascist revolution was FOR the preservation of certain liberties," as he wrote in *Jefferson and/or Mussolini*,[7] a work which Williams reviewed very enthusiastically in *New Democracy*, claiming that Pound "has never done a better piece of writing."[8] In the course of the review, Williams writes in a distinctly Poundian vein:

In the tremendous task of bringing credit into line as the only means for effective distribution of world wealth, lies the hope of the future. Pound has realized this before all the widely touted professional economists and makes it the basis of what he has to say. Who is it that wants us to believe that we are in for a hundred years of bloody and destructive wars? Who is it that wishes us to believe that the U.S. is sinking under a burden of debts? None but those who wish to profit by wars or who have credit to lend at 6% while they hold tax-free bonds *from the government* at an additional 1½ or 2 or 3%. The world has gone in for stupidity [on] a large scale and we crave to be hypnotized and raped. There is no millenium for sheep.

113

And he was, if anything, even more emphatic when he wrote in April 1936—again for *New Democracy*—a piece called "A Social Diagnosis for Surgery" under the by-line "A Poet-Physician on the Money-Cancer." This essay begins, "The unmitigated fools! can they not see, they who possess bank credit, willingly or unwillingly, as a private instrument, that their capitalism is dying rapidly of a disease of which the cure is known? This is not a question of radicalism or conservatism but of surgery, of a growth to be extirpated that is eating out their viscera. . . . The disease is usury. The capitalistic world is bound headlong for disaster of the direst sort unless that in its guts . . .has been removed."[9]

During the 1920s in America, many middle- and upper-class WASP citizens in positions of power and influence in their communities, institutions, businesses were—with the support and approval of the majority of the WASP community—actively involved in depriving Jews of their rights and liberties and in publicizing in the most blatant way the ugliest of anti-Semitic attitudes and stereotypes. Clubs, hotels, and resorts were often closed to Jews; they were frequently excluded from universities and medical schools; and they were routinely discriminated against in hiring and in housing. A. Lawrence Lowell, president of Harvard, "urged the Corporation to adopt a quota system to solve the 'Jewish Problem.' " At the beginning of the 1920s Nicholas Murray Butler "cut down the proportion of Jews at Columbia from 40 to around 20% within two years."[10] Jews were largely excluded from tenured positions in good universities in almost all disciplines and "no Jew ever held a tenure appointment in any English department at the 'big three' until the Second War."[11] There was widespread support for the eugenics movement and for the restriction of immigration. In 1914, Edward A. Ross published his influential attack on immigration in *The Old World and the New,* and "most of the leading social scientists of [his] generation . . . either directly or indirectly gave aid, counsel or moral support to the work of the Immigration Restriction League."[12]

As E. Digby Baltzell reminds us, "In [1924] President Coolidge, who had previously written an article on the dangers of race-pollution for *Good Housekeeping* magazine, called for some final and permanent restrictive [immigration] legislation in his annual message to Congress," and signed such a bill into law later that year. Baltzell continues, the bill "ended the dream of America as a land of hope and opportunity for the toiling and oppressed masses of the Old World. It was indeed the end of an optimistic and humanitarian epoch in American history.

Yet this so-called Nordic victory was certainly a popular triumph, supported by the vast majority of the American people of all classes and various economic interests."[13]

Pound, living in Europe, cannot be implicated in this ugly triumph of meanspiritedness and, as we can tell from his writings, he was not raised with the WASP establishment's offensively condescending attitudes toward the immigrant. Although their names are often mentioned together in discussions of anti-Semitism among American writers, Henry Adams' snobbish, spiteful, and resentful feelings are completely lacking in Pound. Pound himself unwittingly prepares his own best defense in the pages of *Patria Mia*. His enthusiastic optimism about the contribution that he believes the new immigrants will make to the vitality of American society shows that he has nothing in common with the nativists. It is precisely this instinctive optimism and generosity of spirit that too many critics of Pound are ready to overlook or deny, that is the hallmark of his personality, and that must be acknowledged by anyone claiming to offer a fair appraisal of him. His reaction to the disruptive effect of the massive "new immigration" is to be encouraged by the fact that "uncertainty of standards" is often a symptom or forecast of a renaissance. He takes as one of the signs of a renaissance for the "American medieval system"

the surging crowd on Seventh Avenue. . . . A crowd pagan as ever imperial Rome was, eager, careless, with an animal vigour unlike that of any European crowd that I have ever looked at. There is none of the melancholy, the sullenness, the unhealth of the London mass, none of the worn vivacity of Paris. . . . One returns from Europe and one takes note of the size and vigour of this new strange people. They are not Anglo-Saxon; their gods are not the gods whom one was reared to reverence. . . .[14] . . . The sort of man who made America is nomadic. . . . Out of races static there came in the beginning the migratory element, and generation by generation this divided itself into parts, static and migratory, and the former was marooned and left inert, and the latter pushed on to new forests, to mines, to grazing land. . . . The static element of the Anglo-Saxon migration is submerged and well nigh lost in the pool of races which have followed them. . . . People marvel that foreigners deluge America and "lose their own individuality almost at once"; that "their children all look alike." It must be considered that the men who come to America from Hungary, or from Sweden, Dravats, Slavs, Czecs. [sic], Italians, Germans, are men of similar tastes and similar intentions. Irish or Russian Jew, the man comes with the determination to improve his material condition.[15]

His position on the mixing of the races is certainly very far from that of the American eugenicists:

The Englishman, in dealing with the American, forgets, I think, that he has to do with a southerner, a man of the Midi. He thinks, erroneously, that the United States, once a set of his colonies, is by race Anglo-Saxon. New York is on the same parallel with Florence. Philadelphia is farther south than Rome. It is certain that the climate has about as much to do with the characteristics of a people as their ethnology. And especially if the race is mongrel, one stock neutralizing the forces of the other, the climate takes up its lordship and decrees the nature of the people resulting.[16]

Pound's comments on Roosevelt in the radio speeches are often referred to as particularly strong evidence of his instability but always with no mention of the virulence of opposition to Roosevelt in America itself. Pound was not initially hostile to Roosevelt and only became so in response to what he saw as the President's responsibility for America's entry into the war. As was always the case, Pound's primary motive for hostility was his conviction that war must be avoided at all costs. In contrast, the haters of Roosevelt in America were frequently motivated by feelings that were not capable of any justification. Baltzell concludes that "the hatred of Roosevelt, shared by the majority of the WASP establishment, was surely due to deep-seated caste values and an irrational fear, if not horror, of social and racial equality."[17] He refers to George Wolfskill's judgment in the history of the American Liberty League that "the hatred of Roosevelt had far deeper origins than mere economics, as anyone who dined out in polite society at the time knows—anyone, that is, who remembers being called a Jew- or nigger-lover for making even a mildly favorable comment on 'That Man, Rosenfelt.' "[18] And Baltzell finds Eric Goldman making this point in his *Rendezvous with Destiny*, "For quite a while I have lived in a commuter community that is rabidly anti-Roosevelt and I am convinced that the heart of their hatred is not economic. The real source of the venom is that Roosevelt challenged their feeling that they were superior people, occupying by right a privileged position in the world."[19]

Pound himself is never guilty of this "anti-Semitism of the privileged." His commitment to reform, no matter how impractical it came to seem, was always thoroughly sincere, and this, together with his natural optimism, altruism, and generosity of spirit, made him incapable of the selfish and self-righteous commitment to repression found in the new class of establishment anti-Semites of the 1920s.

Embittered and embattled in the face of what they chose to see as a threat to their ascendancy and privilege, these influential voices in academia, business, and politics provided both a rationale for and a means by which to act upon their deliberate aversion to the Jews as a race. Pound, who would have found this new variety of American

anti-Semitism offensive, because of his European vantage point, was
not aware of its real nature. When he does finally stoop to anti-Semitism
once war comes, he recurs to the slogans of the old-style, Populist
anti-Semitism of the thwarted agrarian reformers of the 1890s. This has
nothing to do with the theories of the racial degeneracy of the Jews,
popularized in the 1920s, but centers on the idea of Jewish control
of international finance. As John Higham explains in *Strangers in the
Land*, the ancient stereotype of the associaton of Jews with gold was
given a new emphasis with the agrarian movement's attack on the gold
standard and campaigns for free silver in the 1890s, so that we find
William Jennings Bryan accusing President Cleveland of "putting the
country in the hands of the English Rothschilds."[20]

Pound's own family history and the roots of his commitment to
social reform lie very much in this period of American reformism.
It is no coincidence that when he spoke over Rome Radio, Pound
referred from time to time to his grandfather, Thaddeus Pound. He
ended his May 4, 1942, broadcast with the comment: "This is my war
all right, I have been in it for 20 years. My Grandad was in it before
me." In another speech of the same year he says that his radio talks are
based on facts that

mostly antedate the fascist era and cannot be considered as improvisations
trumped up to meet present requirements. Neither can the beliefs of
Washington, John Adams, Jefferson, Jackson, Van Buren, and Lincoln be
laughed off as mere fascist propaganda. And even my own observations date
largely before the opening of the present hostilities, as do those of my
grandfather expressed in the U.S. Congress in 1878. I defend the particularly
American, North American, United States heritage. If anybody can find
anything hostile to the Constitution of the U.S.A. in these speeches, it would
greatly interest me to know what.[21]

It is clear that Pound saw himself as following in his grandfather's
footsteps, as indeed he was and—in an important sense—had always
been. His decision in 1922 to write the history of his family showed his
interest in his activist forebears, but at that stage he was resisting the
idea of following their example: "It is one thing to feel that one could
write the whole social history of the United States from one's family
annals, and vastly another to embark upon any such Balzacian and
voluminous endeavour." He told how he had "received personal and
confidential reports"—at a very early age—"about ancestors such
as Joseph Wadsworth, who stole the Connecticut Charter and hid it
in Charter Oak, to the embarrassment of legitimist tyranny." He
admitted to having felt only "a certain intellectual interest in stealing

charters pro bono (very romantically) publico" but claimed "my interest had suffered etiolation . . .that is, to the extent that one had no intention of allowing these things to obtrude upon one's own future action even though one may in the safety of twenty years lapse admit their value as literary capital—in part."[22] Yet they were destined most definitely to be more to him than just literary capital.

The whole of *Indiscretions* is written in an arch manner appropriate to the persona of the aesthete he had chosen for his public appearances during his London years. He had, of course, been every bit as activist in literary matters as his grandfather had ever been in politics and strenuously earnest on both economic and poetic matters (as he was always to be), but he needed some protective camouflage to move around unscathed under the rather supercilious eye of Wyndham Lewis. A condescending but good-natured facetiousness had proved quite serviceable. But a strong moral earnestness and an extraordinary degree of naivety was in the blood and, even as he was writing *Indiscretions*, the social activist was feeling increasingly constricted by the persona of the aesthete and the hedonist—as *Hugh Selwyn Mauberley* clearly shows.

Although, as he wrote *Indiscretions*, Pound claimed to be seeing his family history as no more than literary capital, the very fact that he chose to write about this material shows that it was of more than incidental interest to him. His decision, a year later, to go to Italy shows that in deciding to write *Indiscretions*, he was in fact returning to his roots to re-orient himself and to cast off the mask of the very persona behind which he had chosen to write the work. In Italy he found hopeful signs that the economic and social reforms to which he had become increasingly commited had a chance of being implemented. He did not need the aesthete's mask as he had in England and France, and we can now see him clearly as a social activist of a distinctly American variety and with marked family characteristics.

It is possible to use the *Indiscretions* descriptions of his father and grandfather to make a composite picture of the poet himself. Thaddeus, auburn-haired like his grandson, was known for his campaign oratory which gave him what a reporter described as a "blood and thunder popularity that pushed him to the front at Republican Party Conventions." "It has been my wont," a Wisconsin newspaper reported him as saying, "to participate more or less actively in the persuasive work incidental to presidential campaigns. . . . Orators for months have thundered the land with arguments, logic, statistics, and history, while the press deluged every fireside with oceans of political literature." His grandson rather had the edge over him in matters of metaphor, but the two of them clearly shared a conviction of the power of oratory and a strong attraction to the orator's role. They also shared a strong concern for fiscal matters. The following certainly has a Poundian ring to it: "The constitution provides that Congress shall 'have the power to coin money and fix the value thereof.' There you have it in a nutshell. . . Now the monstrous proposition is presented . . . to turn the mints of this republic over to the owners of bullion . . . for their free use to convert silver into legal tender dollars, and pocket the . . . difference between the commercial and coin value of metal so coined. . . . [It is the Government's duty] not [to] consent . . . either to the whim, caprice or interest of any man or class of men."[23] This could be Ezra Pound speaking, but it is in fact his grandfather.

Homer and Isabel themselves provided their son with a very concrete model for social activism in the missionary work among Italian immigrants in the slums of Philadelphia that they undertook for the Presbyterian Church. Pound appreciated the value of what they were doing and helped in the work on occasion, as we see in the second of a series of four articles published under the title "Through Alien Eyes" in the *New Age* of January and February 1913. In the course of describing the South 10th Street Mission, Pound writes:

Children came there to learn wood-carving and modelling, and to give plays on a stage in the basement. . . . These Italians are for the most part sturdy peasants who make a living by working on railroads and as masons. . . . They come to the "church" for relaxation, for amusement, it is a decorative feature in their lives. . . . On the opposite corner there is an institution maintained by the Jews. Here you would find children huddled together, learning every sort of trade—shoe-making, the various specialities of tailoring, etc. . . . This wise and provident people, receiving its emigrants from Russia, from the afflicted districts, takes measures to prepare them as swiftly as possible to make their way among new surroundings, to acquire—and they do acquire—and buy up land and become rich in due season. . . . I point out the Jewish system of training as the wise means devised by one section of the poor, one nation of our country, to gain advantage over the rest . . . if any work is done "interdenominationally" the Jew overruns it and gradually pushes out the others. . . . Acquisitive, he wants "culture," or anything else that he can get, free; and he has the foresight which is more or less lacking among the simpler, more sensuous emigrants. It is obvious . . . that an intelligent "lower class" would by instinct wish to learn trades and industries rather than "book learning." And it is obvious that this is a wise instinct, and that a sincere Government would try to give them facilities for acquiring such knowledge. . . . My impression of the few missions I've seen [in London] is that they are the old sort that teach the children to sing psalms and to honour their landlord.[24]

To the extent that this is anti-Semitic it clearly involves a passive voicing of prejudice without personal animus and with a lack of self-consciousness which would be impossible today. He concedes the wisdom of the Jewish approach to the training of the young, yet it is clear that his sympathies lay with the less calculating Italian peasants whose easy-going ways, he felt, put them at something of a disadvantage in the immigrants' struggle for economic security. Behind these comments may well have existed a sense that the Italians were mainly at a disadvantage in having a much less well-organized support system at their disposal than the Jews. By 1885, one year after its founding, the Association of Jewish Immigrants at 931 South 4th Street was able to provide shelter for 848 persons and, in the same year, it had processed 900 job applications.[25] This is, of course, something of a reflection on the services offered by the Presbyterian Mission which, although well-intentioned, were by comparison rather ineffectual.

There is certainly no hint of hatred of Jews in this series of articles, but we do find signs of a predictable and largely unselfconscious anti-Semitism of a variety common in America of the 1880s and 1890s when Pound contrasts to the heroic figure of the striking British coal-miner a hypothetical British "shop-keeping type" of the future who "will have the large buttocks of the Jew [and] the curious out-turning feet, and this will be surmounted by a bowler hat and a chest of the dimensions of those which one sees hovering about Eustace Miles' restaurant." Peter Gay claims that even in the case of Germany there was a radical difference between nineteenth- and twentieth-century anti-Semitism:

[N]ineteenth century anti-Semitism, however unpalatable even at the time, however pregnant with a terrifying future, was different in kind from the twentieth-century variety. It belonged in a coarse, remarkably crude culture, a culture in which cruel ethnic jokes—jokes that would make us cringe today—formed the staple of innocuous, even benign humor, and unfeeling ethnic caricatures—caricatures we have learned to identify with the lethal stereotyping of the Nazis—were common coin.[26]

Nineteenth-century, unselfconsciously racist attitudes were unquestionably a part of Pound's childhood, as is clear from several of the large number of items in Carl Gatter's collection of Poundiana in the University of Pennsylvania library. In the article from the *Jenkintown Times-Chronicle* for May 30, 1896, for example, we read: "Just no more Italians in Wyncote. Is our budding hope that this place will be entirely aristocratic squelched?" Mr. Gatter records that "In the mid-nineties, the popular Beechwood hostelry, close to our Jenkintown-Wyncote railroad station, announced that is was discontinuing the boarding of Jews." When he is interviewed by Mr. Gatter, Edward Hicks Parry (who knew Pound as a boy) says, in reaction to Pound's description of his anti-Semitism as a "stupid suburban prejudice," that "Pound never [spoke] a truer word. This was true. 'Oh! he's Jewish' was a common expression." But we cannot assume that this kind of *pro forma* anti-Semitic comment necessarily "influenced people's treatment of individual Jews." Homer and Isabel Pound, for example, rented their house in 1902 and 1903 to Mr. Hackenburg, President of the Jewish Hospital Association.

121

Pound had assimilated unselfconsciously racist sentiments from the local, so-called "genteel" community, but his habit of expressing these in a kind of old-boy tough-talk in letters was a personal idiosyncracy—an exaggerated parade of bravado used to disguise his selfconsciousness, not about racism but at expressing himself confidentially to family and friends. We find that he uses this kind of slang habitually and from a very young age in letters, occasionally in the *Cantos,* increasingly in his prose writings of the 1930s, and finally in the radio broadcasts. When this slang is racist it clearly does not involve anti-Semitism alone. For example, in a letter to Williams of February 3, 1909, he writes: "As for your p'tit frère, I knew he'd hit the pike for Dagotalia,"[27] and in the *Cantos:* "and this was due to the frog and the portagoose / Gerbillon and Pereira";[28] "and the chink grandees took him down the canal" (61 / 337); "The Pollock was hooked by false promise" (105/740); "Edishu added a zero to the number of Krauts murdered in Poland" (103/734); "and the dog-damn wop is not save by exception / honest in administration anymore than the briton is truthful" (77/470). The range of the abuse does not make it any more excusable, but it does suggest that when Pound uses the work "kike" we should not assume that it carries the weight of a Nazi-style hatred.

The examples of his father, mother, and grandfather had impressed upon him his duty to be actively involved in social reform, but he was not able to put himself forward with the painlessly unselfconscious ease that he singled out as a marked trait of his father's. He credited his father with inheriting a knack for gaining access, against regulations, to centers of power which were by rights closed to the general public. He wrote in *Indiscretions:* "Thaddeus thus bequeathed to his son, my father, the naive Euripides Weight, a certain sophistication, a certain ability to stand unabashed in the face of the largest national luminaries, to pass the 'ropes,' etc., designed for restricting democratic ingress and demoralizing the popular enthusiasm at processions."[29]

As we see from his attempts to influence the economic policies of Roosevelt and Mussolini, Pound was not deterred by his self-consciousness from addressing himself directly to "the largest national luminaries" and the reason for this is yet another trait which he found in his father and grandfather and which was the key to his ill-fated reliance on the good faith of Mussolini—an astoundingly thoroughgoing naivety.

It is hard to exaggerate the degree of Pound's own naivety, and we cannot begin to make a fair assessment of his motives until we realize this. We see it, not so much in the tenets of his economic theories which were not in themselves illogical or necessarily impractical—after all, Keynes himself has said, "I believe that the future will learn more from the spirit of Gesell than from that of Marx"—but in his confidence that they would be adopted. He assumed that a country's economic system could be completely reorganized in a direct and straightforward way as soon as the country's leader could be convinced of the merits of the reorganization. His task, as he saw it, was simply to convince the leader that such a change would be worthwhile. Pound's native naivety is abetted in this by another legacy which Pearlman reminds us of when he describes Pound as "the type of optimist so common at the turn of the century in an expansionist America almost incapable of self-doubt."[30]

The most dangerous error that Pound's naivety led him into was his reliance on the good faith of Mussolini. The public announcements, the social reforms, and the propaganda films of the first thirteen years of Mussolini's rule presented a version of fascist goals and ideals that corresponded so closely to Pound's own vision of social change that, given his naivety and the strength of his desire for social reform, it is not surprising that he accepted the fascist propaganda in good faith. The alternative to trusting Mussolini would be profoundly depressing to Pound. It would mean an end to all possibility of a sound economic system and of preventing the economic depressions that led to war. It would mean abandoning the cause that he had devoted his energies to for over twenty years. It would mean giving up hope. Rather than do this he resorted to self-deception, putting the most favorable interpretation on what was questionable in the Duce's actions and rationalizing or ignoring what, according to his own principles, he would otherwise have condemned outright—the fascist armed squads, the invasion of Ethiopia, and the alliance with Hitler, whose propaganda he had dismissed as late as 1933 as "hysterical . . . yawping."[31] He convinced himself that Mussolini wanted peace and that Hitler was only a front for the men who really caused the war—the international bankers who planned the Second World War "to create debt." His firm belief in this theory constituted a genuine psychosis which persisted throughout all his years in St. Elizabeths even though his thinking on other subjects was quite rational.

I believe that this was a genuine act of self-deception on Pound's part and not the result of callousness or cynicism. The anxieties and frustrations generated by it were all internalized and produced a kind of confusion that the poet could neither understand nor entirely suppress or control. The strain of this self-deception was severe, and as the voice of his suppressed misgivings grew louder, he was reduced to being more and more emphatic in trying to shout it down or drown it out. We see this in his increasingly impatient dogmatism which would give way from time to time to bursts of defiant anger. There had been no occasion for anger as long as he could convince himself that reform was still a possibility and war could be avoided. Once both of these hopes were dashed, his anger rose, and rather than direct it at Mussolini for his duplicity and at himself for his gullibility and self-deception, he chose a convenient scapegoat—the "International Jewish Conspiracy to start wars." As despicable as Pound's recourse to this pernicious theory is, we are not justified in accusing him of parroting Mussolini's or Hitler's propaganda when he asserts it. This is an idea that had been current since before the First World War and had been advocated much more emphatically and generally in America than it ever was in Italy. It had been dinned into the national consciousness for seven years under the imprimatur and hence with the implicit blessing of Henry Ford through the pages of the *Dearborn Independent* and even after 1927 through the four books of articles excerpted from that newspaper. As late as September 1941, it had been announced to an audience of 7,500 people by the great American hero, Charles Lindbergh.

It is, of course, almost impossible for us to read the transcripts of Pound's radio speeches in the spirit in which he delivered them. The anti-Semitic passages, when they occur, are brief and yet it is almost inevitable that the strength of our revulsion at reading them will have the effect of drowning out the content of the rest of the speech, which we are likely to think of as mere temporization—nothing more than a spurious kind of drapery over the otherwise naked ugliness of the real content, hatred. But if, in the interest of understanding how Pound's mind might have been working at this stage, we make an effort to suspend our anger, we can notice that by far the greater part of each of the speeches—and the entirety of some—is an earnest recapitulation of fundamental economic and cultural points which

123

were Pound's serious and emphatic concern and had been for twenty years.

Pound's rather laborious spelling out and reiteration of basic points is clearly something very different from the unrestrained and fluent tirade of the anti-Semitic demagogue that we would expect from Pound if his anti-Semitism was, as Pearlman claims, an outpouring of long-suppressed envy and virulent hatred and if he had jumped on the Nazi bandwagon, as so many people have assumed. As Leonard Doob observes in the brief commentary on the style and techniques of the speeches, "With two exceptions, [Pound's] appeal seemed to be what might be loosely called intellectual rather than emotional. . . . On an intellectual level he almost always made flat, unqualified, undocumented statements that might be easily understood."[32] A friend of H.D.'s who heard Pound's talks when she was monitoring BBC foreign broadcasts similarly had a sense of his lack of emotional engagement with his listeners. H.D. remembers that her friend "said the effect was baffling, confused, confusing, and she didn't feel that the 'message,' whatever it was, was doing any harm or any good to anybody. It had, in a way, nothing whatever to do with us and the 20,000 victims of the first big air attacks and the fires in London."[33]

When the speeches in their entirety are dismissed, as they usually are, as "ravings," this is likely to imply a comment on their form as well as their content. Yet we cannot automatically assume that their form, idiosyncratic as it is, is involuntarily symptomatic of a deranged mind. This was a deliberate style of address that Pound had evolved. It is clearly anticipated in *Guide to Kulchur,* and we find that the form of a piece like "Hands off Alberta" in the *New Democracy* of November 1935 is virtually identical to that of the radio speeches. In his "Department of Prose and Verse" which follows Pound's "Alberta" essay—and which is auspiciously called "New Directions"—James Laughlin gives a very clear and accurate explanation of Pound's purpose in using this form: "Nothing in it is accidental. The staccato paragraphing, the rough diction, the sound effects, the distorted spelling, the typographical stunts, the anecdotes & allusions, the shouting & swearing are all there for a purpose: to shatter the reader's mental slumber and *make* him absorb the content."[34] When he used these techniques in the broadcasts, it was with this same purpose, and when he exaggerated even more strongly his old-boy, cracker-barrel persona, it was because now he needed not simply to catch a reader's eye but to seize and hold the attention of the potential listeners as they turned their radio dials. It is true, of course, that there were particular dangers for Pound in using this style. At a time when his contact with the reality around him was becoming increasingly tenuous, the habit of asserting without proving and of juxtaposing without specifically connecting allowed him to hide from himself the impossibility of demonstrating the truth of what he was contending about Mussolini's good faith.

Paradoxically, the aspect of the broadcasts that seems to us now most strikingly offensive—Pound's use of the word "kike"—in that it is the expression of a less virulent nineteenth-century form of American anti-Semitism, is in fact less sinister than his references to the existence of an "International Jewish Conspiracy." This idea had been the stock-in-trade of American anti-Semites for the previous twenty years, but Pound had, up until then, avoided it. The fact that at this stage he gave his assent to this paranoid theory shows that his self-deception about Mussolini's good faith was taking its toll on his state of mind. His subconscious awareness that he was no longer being honest with himself generated a mounting sense of distress and confusion; his angry outbursts betrayed a barely concealed note of panic. On occasion he openly admitted his confusion. Broadcasting in March 1942 he said: "I lose my thread some times. So much that I can't count on anyone's knowing. Thread as they call it of discourse." In July of that year he said: "after a hundred broadcasts it is STILL hard to know where to begin. There is so MUCH that the United States does not know. This war is the fruit of such vast incomprehensions, such tangled ignorance, so many strains of unknowing. I am held up, enraged, by the delay needed to change a typing ribbon, so much is there that OUGHT to be put into the young American head. Don't know which, what to put down, can't write two scripts at once. NECESSARY facts, ideas, come in pell-mell. I try to get too much into ten minutes."[35] It is probably no coincidence that in this speech, in which he openly confronted the pressure of his confusion, there are no anti-Semitic references at all.

As I mentioned before, Pound was fundamentally both by instinct and by inclination a very forthright person who could not lie to himself with impunity. The particular paranoid strategy that he had chosen when he had recourse to the idea of an "International Jewish Conspiracy" took its toll on him and increased rather than alleviated, his painful confusion. To evade the truth as he had done was, in Pound's eyes, a very serious matter, one for which he would eventually judge himself harshly, but it would be a long time before he was able to see what he had done.

There are several reasons for this delay. Although he was guilty of lying to himself about some of Mussolini's actions, his motives had been positive rather than negative in that he had done so to be able to continue to believe that his ideal of economic and social reform could still be realized, that a Second World War could be prevented, and then that America could be kept out of the war. He sensed that he was guilty of something but it was not possible for him to understand exactly what, and it was very clear to him what he was not guilty of. He knew beyond a shadow of a doubt that it had never been his intention, consciously or subconsciously, to betray America—that all his efforts had been intended to save his country from war and its people from exploitation by manipulators of money. It seems very likely that his certainty that the charge of treason was unjust, in fact, acted as a distraction from or an excuse to postpone the difficult process of self-examination that would be necessary if he were ever to discover exactly where his guilt lay. This would help to explain the sense that some visitors to St. Elizabeths had that at times he almost seemed relieved to be there.

After long imprisonment, he returned to Italy, but what in one sense was obviously a new freedom was in another sense the end of a reprieve. Back on Italian soil, no longer being punished for the crime of treason of which he knew himself to be innocent, he no longer had an excuse to postpone confronting the guilt of his self-deception. Within a year he began to suffer from extreme depression. His physical condition deteriorated rapidly, aggravated by his frequent refusal to eat and he was overwhelmed with feelings of remorse and self-accusation. During the years of his self-imposed silence, he did undertake the self-examination that he had postponed for so long and, although he continued to be very much troubled by remorse and self-doubt, at times he was able to attempt what I have tried to do here on his behalf—"To confess wrong without losing rightness." (116/ 797)

Notes

1. Hilton Kramer, *New York Times*, January 22, 1981.

2. I believe that we are now finally at a point sufficiently distant from World War II that we can undertake the thorough and accurate anatomizing of anti-Semitism that is necessary. The recent proliferation of Holocaust studies shows that this process is already well under way. The following comments on anti-Semitism are a summary version of a more detailed analysis of the subject that forms part of my forthcoming book, *The American Ezra Pound*.

3. Daniel Pearlman, "Ezra Pound: America's Wandering Jew," *Paideuma* (Winter 1980).

4. Meir Michaelis, *Mussolini and the Jews: German-Italian Relations and the Jewish Question in Italy, 1922–1945* (Oxford: The Clarendon Press, 1978), p. 55.

5. Ibid., pp. 51, 115, 119.

6. Ibid., pp. 302, 304–11, 352.

7. Ezra Pound, *Jefferson and/or Mussolini* (New York: New Directions, 1970), p. 127.

8. Williams Carlos Williams, "Jefferson and/or Mussolini," *New Democracy* (October 1935), 61.

9. Williams Carlos Williams, "A Social Diagnosis for Surgery," *New Democracy* (April 1936), 26.

10. E. Digby Baltzell, *The Protestant Establishment: Aristocracy and Caste in America* (New York: Random House, 1964), pp. 210, 211.

11. Ibid., pp. 211, 212.

12. Barbara Miller Solomon, *Ancestors and Immigrants: A Changing New England* (Cambridge: Harvard University Press, 1956), p. 38.

13. Baltzell, *Protestant Establishment*, p. 203.

14. Ezra Pound, *Patria Mia*, in *Ezra Pound: Selected Prose, 1909–1965* (New York: New Directions, 1973), p. 104.

15. Ibid., pp. 108, 101.

16. Ibid., pp. 101, 102.

17. Baltzell, *Protestant Establishment*, p. 248.

18. George Wolfskill, *The Revolt of the Conservative: A History of the American Liberty League, 1934–1940* (New York: Houghton Mifflin Co., 1962), p. 102.

19. Eric Goldman, *Rendezvous with Destiny* (New York: Vintage Books, 1956), p. 289.

20. John Higham, *Strangers in the Land: Patterns of American Nativism, 1860–1925* (New York: Athenaeum, 1978), p. 94.

21. Ezra Pound, *Ezra Pound Speaking: Radio Speeches of World War II*, ed. Leonard W. Doob (Westport, Conn.: Greenwood Press, 1978), pp. 120, 393.

22. Ezra Pound, *Indiscretions*, in *Pavannes and Divagations* (New York: New Directions, 1958), p. 6.

23. These quotations are taken from newspaper clippings in Homer Pound's scrapbook. In most cases the dates and names of the newspapers have not been included.

24. Ezra Pound, "Through Alien Eyes," *New Age* (1913), 276.

25. Rufus Learsi, *The Jews in America* (New York: The World Publishing Co., 1954), pp. 131–35.

26. Peter Gay, *Freud, Jews and Other Germans: Masters and Victims in Modernist Culture* (Oxford University Press, 1978), p. 15.

27. Ezra Pound, *The Letters of Ezra Pound*, ed. D.D. Paige (New York: Harcourt, Brace and World, Inc.), p. 7.

28. Ezra Pound, *The Cantos of Ezra Pound* (New York: New Directions, 1973). Citations in the text give the number of the canto, followed by the page number in this edition.

29. *Indiscretions*, p. 15.

30. Pearlman, "America's Wandering Jew," p. 470.

31. Ezra Pound, *Jefferson and/or Mussolini*, p. 127.

32. *Ezra Pound Speaking*, pp. 438–40.

33. *End to Torment* (New York: New Directions, 1979), p. 48.

34. James Laughlin, "Department of Prose and Verse," *New Democracy* (November 1935), 120.

35. *Ezra Pound Speaking*, pp. 57, 192.

Part Three

William Carlos Williams

6. The Ideas in the Things

Denise Levertov

There are many more "ideas" in William Carlos Williams' "things" than he is commonly credited with even today; and this is true not only of *Paterson* and the post-Patersonian, clearly meditative poems in triadic lines, but also of a great deal of his earlier work. Because he did write numerous poems that are exercises in the notation of speech or in the taking of verbal Polaroid snapshots, it is assumed that many other short- or medium-length poems of his are likewise essays in the non-metaphorical, the wholly objective. And because he said (in his "Introduction" to *The Wedge*, 1944), "Let the metaphysical take care of itself, the arts have nothing to do with it," it is forgotten that he immediately followed those words with these: "They will concern themselves with it if they please." It is not noticed that he himself frequently *did* so please. Williams, for much of his life, did take on, it is true, the task of providing for himself and others a context of objective, anti-metaphysical aesthetic intent in order to free poetry from the entanglement of that sentimental intellectualism which only recognizes the incorporal term of an analogy and scorns its literal, sensuous term. This view denies the equipoise of thing and idea, acknowledging only a utilitarian role for the literal (as if it were brought into existence expressly and merely to articulate the all-important abstract term), rather than perceiving concrete images as the very *incarnation* of thought. This view insults the imagination, for the imagination does not reject its own sensory origins but illuminates them, and connects them with intellectual and intuitive experience. Williams, working against that insult to imagination, needed to assert and reestablish a confidence in the actuality and value of observable phenomena and a recognition of the necessity of sensory data to the life and health of poetry. But by so doing he incurred much misunderstanding from his admirers (not to speak of his detractors) and, I suspect, endured a good deal of (mainly unacknowledged) inner conflict; for he was frequently obliged to betray his stated principles in favor of the irresistible impulsion toward metaphor, which is at the heart of *poiesis*.

I find it interesting to sort out, in the *Collected Earlier Poems*, those poems which are indeed snapshots, descriptive vignettes, notations of idiom and emphasis (as are some of the very late short poems also) from those which have unobtrusively the resonance of metaphor and symbol.

The mystery and richness of *further significance* which such poems of his possess is akin to what R. H. Blyth delineated for us in his commentaries on Japanese haiku. The allusive nature of the Zen art, possible only in a culture alert to the ubiquity of correspondences and familiar with an elaborate symbology, has of course no exact parallel in twentieth-century America; yet Blyth could have been evoking the art of Williams when he quoted this haiku by Kyoroku,

> *even to the saucepan*
> *where potatoes are boiling—*
> *a moonlit night.*

and commented, "It is only when we realize that the moon is in the saucepan with the potatoes that we know the grandeur of the moon in the highest heaven. It is only when we see a part that we know the whole."

Readers who come to Williams' pre-Patersonian or pre-*Desert Music* poems with the expectation of simple depictive Imagism or of a classic, ascetically single-visioned objectivity (which was not in fact the stated aim of the Objectivists, incidentally) miss these resonances, that sense of discovering, in a vivid part, the adumbration of an unnamed but intensely intuited whole; they forego the experience of becoming aware, precisely through the physical *presentness* of what is *de*noted, of the other presentness—invisible but palpable—of what is *con*noted. They come to the poems solely for the Things; but inherent in the Things are the Ideas.

I'd like to present two examples along with a running commentary on what I believe is to be found beneath their surfaces.

"The Farmer," the third poem from *Spring and All* (a series detached from its prose context in *Collected Earlier Poems* [1951, pp. 241-87]), is not a depiction of a farmer that compares him to an artist, but vice versa. Read thus, as a portrait of the artist, each of its images has a double meaning. The literal *is there*, vivid in every detail. But climate, landscape, everything takes on *along with* (not instead of) its denotative significance a symbolic one. The poet is a *farmer,* one who tends the land of language and imagination and its creatures, who makes things grow, poem-things, story-things, not out of nowhere but out of the ground on which he walks. At present the rain is falling, the climate is cold and wet, as was the critical climate of the time for Williams the poet; he is exposed to that wet and cold, and his fields—the fields of his art—are apparently empty. But he's trudging around *in* that climate and *in* the fields of language, calmly, hands in his pockets, intent on imagining the future poems; and the rain prepares the soil and the seeds. "On all sides / the world rolls coldly away"—he's left quite alone with his imagination. The orchard trees are black with the rain, but it is spring (the preceding prose has announced, "Meanwhile, SPRING, which has been approaching for several pages, is at last here," and the poem states that it is March). Soon those trees (the deep-rooted anatomy of what grows from his terrain) will be white with blossom: there are implied poems in this superficially unpromising landscape; and the very isolation in which the poet is left by the world gives him "room for thought." His dirt road (his own road among his fields) is sluiced (and thus deepened) by the rain that will help the seeds to sprout. He's not a small, lost figure in nature, this artist farmer—he "looms" as he moves along past the scratchy brushwood that, trimmed and dried, will make good tinder. The poet is *composing* as he goes, just as a farmer, pacing his fields on a Sunday at the end of winter, composes in his mind's eye a picture of spring growth and summer harvest. He is an *antagonist*—but to what? To the hostility of the environment, which, however, contains the elements that will nourish his crops. And in what sense? In the sense of the struggle *to* compose—not to *im*pose order but to *com*pose the passive elements into a harvest, to grow not tares but wheat.

"A Morning Imagination of Russia" is a poem I'm very fond of and which, besides being full of implication and resonances, has many of the qualities of a short story (indeed, as well as being *set* in Russia, it has a flavor or tone quite Chekhovian); it is a part of *The Descent of Winter* (*Collected Earlier Poetry,* pp. 305-108). Webster Schott's selection from Williams' prose and poetry, *Imaginations,* restored the full context of that series as well as of *Spring and All;* and Schott, unlike some of Williams' critics, doesn't treat him as wholly lacking in thought. Nevertheless, intent upon an enthusiastic but careless reading of this poem, which sees it as speaking figuratively, of Williams own situation vis-à-vis American poetry, Schott misses the clear drama of its narrative. He quite unjustifiably claims that it depicts *Williams himself on an imaginary visit* to Russia after the revolution, whereas (however much he may be a projection of the poet's sensibility) it seems to me quite clear that the protagonist is not intended as a persona but as a fictive personage, a member of the intelligentsia who is casting his lot with the masses. The time is very early in the revolution. Nothing has yet settled down. No new repressive bureaucracy has yet replaced the old oppression—the whole atmosphere is like that of a convalescent's first walk in pale sunshine after a time when bitter storms in the world outside paralleled his inner storm of fever and life-and-death struggle. It begins:

> *The earth and the sky were very close*
> *When the sun rose it rose in his heart*

The dawn is, equally, an actual one and the dawn of an era. And he feels one with it.

> *It bathed the red cold world of*
> *the dawn so that the chill was his own.*

The red is the red of sunrise *and* of revolution.

> *The mists were sleep and sleep began*
> *to fade from his eyes . . .*

The mists are both morning mists and the mists of the past, of pre-revolutionary sleep. His consciousness is changing.

> *. . . below him in the*
> *garden a few flowers were lying forward*
> *on the intense green grass where*
> *in the opalescent shadows oak leaves*
> *were pressed hard down upon it in patches*
> *by the night rain . . .*

The beauty of flowers and grass, opalescent shadows, patches of rain-soaked dead oak leaves, is vividly evoked. It can all be read with validity as pure, precise description. But it too has a doubleness; the whole scene has been through a night of storm, the flowers are bowed forward by it, the grass is more vividly green than it would have been without it, but parts of the grass are hidden and half-smothered by the fallen brown leaves. All this is the counterpart of his own experience and of events in the historical moment. The flowers and common grass of his own life are more vivid and yet almost

broken—and some of his life is gone, is fallen, like the leaves, gone
with the lives and the ways of living fallen in wet and revolution.

> *. . . There were no cities*
> *between him and his desires,*
> *his hatreds and his loves were without walls*
> *without rooms, without elevators*
> *without files, delays of veiled murderers*
> *muffled thieves, the tailings of*
> *tedious, dead pavements, the walls*
> *against desire save only for him who can pay*
> *high, there were no cities—he was*
> *without money—*

> *Cities had faded richly*
> *into foreign countries, stolen from Russia—*
> *the richness of her cities.—*

Here, deep in rural Russia, deep into the attempt to construct a new
society, he is not impeded by the complexities of urban, Westernized
Russia. His nature—his desires, hatreds, loves—is out in the open; and
the "city" here clearly stands for more than an architectural and
demographic agglomeration, but for the money values of capitalism.
He has no money—but here and now he does not need it. All the
desirable content of Russia's cities has been stolen away, gone West
with the emigrés.

> *Scattered wealth was close to his heart*
> *he felt it uncertainly beating at*
> *that moment in his wrists, scattered*
> *wealth—but there was not much at hand.*

The "scattered wealth" he feels (scattered like money and jewels
dropped by fleeing thieves) is his own and Russia's—it has not been,
and cannot be, wholly robbed, absconded with. He feels that, feels
it close. But also he feels a tickling wave of nostalgia:

> *Cities are full of light, fine clothes*
> *delicacies for the table, variety,*
> *novelty—fashion: all spent for this.*
> *Never to be like that again:*
> *the frame that was. It tickled his*
> *imagination. But it passed in a rising calm.*

He feels a nostalgia for all which (for now, anyway, and perhaps forever)
must be given up for the sake of the new thing yet to be defined. The

old context, the frame, gone. But now *"this"*: the "few flowers," the vividness he will know.

But that wave of nostalgia passes in a *rising* calm—not the sinking calm of resignation, but a lift of the spirits.

> *Tan dar a dei; Tan dar a dei!*
> *He was singing. Two miserable peasants*
> *very lazy and foolish*
> *seemed to have walked out from his own*
> *feet and were walking away with wooden rakes*
> *under the six nearly bare poplars, up the hill*
>
> *There go my feet.*

Singing with lifted spirits (singing, one notices—and there is an irony in this—that medieval refrain we associate with spring, love and courtesy, ancient forests, knights errant, and troubadours), he feels as much one with the peasants he watches from his window as he had with the chill red dawn. He sees them as lazy and foolish, as well as miserable, just as he might have done from the viewpoint of pre-revolutionary class privilege: he does not idealize them; but the difference is that now he identifies with them, lazy and foolish as they are, and with their task—to rake away rubbish, perhaps dead leaves—to which they must go *uphill*. "There go my feet."

> *He stood still in the window forgetting*
> *to shave—*
> *The very old past was refound*
> *redirected. It had wandered into himself*
> *The world was himself, these were*
> *his own eyes that were seeing, his own mind*
> *that was straining to comprehend, his own*
> *hands that would be touching other hands*
> *They were his own!*
> *His own, feeble, uncertain . . .*

In this new world—around him and within him—he finds ancient roots, not the immediate past which has been razed but the *"very old past,"* taking new directions. Identified with what is happening historically, he feels himself a microcosm; the proposition invites reversal—it is not only that he is intimately and intensely involved but that just as his mind strains to comprehend, so the mind of the peasants, the mind of all Russia collectively, strains to see and comprehend. His hands, reaching out to touch others, are feeble and uncertain, though; and so are the hands of the multitude.

> *. . . He would go*
> *out to pick herbs, he graduate of*
> *the old university. He would go out*
> *and ask that old woman, in the little*
> *village by the lake, to show him wild*
> *ginger. He himself would not know the plant.*

137

He will go humbly, as pupil of the old peasant, the ancient root wisdom, not as teacher of others.

> *A horse was stepping up the dirt road*
> *under his window*

—a live thing moving on unpaved earth: not merely a descriptive detail but a metaphor.

> *He decided not to shave. Like those two [the two peasants]*
> *that he knew now, as he had never*
> *known them formerly. A city, fashion*
> *had been between—*
>
> *Nothing between now.*
>
> *He would go to the soviet unshaven. This*
> *was the day—and listen. Listen. That*
> *was all he did, listen to them, weigh*
> *for them. He was turning into*
> *a pair of scales, the scales in the*
> *zodiac.*

This is evidently the day of the regular meeting of the local soviet, which he is attending not for the first time, as one can gather from the syntax, and it is also the day of a new access of consciousness and resolve, a *first* day in some sense. He puts his university education at the service of the community. Perhaps he weighs physical supplies— grain, fertilizer, medicines—bringing specific professional skills into play: that's not specified. But there's more to weighing than that. He not only feels, with a mixture of humility and amusement, that he becomes his function, becomes a pair of scales, but that they are the zodiacal scales, charged with moral, mythical, and psychological symbolism.

> *But closer, he was himself*
> *the scales . . .*

That is, not only did his work of weighing transform him into a function, but he was anyway, intrinsically, an evaluator, he realizes.

> *. . . The local soviet. They could*
> *weigh . . .*

That is, in his new sense of identification with his fellows, others too are intrinsically, as humans, evaluators.

> *. . . If it was not too late.*

That is, if too much damage had not already been done, too much for the revolution to have a future after all, too much for that human ability to measure for themselves to evaluate justly, to manifest itself among the many.

> *. . . He felt*
> *uncertain many days. But all were uncertain*
> *together and he must weigh for them out*
> *of himself.*

His "weighing" is a service he performs as an intellectual, contributing his ability to listen closely, which has been trained by education; but his judgments must be made out of a commitment, a center in himself, and not merely abstractly, which would be perfunctory. It is "out of himself," his very substance, that he must act.

> *He took a small pair of scissors*
> *from the shelf and clipped his nails*
> *carefully. He himself served the fire.*

He reasserts his education, maintains his standards of hygiene and decent appearance. But to attend to the fire in his hearth himself— this is new for him. To use his hands, with their clean, clipped nails. And that fire: it is literal, and it is the fire of life, hope, revolution. Now he soliloquizes:

> *We have cut out the cancer but*
> *who knows? perhaps the patient will die*

He reiterates his own realistic uncertainty. Then he proceeds to define

the "patient," which is not solely Russia, a country in the throes of
total reorganization:

> *the patient is anybody, anything*
> *worthless that I desire, my hands*
> *to have it—*

lines which I would gloss thus: anybody, anything albeit considered
"worthless" that I desire—my hands *desiring* to have it. That is to say,
the "patient" is the sum of things that—though the world think them
tawdry, assigning them no value—Williams consistently sees as having
the glitter of life: cats' eyes in the dark. Beautiful Thing. "Melon
flowers that open / about the edge of refuse / . . . the small / yellow
cinquefoil in the / parched places." Or those starlings in the wind's
teeth. And, too, the "patient" whose survival is in question is desire
itself, the desire to touch that aliveness with bare hands,

> *—instead of the feeling*
> *that there is a piece of glazed paper*
> *between me and the paper—invisible*
> *but tough running through the legal*
> *processes of possession—*

That glazed top sheet, a transparent obstacle to touch, covers the surface
even of the documents that proclaim possession of what is desired,
and thus cancels out the *experience* of possession.

> *—a city that*
> *we could possess—*

that is, *my hands desire to have a city that we could possess.* (The syntax is
clearer here if instead of dashes before the word "instead" and after
the word "possession" we enclose those lines in parentheses.) A city,
then—unlike the cities that have "faded richly / into foreign countries"
and were only to be enjoyed by those who "can pay high"—that
would embody an accessible life.

> *It's in art, it's in*
> *the French school.*

> *What we lacked was*
> *everything. It is the middle of*
> *everything. Not to have.*

Here both "it's" refer back to the "patient" in the sense of that quality

of immediacy which, in the prose passage immediately preceding
"A Morning Imagination of Russia" in the *Descent of Winter* sequence
and dated only one day before it, Williams had said was the very goal
of poetry: "poetry should strive for nothing else, this vividness alone,
per se, for itself," and further, "The vividness *which is* poetry." So,
"*It's* in art, in the French school"—here he draws on his own educated
knowledge and experience, on all that make him different from those
two "miserable, lazy, and foolish" peasants—and also "*It* is the
middle of everything"—*it* is not *only* in art but in all kinds of things,
common experience, and here he reasserts his sense of brotherhood.
But "What we lacked was everything . . . *Not to have*," was what, till
now, we experienced. I am reminded here of Wallace Stevens' lines,

> That's what misery is,
> Nothing to have at heart:

Both the intellectual, because of his sense of that invisible wall of glazed
paper between him and life, and oppressed and ignorant people have
hitherto been cut off from the "everything" in the middle of which
are found the sparks of vivid beauty; they have experienced only *not
having*, absence.

> We have little now but
> we have that. [The "it," the sparks, the poetry.]
> We are convalescents. Very
> feeble. Our hands shake. We need a
> transfusion. No one will give it to us,
> they are afraid of infection. I do not
> blame them. We have paid heavily. But we
> have gotten—touch. The eyes and the ears
> down on it. Close.

The whole people are convalescent from the convulsions of revolution.
The transfusion they need is not forthcoming—seen historically, this
would have meant international support for their experiment instead
of an economic and psychological blockade. But other nations, other
governments, were scared. The protagonist, like a true Chekhovian
character, says he can't blame them; he sees what scares them, and
why—he is not doctrinaire. And he recognizes that a great price has
been paid and will perhaps be further exacted. But what has been
gained is precisely what he has desired: touch itself. Williams the doctor
knew how the touch of hands could diagnose, cure, bring to birth;
his fictive Russian knows the imagination as an intimate form of touch
without which all is dull, hopeless, ashen. What he celebrates here,

at the end of the poem, returning to its opening, when earth and sky are close, known, touched with the imagination—is the sun rising in his heart.

The prose which immediately follows the poem and is dated four days later, begins with the words, "Russia is every country, here he must live. . . ." And a few pages further on Williams breaks off from diverse topics to return to the protagonist of the poem, in these sentences, "—He feels the richness, but a distressing feeling of loss is close upon it. He knows he must coordinate the villages for effectiveness in a flood, a famine." I see two ways of reading that, and they are complementary, not conflicting. If, as I've been doing, one reads the poem without disregard for its narrative reality, the truth of its fiction, and thus the universality of the poem's Russia— "every country; here he must live"—then the richness that "he," the protagonist, feels is the richness of new beginnings, the reassertion of the "very old" past and also the democratic "everything" of human experience; while the "distressing feeling of loss" that comes close upon it concerns the equally real subtleties, nuances, desireable complexities, that "scattered wealth" he earlier felt "beating at his wrists," which as yet we have not figured out how to attain in any social system without a sacrifice of justice and mercy. But one can also read "A Morning Imagination of Russia" somewhat as Webster Schott chose to do, that is, as a parable of Williams' poetic struggle in the 1920s (it was written in 1927). According to the first reading, the hero's recognition of the need to "coordinate the villages for effectiveness in a flood, a famine," reminds one of Chekhov's letters in the early 1890s when he was an unpaid local medical inspector during the cholera epidemic. If one looks beyond the Russian scene (set just a few years before *The Descent of Winter*) to an analogy in Williams' own struggles to establish a new sense of poetry and the imagination in the American 1920s, we may see in those words about coordinating the villages an almost Poundian missionary spirit, for then one takes the "villages" to be outposts of intelligent poetry and the flood or famine as aspects of the hostile or uncomprehending world of readers, critics, other poets, and the public at large. Webster Schott, reintroducing *The Descent of Winter* in 1970, saw it *entirely* as Williams' struggle "to verbalize a theory of contemporary poetry" and "to realize a clear conception of himself as an artist." That is partially true; but when Williams wrote the words "We have paid heavily. But we/ have gotten—touch," he was not speaking in a vacuum, as if from an airtight aesthetic island in which the political images with which, in "A Morning Imagination," he had chosen to work, had no meaning *except* as

141

metaphor, as figurative ways to speak about literature. Those images work as Chekhovian narrative description; they work as implications of political ideas; *and* they work as analogies for the poet's need to act in society, humbly and with an understanding that in trying to serve the commonweal he will serve also his own need for intimate experience of the living mystery. Ideas without Things are vaporous, mere irritants of the detached and insensate intellect; but Things abound and are chockablock with the Ideas that dance and stumble, groan or sing, calling and beckoning to one another, throughout the decades of his poetry.

7. William Carlos Williams in the Forties: Prelude to Postmodernism

Paul Christensen

William Carlos Williams confronted his life's work twice in a four-year span—once, when the Objectivist Press (three years late in publication) issued Williams' *Collected Poems 1921–31* (1934), and again in 1938, when New Directions issued the *Complete Collected Poems*. Twice critics had the chance to measure the achievement of Williams the poet, and the general consensus in both rounds of discussion was that he was a good but minor writer, a lyric poet of technical sophistication—only a "major" poet had "ideas." As Paul Mariani observed, the critics assailed Williams because "his poetry lacked a central, all-informing myth." Williams finally talked back to his critics in a little essay in *New Republic* (January 11, 1939): "I'm not important but I'm not insignificant. Boy! that's pretty cagey shootin'. . . . Tell [Phillip Horton] to go wipe his nose."[1] Williams only mentions that the collections came out in his *Autobiography*; but in *I Wanted To Write A Poem* (1958), he told Edith Heal, his bibliographer:

The *Collected Poems* [1938] gave me the whole picture, all I had gone through technically to learn about the making of a poem. I could look at the poems as they lay before me. I could reject the looseness of the free verse. Free verse wasn't verse at all to me. All art is orderly. Yet the early poems disturbed me. They were too conventional, too academic. Still, there was orderliness. My models, Shakespeare, Milton, dated back to a time when men thought in orderly fashion. I felt that modern life had gone beyond that; our poems could not be contained in the strict orderliness of the classics.[2]

144

Certainly, Williams had been assessed unfairly. Critics had mistaken his work as a lifelong effort to acquire the minimal language of Imagism; they had not perceived the steady refinement of his attention to the structure of objects, or the delicate nuance of patterns that play over the surface of his verbal collages. One critic called his poems an "exercise in spiritual hygiene." Everyone seemed to think the narrow little poems of the canon strange against the garrulous, polyglot culture of America. Life had an eerie stillness to this poet's eye; he had sorted the world into curious little bundles of particulars and he searched for clues to their collective integrity. The language of Williams' poetry is tense, nervous, abrupt, tough, utterly conscious, and aware. Williams was deeply distrustful of the mind's unruly habits, its tendency to drift off, digress, dream, distort; mind is mute here, as though all thought occurred in the very eye focused on the particulars of life. The critics felt the chill of the work and uttered their faint praise.

Williams himself did not feel triumphant about the work; he saw the achievements of skill and technique, but the world was different now, and these poems did not account for it. He was fifty-five years old in 1938; with the *Complete Collected Poems* before him, he felt the need to start over again, to originate a new poetic that would satisfy his sense of the changed world. There was no one of his time in whom to confide this feeling of dissatisfaction; he may have admired Charles Henri Ford, but privately distrusted the flamboyant swagger of his surrealist, jazzy lyrics; of surrealism itself, he, like other leftists of the age, scorned it all as a "flight from life."[3] Pound was in Italy, and their correspondence had languished; their friendship was nearly broken over the then rumored broadcasts he was making for Rome Radio. "What the hell right has he to drag me into his dirty messes?"[4] Others of his generation were still writing, but the original force of their era was lost. Looking back to those years, in his *Autobiography* Paris seemed a vanished Brigadoon, the brilliant talents of the era dead or scattered:

. . . Pound confined to a hospital for the insane in Washington; Bob McAlmon working for his brothers in El Paso; Hemingway a popular novelist; Joyce dead; Gertrude Stein dead; Picasso doing ceramics; Soupault married to a wealthy (?) American; Skip Cannell—who after divorcing Kitty married a French woman, *disparu!*; Nancy Cunard still alive, thin as paper as she is; Bill and Sally Bird, unable to stand the Paris weather any longer, removed to Tangier; Sylvia Beach, who had been cleaned out by the Germans, living upstairs from her famous Twelve rue de l'Odéon. Clotilde Vail dead; Brancusi too old to work; Stieglitz dead; Hart Crane dead; Juan Gris—at one time my favorite painter— long since dead; Charles Demuth dead; Marsden Hartley dead; Marcel

Duchamp idling in a telephonless Fourteenth Street garret in New York; the Baroness dead; Jane Heap dead; Margaret Anderson, I don't know where; Peggy Guggenheim, active at least, in Venice keeping a gallery for modern pictures in which it is said she hardly believes; Steichen a director at the Modern Museum; Norman Douglas writing—but I think not; T. S. Eliot a successful playwright; Auden, E. E. Cummings, Wallace Stevens—alive and working; Marianne Moore translating *Les Fables* of La Fontaine . . . Harold Loeb— where?—but back in Wall Street; Ford Madox Ford dead; Henry Miller living with his wife and children on a half-mile-high mountain near Carmel, California, from which he seldom descends. Lola Ridge dead; Djuna Bannes living in poverty somewhere, not, at least, writing; Bob Brown, having lost his money, surviving in Brazil, Carl Sandburg turned long since from the poem; Alfred Kreymborg a member of the Institute of Arts and Letters; Mina Loy, Eugene O'Neill—more or less silent.[5]

A world shrouded in mists; the very one in which he had become the artist, of which the *Complete Collected Poems* was his testament. The next chapter of the *Autobiography* tallies up the last living links with his past, which he calls "Friendship," and where he is easily moved by memories. But he survives all that, and announces the change in his life in the next chapter, which prints the bulk of Charles Olson's essay, "Projective Verse," the manifesto of the new revolution in poetry, in which Williams could find many of his own ideas of the 1940s brilliantly understood and deployed for a new generation.

In a decade of war and political turmoil, Williams had undergone a profound transformation of his values and ideas as a poet; he attacked the fundamental issue of his own poetry—its perception of reality—in order to free himself from his own immense will to be elemental and direct in language. Beginning in 1939, we find Williams testing his principles in published essays, finding that art often grew by radical negation of its own tenets; he talked of the other arts, but it was his own he was arguing with—and the key terms of a new tenet for poetry were *profusion, inclusion,* the *ill-assorted.* War had altered all: the United States could no longer pretend to neutrality by 1939; Europe's best minds had been flooding into the country from 1930 on, bringing with them a bold new sensibility in art and science that immediately challenged domestic thought; the disappearance of his own generation of genius isolated Williams and forced him onto new ground. These converging influences made a poet of late middle age into a changeling, a uniquely different voice of postwar American poetry.

Objectivism was an art of design, of the deliberate, calculated placement of elements to make a whole. It was the effort to arrange parts so that they created their own environment and context, in which the combined result would be as sufficient as any "form" or "object" in nature, a tree or hillside. One needed to remove all vagueness and subjectivity from such composite works in order to create the feeling of its wholeness and self-sufficiency. Nuance and subtlety came through the interaction of the parts within the whole; the peculiar contours of each object, as they intersected and juxtaposed with one another, brought forth certain subtle perceptions, "gestalts," giving the otherwise still and isolated composition delicate movements along its interstices and in its overall configurations. The Objectivists perfected the unformulated stance of Imagism, which had set out to correct the habit of poets to lose themselves in their sentimental ruminations rather than "look" directly at the world. But in Objectivism, it might be said, the poet had finally begun to arrange nature in controlled spaces as rigorously as had Cézanne and the Cubists; where Imagism had sought rhymes among mental categories and among random shapes in life (apple boughs/subway tunnels), Objectivism wished to make the combinations of elements deliberate, planned, methodical, like an experiment in physics. It was their effort to order nature by no other means than color, sound, and contour; left out of the Objectivist "picture" were any binding powers of ideology and emotion; if such survived, it was by the object's own powers of inference and latent symbolism. It was an esthetic that wanted to prove that nature was coherent and meaningful without imposing upon it the formation of idea and feeling. It was an art that by its very simplicity and aloofness reacted against the confused politics of its era; but in its firm control over its materials and speech, it may also have breathed in the atmosphere of Will of the fascist decade.

146

This is the art Williams knew he had created successfully, perhaps better than anyone else had done; the collected poems showed the grasping of a technique in verse, and yet the technique must have seemed to him at times to have been won too handily. In Objectivism, one conquered meaning by keeping out the mind's own wanderings; measure in the Objectivist poem was largely achieved by freezing still the elements that needed to be arranged and made whole. A deeper, truer measure would have to include the whole poet in its formal symmetry, in which his ragings and desires, his dreams, and his fantasies would be bound into the form of the poem but in a way that gave them both freedom and participation in the design. In other words, it must have occurred to Williams throughout the next decade, the 1940s, that his task was to include the truth of the poet's own

imagination in the poem, otherwise the poem enclosed too little too
well. His struggle throughout the decade was to find how one could
bring in the ruminative mind and still bind it up with actual life in a
disciplined, formal construction. It would require him to rethink his
esthetic, to coax himself to break down his censure of the "trivial,"
accidental, and distorted that were as true of life as were the hard-
shaped particulars; more difficult would be to set the poised elements
of the poem into motion, in order to shift language from "record"
to "narrative," which aroused the mind into expressing its whole process
in language. Williams was looking for a way to go behind Imagism
to rediscover usable lyric principles without losing the mode of
disjunctive sequence on which he depended as a constant of his art.

147

   Objectivism was a winter-hard portrayal of reality; one sees the
ice and glare of winter in much of Williams' early poetry; he associated
order with the boney, bare landscapes of New Jersey in March. In
Williams' most famous short poem, "The Red Wheelbarrow," Jerome
Mazzaro finds that emotions have crystallized into facts, like "Villon's
frozen ink pot at the conclusion of the *Petit Testament*."[6] But Mazzaro
goes on to give the background of Williams' poem from Williams' own
account of it in "Seventy Years Deep," as his "affection for an old
Negro named Marshall. He had been a fisherman, caught porgies off
Gloucester. He used to tell me how he had to work in the hold in
freezing weather, standing ankle deep in cracked ice packing down
the fish. He said he didn't feel cold."[7] It was in Marshall's backyard that
Williams found the scene of his poem, the wheelbarrow *glazed* with
rainwater, the white chickens like—snow? Williams depicted nature
without Kora; his clear language was the poised geometry of a
snowflake, shards of description bound like an ice crystal on the empty
landscape:

> *A tramp thawing out*
> *on a doorstep*
> *against an east wall*
> *Nov. 1, 1933 . . .*
> ("The Sun Bathers," CEP, p. 7)

In a brief poem near the end of the *Collected Earlier Poems* (cited as
CEP) Williams put the task ahead of him in terms of the myth his poetry
had been elucidating all along—that Kora must be rescued from hell
in order to create paradise, and that rescue and renewal meant returning
to the distrusted thing, the *chaotic* imagination:

Descent

From disorder (a chaos)
order grows
—grows fruitful.
The chaos feeds it. Chaos
feeds the tree.

(CEP, p. 460)

148

Clear, crisp, hard, accurate: winter words, a winter rhetoric for poetry, because the age itself was cold. Williams had renounced free verse in 1924, in his poem "This Florida," as shapeless, "flowery," coming from a world besotted on lush weather, the warm sun of those "escaping winter." Florida was Stevens' landscape of the imagination, where the palms of the mind sprouted luxuriantly along the coast— Williams rejects it all as if to say he could find the truth only in the orders of winter. A year later, Eliot renounced his own past in "Ash Wednesday," which too accepts a world without Kora. Perhaps the prosperous Roaring Twenties seemed a false summer in which to luxuriate; only a poet in wintry Hartford could appreciate the formless exuberance of its tropical weather. But the free verse poets were through with the disorder of unmeasured speech. Winter would come anyway in 1929, perhaps deepening the convictions of all those who distrusted this "easy" harvest of pleasure and wealth. One wanted to discover the bones of reality behind the plumes and fronds and other summer disguises: what were the structural joints of the scene; what was the geometry of nature? Williams could think of art then only as a stripping away of the clothing, even of the flesh of life, which could be carried out to a certain extent in the novel but which only the poem dares to achieve completely:

"The novel is in effect a strip-tease. You take off a chapter at a time, beginning with the front. As you get deeper your subject begins more and more to reveal itself . . . but if and when you get down to nothing more than the sheer (nylon) panties or shall we say, jock strap, slip a finger under the edge and snap it off—we have, hopefully, the poem."

An old, deep conviction against the romantic then came to the surface of his little college talk:

"You see," I went on, "there are no primitive novels. It began, barely, with the poem. You do not get the novel until you begin to hide the cruel nudity; until you get clothes."[8]

   The well-made poem cut through all that clothing of an age to
find the reality beneath it, the naked body; Williams was very nearly
saying that poetry was a kind of fire of righteousness raging against
the gaudy refinements of a vain era—the way "Henry James' work"
ushered in the "classic age, the poem." Was James the decadent last
voice of the Gilded Age? Was Fitzgerald the voice of Ziegfield's
Follies, of Gatsby's terraced limousine? Did the poem expose the glacial
symmetry of bone under the silks of a decadent excess? Then Williams   *149*
must have read Pound's dicta of Imagism as a break with the moral
decadence of the nineties as much as a corrective to the sermonizing
of Victorian poetry. Imagism was a bony sculpture beneath the silks
of Symons, Beardsley, Dowson, Le Gallienne, Yeats. Florida was another
landscape of *florid* excess, a land without the purgative ice of winter—
the Objectivist season. We know he feels these things because earlier
poems gradually lead up to this rejection of Florida as a landscape
of poetry:

> raw Winter's done
> to a turn—Restaurant: Spring!
> Ah, Madam, what good are your thoughts
>
> romantic but true
> beside this gaiety of the sun
> and that huge appetite?
>
> Look!
> from a glass pitcher she serves
> clear water to the white chickens.
>
> What are your memories
> beside that purity?
>
>   ("Brilliant Sad Sun," CEP, p. 324)

The poems after "This Florida" recede from flourishes of language
and thought, looking for those details in nature that are lone against
the sky, like the tree's "eccentric knotted/ twigs/ bending forward/
hornlike at the top" in "Young Sycamore."[9] Williams surrounds his
rejection of Florida with poems about New England's "iron girders,"
metal bones, and how the "round sun" smoothes the "lacquer" of
a tethered bull until "his substance" is as "hard as ivory or glass."[10]
   The long years of Objectivism represent the perfecting of a poet's
eyes, which, like Cézanne's, could see the buried symmetries of reality,
the submerged joints, angles, balances, bare lovely structures of an
otherwise deceitfully whimsical, "busy" foreground of abundance. But

by 1938, that vision of the world closed with the appearance of the
Complete Collected Poems. The tense counterbalances of power in the
political world had collapsed into channels of frightening motion:
in 1935, Mussolini launched an attack against Ethiopia, subduing it
to the Italian Empire; in 1936, Hitler advanced into the demilitarized
Rhineland, while at the same time civil war burst in Spain; and in
October 1937, Roosevelt delivered his "quarantine speech," arguing

150 that American neutrality was no safeguard against the contagion of
war. A violent tide of war seemed to release from many points at once
the pent-up energies of hostility, resentment, and aggression left
unspent from World War I. All Europe was set in motion, and its vortex
pulled at the United States by the end of the decade. Williams would
find his methods of writing shattered and replaced:

> *To make a start,*
> *out of particulars*
> *and make them general, rolling*
> *up the sum, by defective means*

A boiling river of contents swept away the delicate skeletal symmetry
of reality, so that

> *(The multiple seed,*
> *packed tight with details soured,*
> *is lost in the flux and the mind,*
> *distracted, floats off in the same*
> *scum)*
>
> *Rolling up, rolling up heavy with*
> *numbers*

The winter stillness of Objectivism had become a violent watery world:

> *Rolling in, top up,*
> *under, thrust and recoil, a great clatter:*
> *lifted as air, boated, multicolored, a*
> *wash of seas—*
> *from mathematics to particulars—*
>
> *divided as the dew,*
> *floating mists, to be rained down and*
> *regathered into a river that flows*
> *and encircles:*

> *shells and animalcules*
> *generally and so to man,*
>
> *to Paterson.*
>
> *("The Preface,"* Paterson, *1946)*

Getting to the water world of *Paterson;* a postwar poem, required deliberate, bold steps; Williams was a thorough and meticulous reasoner. Like Pound, he would begin to remake himself by reexamining literary history. In 1939, Dorothy Norman and Edward Dahlberg had started up their review called *Twice A Year,* in the first number of which Charles Olson's essay "Lear and Moby-Dick" appeared, a piece of deft scholarship linking together works about powerful personae forced to submit to change; water works. Among the other essays was a longish piece by Williams entitled "Against the Weather: A Study of the Artist."[11]

> The weather changes and man adapts his methods that he may survive, one by one, in order to be there for agreements later.

It was necessary, he felt, to repudiate the strictness of order in the arts because in life order had become a deadly strategy of fascist control. "The natural corrective is the salutary mutation in the expression of all truths, the continual change without which no symbol remains permanent. It must change, it must reappear in another form, to remain permanent. It is the image of the Phoenix" (Selected Essays [SE], 208). It is also the image of the river. "We live," he wrote grimly, "under attack by various parties against the whole. And all in the name of order!"

> The understanding of Walt Whitman is after the same nature. Verse is measure, there is no free verse. *But* the measure must be one of more trust, greater liberty, than has been permitted in the past. It must be an open formation. Whitman was never able fully to realize the significance of his structural innovations. . . . And so about a generation ago, when under the influence of Whitman, the prevalent verse forms had gone to the free-verse pole, the countering cry of Order! Order! reawakened. That was the time of the new Anglo-Catholicism.
> The result was predictable. Slash down the best life of the day to bring it into the lines of control.
>
> (SE, 212)

"Obviously the artist cannot ignore the economic dominance in his time," he wrote. "He is all but suppressed by it—which should mean something—but never converted. On the contrary he attacks and his attack is basic, the only basic one." Exclusion of life from the structure of the work of art, for any reason, is the lust for power over the materials and not the expression of man's actual existence, his truth.

The responsibility of the artist in face of the world is toward inclusion when others sell out to a party.

(SE, 211)

Pound and Eliot, in Williams' eyes, had been seduced into the very exclusions on which the fascists depended to organize the new warring states of Europe. It therefore remained for the artist to become a revolutionary, for it was through his structure of verse that "he builds a structure of government." Thus, "the creation which gives the artist his status as a man" comes only when he seizes his major opportunity, "to build his living, complex day into the body of his poems." Man is an *urb*, into whose ear the river pours as he dreams, and his creation will be citizens of the dream in acts of daily living.

Unless he discovers and builds anew he is betraying his contemporaries in all other fields of intellectual realization and achievement and must bring their contempt upon himself and his fellow artists.

(SE, 217)

Williams recalled, in going over the 1938 *Collected Poems*, he found " "many brief poems, arranged in couplet or quatrain form. I noticed also that I was peculiarly fascinated by another pattern: the dividing of the little paragraphs in lines of three." In rewriting some of his poems, "in the attempt to make [the poem] go faster, "the quatrain changed into a three line stanza."[12]

In "Against the Weather," he seizes upon the difference in rhyme schemes of Juan Ruiz' *Libro de Buen Amor* and Dante's *Divina Commedia*; Ruiz' epic had fashioned a "flat-footed quadruple rhyme scheme" which broke with the dogmatism of Christian trinity; the fourth rhyme was the devil, now mortared into the sensibility of the Middle Ages; the pagan world, so long excluded from the art of Europe, suddenly took its place in the fourth angle of the poem's building unit; Dante's poem, composed in *terza rima*, remained enslaved to the trinitarian vision of Catholicism, and it was only by the sheer force of the poet's deep sensuality that the poem is saved from the oblivion of mere propaganda. Ruiz' vision is due in part to his residence in Spain, where he was safe from the immediate censure of Rome; but both poems are important signals of a tension about to be released—each takes in the forbidden pagan vision and weaves it through the Christian order of reality. Williams detects in both epics an "undercurrent, a hidden—mystical—quality" which fused together the Christian and pagan minds, setting all the arts free into that ultimate confluence, the Renaissance. He could only think of the release in river terms, of an "Undercurrent," a merging of separate streams from which flowed a deep, universal freedom of thought and expression.

Williams is a shrewd polemicist of his own cause; note where he takes his evidence, in the fundamentals of measure and symmetry in a poem; not in vision and style, but in handiwork, where a poet must count and order his syllables. Thus, it was through a poet's structure that he freed all else about himself—through line length, syllable counts, rhymes, if necessary; such symmetry as Ruiz had employed broke open the poem to a new reality. "This," Williams argues, "is the essence of what art is expected to do and cannot live without doing." Even so, Williams secretly enjoyed the wild struggle of Dante's *terza rima* more than he admired the "flat-footed quadruple rhyme" of the *Book of Love;* Pan fought to be among the holy trinity, a battle raging *in* the poem. Eliot's *Four Quartets* (1943) would make the number four a suspect quantity, even though, as Williams wrote to Henry Wells in 1955, "I found myself always conceiving my abstract designs as possessing four sides. That was natural enough with spring, summer, autumn and winter always before me." The "trinity," or three-line stanza, "always seemed unstable, it lacked a fourth member, the devil."[13] But it was instability that created the motion of thought, the thawing of relations, which Imagism and Objectivism both had depicted as fixed like shards of ice. Those quadruple rhymes of Ruiz, Williams cannot help saying, rose "like masonry" to build a structure; in Dante, the struggle was between an old inherited faith crumbling into tryanny and an energy to welcome in the alien and new, felt in the dissonant new rhyme of the "fourth line," where Pan emerged, laughing, erotic, disorderly. The clean masonry lacked that light foot, the dance of the intellect in uncertainty and the new. The tercet made the poem go "faster," possibly because thought was in trouble, the measure off balance, the stream of thinking moral and imprecise, altered to the disquieting ambiguities of reality and not to clarify outlines. The tercet, the "triadic" stanza as Williams called it, was a structure for measuring the relativity of reality, especially during a war. In *Paterson*, one finds an elaborate triadic structure governing the poem, from its books (6) to book parts (3) to the measure Williams hits upon in Book II, Part III, the triadic stanza, bound only by the "variable foot."

On one point Williams is silent in his essays: was it in fact the *terza rima* of the *Divina Commedia* that brought forth Dante's sensuousness? The very imbalance of a triple rhyme might alert the mind to new realms within the psyche—might, in fact, call forth the bottomless unconscious, with its phantasms of desire, its visions of immaterial unities, its longings, its racial memories, the whole latent store of vitality kept out of the framework of one's guarded consciousness. Dante's inferno is very similar to Hieronymous Bosch's lurid triptychs of the religious universe. Threefold vision perhaps opened consciousness to the divine, the transcendent, as well as to the base and forbidden; it was the rhythm of vision itself and could call forth gods as well as devils—hence, the Christian dogma of trinity. Williams eventually used a modified *terza rima* in one of his most successful poems, "Asphodel, that Greeny Flower." The triadic stanza, which formed much of the poetry of his later life, gradually emerged from the writing of the next few years. Here, then, was a most suggestive dichotomy in poetry, between the absolute premises of faith and the relativity of one's own consciousness, which Williams discovered melting into a general stream of thought in the Middle Ages. It was a paradigm of how art frees itself from its political and social entrapments. He looked among his contemporaries for evidence of this dichotomy in his own time—he wanted to find some immanent confluence of separate streams of thought which would again liberate art from its rigid formulae.

In his introduction to a retrospective of paintings by his old friend Charles Sheeler, Williams perceived a subtle vacillation in the artist's later works: contours, the surface of life, were no longer hard, clear, and well defined, but seemed to dissolve slightly. Sheeler was asking questions about the hidden identity of the images of life, the submerged fixities of their content, and inquiring into the medium which detected these images. Sheeler did not abandon his objectivity, but Williams felt he was lured away from the look of the world as he probed into the immaterial dimension of his subjects: "Sheeler," Williams wrote, "turned where his growth was to lie, to a subtler particularization, the abstract if you will."[14] At the other extreme was the poetry of Charles Henri Ford, which had taken its measure from the rhythms of American jazz and its thought from French Surrealism; Williams is very cautious with this poetry that wildly rejoices in erotic fantasy. But Williams is writing an introduction to this work *as well;* he soberly describes it as "generally dreamlike," an accompaniment "well put together as to their words" of "radio jazz and other various, half-preaching, half-sacrilegious sounds of a Saturday night in June."[15] Ford was trying to merge France and Africa into an American idiom, but Williams will have little of it in so serious a forum as a book's introduction. He will go only so far as to admit such a verse can "revive the senses and force them to re-see, re-hear, re-taste, re-smell and generally revalue" the threadbare moment of reality. Here Williams stood in the middle of the extremes of expression: Sheeler and American pragmatism, Ford and French Surrealism. If a new poetry were to succeed, it is clear these were the separate streams that needed to converge in American art. Surrealism, like jazz, seemed fraught with protest and complaint, and by its seeming recklessness and arrogant disregard of symmetry, bore against restraint, calculation, and limits of any kind. It was only a matter of time before the American government would request the moral support of artists in the war effort, in which Williams saw a deadly alliance of authority and art. This threat drove him to embrace European Surrealism before he could fully digest its political and esthetic implications; now he was its American spokesman, proclaiming the alliance of art with innovation and protest. In "Midas: A Proposal for a Magazine," published in 1941, he argued the resilience of the Surrealists. Their poetry of the immaterial, of the dream, fortified them in their struggle against propaganda and fascist authority; it invigorated their quest for reality, which Williams implies is needed in American poetry. The European poets "dig under," he wrote, "where, hidden in the soil of the mind, divergent excellences may be found." Surrealism had "sapped the war of all intellectual strength before it started," and now "something equally pregnant must follow" in the United States. "The means" of artistic freedom and liberation "were locked up in stupidity, war released them."[16] The image of a pent-up, frozen reality reinvoked his myth of the dialectic of the seasons, of Kora's captivity. Surrealism brought back overwhelming spring, a superabundance of dream foliage and eroticism to the hard, leafless landscape of the prewar years. Here was the "defective means" for "rolling up the particulars" into a torrent of released energies and widening banks of reality.

Many more forces than Surrealism converged upon the last years of the decade to form a movement, perhaps even a wedge, against the stolid pragmatism of American artists. By the late 1930s, American jazz was no longer a racial music but a national art form composed and performed throughout the country; it was now at its most powerful stage of innovation. When Williams occasionally complained of its exuberance, he was perhaps thinking of an earlier stage of Dixieland and Harlem jazz, which e. e. cummings had once affectionately parodied in lyrics like "Jimmy's Got A Goil," to which Williams responded with "Shoot It, Jimmy," their versions of scat singing, possibly. But years later, Williams argued that his sense of the "American idiom" had "as much originality as jazz." In some poems, he remarked elsewhere, "I was following the beat in my mind, the beat of the American idiom."[17]

American theater, which interested Williams deeply (he wrote short experimental plays during the 1930s and 1940s) was in the throes of a slow but profound revolution in dramaturgy and vision. Beginning in the 1920s, the era in which, Alan Downer writes, "most certainties—moral, ethical, and to an extent legal—had given way to uncertainties. It was no longer possible to say with assurance what action was right and what was wrong. All actions had to be freshly examined, all positions freshly argued, all characters and situations freshly analyzed, in the attempt to establish new values and new certainties for the 1920s."[18] Through O'Neill's plays American drama evolved from Naturalism to Expressionism, in which the stage was liberated from the restraints of representation and became an experimental plane for symbolic and abstract projections of the meaning and themes of a play. Dramatic Expressionism is a vehicle for the exploration of the primitive; it is the stage for Freudian conflicts, and, after the example of Bertolt Brecht, who had emigrated to California during World War II, for political protest and ideological conflict as well. The 1930s was a decade of verse drama, of theater as ritual, in which, if anything, the Expressionist stage had become utterly abstract and symbolic. The essential theme of the verse drama was political tragedy. "Distortion served the Expressionists as an X-ray eye for detecting the dynamic essence of their time, the direction in which history was moving. In caricature and nightmare they approached the truth."[19] The Nazi party had purged the German theater of such playwrights, who then emigrated to the United States throughout the 1930s; in essence, Expressionism was to theater what Surrealism was to poetry, or jazz to music. These movements in the arts had all emerged from African art forms, had been expelled from Europe and been transplanted in the United States prior to World War II. But the diaspora of the European intelligentsia during the Fascist decade included practically all branches of science and art in which the spirit of reexamination of reality was being expressed. The arrival of German Gestalt psychologists in the United States, for example, immediately created conflict with American behaviorists, who fought bitterly to prevent Gestaltists from joining their faculties. The same may be said of European physicists, biologists, mathematicians, social scientists (the Frankfurt school in particular), Marxists, and the Bauhaus architects; in sum, the resistant forces of European culture who had been skimmed off and exiled only to concentrate their influences in America's cultural centers; Williams found himself amidst their ferment and could not resist the excitement provoked by their energies and sensibilities. Here was a culture of revolutionaries who had fought their various state authorities and had been punished for their daring visions; they challenged American artists to express themselves with equal freedom and conviction.[20] Here was the "other" stream of thought that was merging with American culture to create a new zeitgeist at mid-century.

157

As Williams put it in "Midas," "A certain number of refugees from the Death in Europe, revolutionary in the full sense, have met others here who welcome them to this country. Together they propose to continue an advance into the present and to publish from time to time a bulletin of their interest" (SE, 241). Philippe Sollers, a founding editor of the Paris journal *Tel Quel*, looked back at the era as a grafting of European thought onto American art:

I see the main graft at the time of the second World War, in the withdrawal and exile of eccentric European personalities to the United States. Let's call it the grafting of the European avant-garde onto the United States, even though the problem is complex, involving Schoenberg and a great many others. . . . Let's also say it was the grafting of Surrealism onto the United States during the war.

To which Julia Kristeva, also of *Tel Quel*, responded:

As to the graft, it unquestionably took place, but it produced something entirely different from what was to be expected. They took Artaud and Duchamp and produced Pollock, which couldn't have happened in either France or Moscow, so that there's something specific and interesting in America.[21]

In 1944, Williams completed a new collection of poems representing his efforts to merge and fuse the different heritages of the era, poems that sought to gather in the various forces alive in the air and to drive them to a single purpose. He called the book *The Wedge*. It begins solemnly: "The war is the first and only thing in the world today." As an artist, he too was at war, but in his own country against the enemies of his own thinking: "this writing," he claimed grimly, is not "a diversion from that for relief, a turning away. It *is* the war or part of it, merely a different sector of the field."[22] In formulating the poetic of his book, Williams stood between his old self and his new, attempting to combine them both into one man. On the one hand, he writes, a poem is a "machine made of words," in which we find the hard, clear, positioned contents of the Objectivist; on the other, it is an "intense expression of [the poet's] perceptions and ardors that they may constitute a revelation in the speech that he uses" (SE, 257). The poet intends to "make clear the complexity of his perceptions" in the medium he has inherited, using words "without distortion which would mar their exact significances." The poem's clarity has now become the means, but the primary intention of the poem is to uncover "the complexity of [the poet's] perceptions." As he wrote several years later, "The objective in writing is, to reveal. It is not to teach, not to advertise, not to sell, not even to communicate. . . . Reveal what? That which is inside the man."[23] It later required him to remark, "In prose, an English word means what it says. In poetry, you're listening to two things. . . . You're listening to the sense, the common sense of what it says. But it says more. That is the difficulty." Sense and more, the fluid "undercurrent" fusing different heritages: American pragmatism, the sense; European Surrealism, abstraction, Expressionism, the "more"? At any rate, these two tracks of content simultaneously unfolding from the "new" poem must be accompanied by "an impetuous rhythm, a Declaration of Independence from every restraint."[24] In 1950, he told Harvey Breit, an editor of the *New York Times*, "Poetry is in a chaotic stage. We have to . . . put ourselves into chaos on purpose, in order to rediscover new constellations of the elements of verse in our time."[25] The poem's parts were suspended in "constellations" bound only by the variable foot, the poem's only gravity. Still, Williams never relinquished his modernist sense that the poem was a struggle to make a mosaic from the parts which must be true to life even in their distortions and abstraction. But now the whole of the poem made its sum the mobilized elements of narrative. In 1961, Williams saw his work as an effort to be "released" from the past to find some fusion of new meters with new thought:

In my language I can find some release with a hard effort, which is invention, hard effort when I want to say something, to speak in some way, to construct a poem that will not be a sonnet and not be a quatrain at all but very sensuous and that wanders over the page in a very curious way that has never been encountered. The poem is here but the metric is here, and they go along side by side—the verbal invention and the purely metrical invention—go along arm in arm looking for a place they can embrace, we'll say, and then they go together. Why, they strike it off. And that's a *poem*! . . . And you can fight and fight and fight a lifetime till you hit a fusion.[26]

In the poems of *The Wedge*, published in 1944, Williams worked hard on "the verbal invention," letting the line go a little soft in order to gather in more words, the foliage to the bare branch. As he did

so, the water images came naturally to his thought, as did the sense
of motion, of wavering ideas and images:

> *What common language to unravel?*
> *The falls, combed into straight lines*
> *from that rafter of a rock's*
> *lip. Strike in! the middle of*
>
> *some trenchant phrase, some*
> *well packed clause.*
>
>   ("*Paterson: The Falls*," CEP, p. 10)

The Wedge is a notebook of preliminary themes and ideas for the making
of *Paterson:*

> *You are lovely as a river*
> *under tranquil skies—*
> *There are imperfections*
> *but a music overlays them—*
>
> *telling by how dark a bed*
> *the current moves*
> *to what sea that shines*
> *and ripples in my thought*
>
>   ("*A Flowing River*," CEP, p. 21)

The theme of the river appears throughout the poems, in passing
metaphors, in images, and as the central motif: "She had come, like
the river / from up country" opens the poem "Eternity"; the shorter
poems of this collection glitter with a new phraseology of "the crazy
weave of the breaking mind" ("The Last Turn") and of how "the
sentence undulates / raising no song," ("The End of the Parade").
The Wedge is a dark book, moving from bitterness at war to the forlorn
sense of spent emotions to the coming again of a hard winter; the
vaguely Surrealist "A Vision of Labor: 1931" depicts a girl, two laborers,
and a dying bishop who are juxtaposed in dream and remain
inaccessible to each other, as if the poet brooded on what it would
require to fuse them together meaningfully. In several of the longer
poems, "Catastrophic Birth," "Burning the Christmas Greens," "To
All Gentleness," and the delicate "Three Sonnets," the theme of
transformation emerges, in which juxtaposition *does* alter and renew.
In "Catastrophic Birth," an erupting volcano is the principle of
historic change, in which "the new opens / new ways beyond all known
ways." It is like birth, but it is also the constant of history: as it
"breathes softly on / the edge of the sky, violence revives and regathers."

There follows "Paterson: the Falls," another force that even though "frozen, / still whispers and moans" of change. But the most brilliant treatment of transformation occurs in "Burning the Christmas Greens," in which the green boughs erupt into "flame red, red as blood, . . . a landscape of flame" from what was once "a promise of peace, a fort / against the cold." Of course these are allegories of the catastrophe of war, but they are also demands of the poet on himself to be changed by what he felt from without. In 1948, he could look back to the war years and see the connection between those poems and their implicit urgings upon him:

> . . . a semiconscious sense of a rending discovery to be made is becoming apparent. For one great thing about "the bomb" is the awakened sense it gives us that catastrophic (but why?) alterations are also possible in the human mind, in art, in the arts. . . . We are too cowed by our fear to realize it fully. But it is *possible*. That is what we mean.²⁷

The Wedge is compelling because the poet's anguish to be "released" pervades his speech; it is a book about war without and the effort to direct some of its violence to a man's thought, in order that he may transform himself. Out of this transformation would come the exuberant, triumphant first book of *Paterson* (1946), with its ecstatic emphasis upon the powerful rushes of water over the head of a man, whose ear gathered in the force of the falls and directed it to his unconscious imagination. Perhaps the wedge of the book is the driving force of the exterior world opening the poet's consciousness, his sensorium, to the "profusion, the Mass—heterogeneous—ill-assorted." Williams' new stance toward this abundant material for poetry was to notice its quantity of particulars more than its structural integrity; the interesting shift in his poetic is just here—originally, Williams found measure in the order of nature, measure taking on a literal meaning of recording the spatial properties of a "scene." But for Williams, measure came to mean a musical tempo that ordered the profuse data of one's speech; measure thus became the tempo of one's thinking struck off in bars. Now Williams could explore the properties of his art—in each "bar" or line of the triadic stanza, one is drawn to the poet's powers to think in sound. The particles of sound become interactive within the line and form patterns of their own beyond immediate sense—in the line, then, one hears the *music* of verse language. The continuity of the speech from line to line, stanza to stanza, enjambed, elided, exposes *rhythm* as well: some of the line cuts are grammatically confusing, but the rhythmic unit is *there*, to be felt visually and aurally. The indentations emphasize the "sweeping" rhythm of the lines through the stanza; the visual order of these triads reinforces the impression that the sound pattern is riverine, a flow of thought punctuated by the slightest silence of the break and the eye's return to initiate the next line. The triadic stanza incorporated control and release at once: control through the deliberate, willful breaks of the flow into segments, and release in the unfettered roaming and near aimlessness of the speech. Here was a fusion at last, between the American's habit to control and to formulate his experience and the European's "pure psychic automatism," thought that was "free from the exercise of reason," as André Breton proclaimed. In 1954, Williams explained his new measure in a letter to Richard Eberhart thus:

> By measure I mean musical pace. Now, with music in our ears the words need only be taught to keep as distinguished an order, as chosen a character, as regular, according to the music, as in the best of prose.
> By its *music* shall the best of modern verse be known and the *resources* of the music. The refinement of the poem, its subtlety is not to be known by the elevation of the words but—the words don't so much matter—by the resources of the *music.* [28]

Nineteen forty-eight is the crucial year in Williams' remaking; not only had he written wisely and deeply on the nature of verse structure and its relation to experience, but he had completed the second book of *Paterson*, where the triadic stanza emerges in Part III with its variable foot rhythm. This astonishing passage begins with a somber vision of the "nul" of the rocky peripheries of the Falls in winter, the landscape of desolation that is abruptly halted with the declaration:

> But Spring shall come and flowers will bloom
> and man must chatter of his doom . . .

The "descent" that beckons is, of course, the descent to the underworld, where Kora is held captive; it is equally a descent into the mind, "inhabited by hordes / heretofore unrealized," which when examined opens the poet to a "world unsuspected." The descent is toward love, toward Kora herself, the Spring of the world and its principle of renewal;

> The descent
>   made up of despairs
>   and without accomplishment
> realizes a new awakening:
>   which is a reversal
> of despair.

These lines, indented and sweeping forward in their disjunctive arcs,

are themselves steps down to hell, the hell that Williams is willing
to enter in order to be renewed. In each line the beat is felt, the beat
of the foot falling on each step of its journey: *Journey to Love* would
follow in 1955, in which the "theory of the variable foot is explicit in
the whole thing." It too is about the renewal of spring, of love, and
of "Asphodel, that greeny flower." The "variable foot" of *Paterson*, Book
II, Part III, was his "sea change," and "from the time I hit on this I
knew what I was going to have to do." *The Desert Music and Other Poems*
developed "the concept I had discovered—the variable foot" and was
followed by *Journey to Love;* both were written in triadic stanzas.

The new measure had brought Williams from modernism to
postmodernism, from a vision of reality as the delicate, frozen
counterpoise of simple objects described in minimal statements to
the flowing rhythms of the triadic stanza of his later years. His
transformation occurred in the heat of war, in the ferment of the
European emigration, in which the whole cultural context Pound had
enjoyed throughout much of his life had suddenly swept over and
liberated Williams' world. Williams was now the hero of a new
generation of poets, who built upon his poetics and who found in
him the desired energy they wished to express in their own work.
Certainly he disapproved of many of the younger poets, particularly
the Beat writers who had mistaken his variable foot for free verse,
but he enjoyed the fruits of his own renewal and success. In the years
immediately following his death, there ensued what Paul Mariani has
called his "canonization," the massive critical reappraisal of the poet
who had sprung forth anew from what was supposedly his
"retirement" following the *Complete Collected Poems* of 1938.

Notes

1. Paul Mariani, *William Carlos Williams: The Poet and His Critics* (Chicago: American Library Association, 1975), pp. 61, 62.

2. *I Wanted to Write a Poem: The Autobiography of the Works of a Poet,* ed. Edith Heal (New York: New Directions, 1958), p. 65. Cited hereafter as IWWP.

3. Dickran Tashjian, *William Carlos Williams and the American Scene: 1920–1940* (New York and Berkeley: Whitney Museum of American Art and the University of California Press, 1978), p. 132.

4. *The Autobiography of William Carlos Williams* (New York: New Directions, 1967), p. 316.

5. *Autobiography,* pp. 318–19.

6. Jerome Mazzaro, *William Carlos Williams: The Later Poems* (Ithaca: Cornell University Press, 1973), p. 85.

7. Ibid., pp. 85–86.

8. *Autobiography,* pp. 368–69.

9. *The Collected Earlier Poems of William Carlos Williams* (New York: New Directions, 1951), p. 332.

10. Ibid., p. 336.

11. *Selected Essays of William Carlos Williams* (New York: New Directions, 1954), pp. 196–218. Cited hereafter as SE.

12. IWWP, p. 66.

13. Mazzaro, *The Later Poems,* p. 79.

14. SE, p. 233.

15. Ibid., p. 235.

16. Ibid., p. 247.

17. "On the Poem," in *Interviews with William Carlos Williams: "Speaking Straight Ahead,"* ed. Linda Wagner (New York: New Directions, 1976), pp. 74–75.

18. "The Revolt from Broadway," in *A Time of Harvest: American Literature—1910–1960,* ed. Robert E. Spiller (New York: Hill and Wang, 1962), p. 47.

19. "Introduction," in *Anthology of German Expressionist Drama: A Prelude to the Absurd,* ed. Walter H. Sokel (Garden City: Anchor Books, 1963), p. xxiii.

20. The full account of the European diaspora is given in *Perspectives in American History* 2 (1968), under the general heading of "The Intellectual Migration: Europe and America, 1930–1960."

21. Julia Kristeva, Marcelin Pleynet, and Philippe Sollers, "The U.S. Now: A Conversation," *October* 6 (Fall 1978), 8, 9.

22. SE, p. 255.

23. Ibid., p. 268.

24. *Interviews,* p. 75.

25. Ibid., p. 60.

26. Ibid., p. 48.

27. SE, p. 287.

28. "A New Measure," in *Modern Poetics,* ed. James Scully (New York: McGraw-Hill Book Company, 1965), p. 72.

163

8. *"Her Heigh Compleynte"*: *The Cress Letters of William Carlos Williams'* Paterson

Theodora R. Graham

In late March 1942, as if responding to his unconscious invocation, an extraordinary Muse appeared at the doorstep of William Carlos Williams' office is Rutherford. Seeking help rather than conferring it, Marcia Nardi was to inspire the poet in completely unforeseen ways. Within two months of their first meeting, she had become inextricably connected with the composition of *Paterson*. By that time Williams had formed in his mind two distinct roles for her, both of which she resisted: the one, in real life, as a late-blooming protégée whose poetry lacked a technical skill in which he might school her; the other, in plans for the epic, as a female version of himself-as-Paterson who, unlike him, had tragically followed the romantic urge to defy social convention. Williams learned to know Nardi's character and voice primarily through the correspondence she initiated after their meeting. The fascination these letters held for him and the manuscript evidence of various schemes he devised for using them in *Paterson* suggest that Nardi herself and Williams' transformation of her into the mysterious Cress were essential to his conception of the poem.

Far-ranging differences exist among critics concerning the nature of Cress's role in *Paterson* and Williams' decision to include so much material from her letters in Book II. While there is general agreement that the letters' "echoing of the themes of divorce and blockage and failure at communication"[1] makes them germane to the poem's major ideas, there remains the question, first raised by Randall Jarrell, of whether or not Williams diminished the force of his writing by relying too extensively on them.

Should so much of this book consist of what are—the reader is forced to conclude—real letters from a real woman? One reads these letters with involved, embarrassed pity, quite as if she had walked into the room and handed them to one. What has been done to them to make them part of the poem . . . ? I can think of no answer except: "They have been copied out on the typewriter." Anyone can object, "The context makes them part of the poem"; and anyone else can reply to this objection, "It takes a lot of context to make somebody else's eight-page letter the conclusion of a poem."[2]

Vivienne Koch commends Williams' artifice in positioning this same long letter after the lyric, "On this most voluptuous night," for in her view it creates an "anticlimactic note of mockery" aimed at Paterson's wish for consummation and renewal.

In effect, Williams makes an ironic attack on himself through the medium of the barely disguised letters. This amounts to a kind of penance, as if the poet were confessing: Here in *Paterson* lie exposed the polar contraries of modern experience. On the one hand, there is the affirmation of art in the poetry; on the other, the mean inadequacies of conduct in the letters. Who is to divine the abyss or construct the modes of reconciliation?[3]

In Roger Seamon's judgment the long letter is a "triumph of the female material, the anti-poetic, over the shape of the poem," its object to rouse Paterson in Book III to subdue Cress "in a violent process which . . . closely resembles the sexual act."[4]

Cress herself has been variously described as a "lacerated and lacerating poetess" and an "emotionally sterilized" woman.[5] In Joel Conarroe's view she suffers "an almost psychotic splitting of personality" and turns Paterson into "a sort of long-distance psychiatrist."[6] Mike Weaver observes, however, that she and other related figures, such as Mrs. Cumming and Alva Turner, are not represented in the poem "because they are neurotic, but because their veracity as thwarted human beings—their unimpaired though distorted vigour—finds expression in action."[7] In a baroque explication, Seamon argues that Williams enacts Cress's defeat in Book III by linking the image of the "dry sand" of her thoughts to the bottle that undergoes metamorphosis in the fire.

. . . a real woman had broken into the poem (in the letters) to "deflower" herself, to strip away the conventional image of female beauty . . . But when this woman became oppressive she was further "deflowered," at first by her own admission, and later by the poet as he reduced her to her most basic elements, wind, fire and water. Out of this second violation came the flame which turned the dry sand into the bottle.[8]

Another, more recent, study takes a contrary position: "Cress' letters . . . directly show up the poet-narrator's pretention; they reveal him as an ordinary, and morally not very scrupulous, man. Yet by containing those very assertions, *Paterson* succeeds, not in 'justifying' Williams himself, but in demonstrating its capacity to speak for more than the sensibility of a single author."[9]

As these interpretations reveal, Cress eludes simple characterization; her letters, changed by Williams in important ways from the originals by Nardi, have an enigmatic power not fully accounted for in studies of the poem. Turning to the extant correspondence between Williams and Nardi and to notes and manuscripts for the first two books, one discovers a complex relationship that for personal and artistic reasons Williams chose to render opaquely. Because in his memories of the letters, Williams' self-projection as Paterson verges on autobiography, knowledge of the details of the Williams-Nardi association and analysis of its literary transmutation can provide a perspective on Dr. Paterson's relation to Cress that the text itself does not easily render. To a young woman who had requested help with a story, Williams wrote in 1949, "remember, as Proust once wrote to Gide, you can say anything so long as you do not say 'I.' You write to reveal, then call it John Henry but surreptitiously reveal yourself."[10] "The poem," he avows in the *Autobiography*, "is a capsule where we wrap up our punishable secrets."[11] In a strict sense Williams' secrets about his relationship to Marcia Nardi were not punishable. However, the ambiguity surrounding Paterson's relationship to Cress is, I hope to demonstrate, a result of Williams' unresolved attitudes toward Nardi, attitudes which reflect ambivalent views he held of women. Seeking emotional support and friendship from someone she considered a fellow poet, Nardi looked to Williams' praise of her writing and his encouragement to breathe new life into her spirit. In her desperate loneliness and poverty, however, she could not perceive the contradictions implicit in the roles she gradually defined for him: as critic and confidant, and at the same time as the loyal and fond hero delivering the lady in distress. Why, one wonders reading the first two books of *Paterson*, had Cress singled out Dr. P. to be her deliverer? Had he, by chance, invited the role?

The correspondence between William Carlos Williams and Marcia Nardi suggests that Cress's prototype needed some version of the mentor-patron Williams was at first ready to be.[12] Two sets of letters

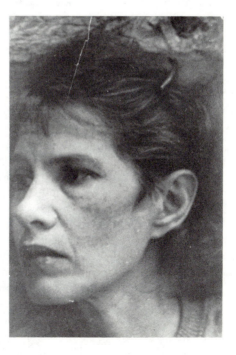

Marcia Nardi, c. 1949. Photos taken
by her husband, Charles Lang
(Courtesy of Miss Nardi).

document the two stages of their relationship; the first, between April 1942 and March 1943; the second, between March 1949 and October 1956.[13] Since only the first period has bearing upon *Paterson*, the following discussion refers exclusively to letters from these twelve months. The later exchange, initiated by Nardi after she had discovered Book II of *Paterson* in a bookstore, records Williams' continued praise of her writing and his efforts to place her poems in *Botteghe Oscura, Poetry,* and other little magazines, as well as his support of her applications for writers' grants. These letters to Nardi are notably different in tone from the earlier set, less formal and reserved, largely, one concludes, because Williams knew she was safely removed from him: married to a painter and living in Woodstock, New York. In late 1942 Williams consciously decided to impose a distance. He was 59, determined to get on with his long poem. Helping her to the extent of her need threatened to become a diversion he could ill afford.

By her own account, Marcia Nardi visited Williams at his invitation on a blustery Sunday evening in March 1942.[14] At the suggestion of Harvey Breit, she had telephoned from New York to ask for advice about gaining her troubled son's release from the Bellevue psychiatric ward. Cut off as a young woman from her disapproving family, Nardi, then 38, was raising her illegitimate son alone in a West 12th Street room, struggling to survive and writing when she could. As early as 1924, when she was just 20, she had published poems in *Measure* and the *New York Herald Tribune Book Review* and had reviewed H. D.'s *Heliodora* for the *New Republic* in 1925.[15] Primarily as a result of the difficulties she experienced as a woman alone with a child during the Depression years, she had not done sustained writing for the nine or ten years prior to meeting Williams. Nevertheless, she was ready to resume serious writing and to develop her own distinctive voice and style. Her first letter to Williams (9 April 1942),[16] parts of which were to become the fragment from Cress in Book I, indicates that—for some reason—she had brought to Rutherford a number of her poems and left them with Williams. While she thanked him for the psychological support that had enabled her to secure her son's release without his intervention, there was still the matter of the poems. This letter discloses, too, that although she had spoken during the visit about certain private affairs, including a recently broken romance with Breit, she had not mentioned her son's illegitimacy nor the problems she faced as an unmarried mother. With one exception, all the letters in this set begin and end formally: Dear Dr. Williams / Sincerely, Marcia Nardi; Dear (or My dear) Marcia Nardi / Sincerely yours, W. C. Williams.

The exception is Williams' second letter to her (13 May 1942), which closes: "Believe me, Your friend / W. C. Williams." What he urged her to believe was that he had found in her letters evidence of an extraordinary mind and talent with language.

> Your letters show you to have one of the best minds I have ever encountered—I say nothing of its reach, which I have had no opportunity to measure but its truth and strength. Your words as I read them have a vigor and a cleanliness to them which constitute for me real beauty. I sincerely and deeply admire you.[17]

169

His first letter (10 April 1942)—responding to her request that he return the poems—had been equally solicitous, inviting her to send him copies of all the poems so that he might work over them. "I'm glad you've been able to solve your personal problems. It has been a privilege to know you."[18] Left without a connection to the literary scene that Breit had briefly provided, Nardi must have felt buoyed by this praise and enthusiasm.

These two letters make clear, however, that Williams was encouraging a *writer.* "Curiously enough, since you ask nothing of me concerning them," his first letter begins, "these poems have in them definitely some of the best writing by a woman (or by anyone else) I have seen in years. They also have plenty of bad writing in them, unfinished, awkward writing." Poetry, he advises, may be therapeutic, the means for her to escape a meager, intellectually arid existence.

> Writing should be your outlet. This may be impossible at the moment, I don't know. It should nevertheless be your constant aim. It is probably the one thing that will give you confidence and relief. Whether or not you can ever bring over into writing the truth that is in your letters and in your thoughts is purely a matter of the technical side. You have the mind. (13 May 1942)

He offered to help her with technique: "and you may believe me I'll always be ready to be of assistance if I can." Moreover, he did not at first ignore her personal difficulties. She had written him (26 April 1942): "I do hope it isn't too presumptuous of me to burden you with all this about my personal life just because of your great kindness in offering to criticize the poems. But it's so hard to separate any one phase of one's life from all the others."[19] He answered: "Your feelings relative to the present object of your misery I find to be altogether correct, more than that, I find them to be distinguished and altogether amazing for one—for anyone." By way of apologizing for the slowness of his response, he mentioned the pressing medical duties of the prior day: "and in the end I lost a baby I was most anxious to save" (13 May

1942). Was there an unconscious connection to Nardi, whom he hoped to save as a woman or as a writer? "There's something here [in your poems] that is not going to be lost if sufficient attention is given to develop and refine it," he wrote her (10 April 1942).

For a brief time Williams' role as critic and adviser was of foremost importance to both of them. Nardi's letter of 26 April demonstrates both naive reservation about Williams' revisions of her poems and persistent self-doubt. Despite job and health problems she had begun to write again. How scrupulous was it, she asked, to accept his suggestions?

170

> Those changes which you pencilled in there make so much difference. They indeed make that poem so much better! But one thing disturbs me, or, rather, raises a problem. Is it quite legitimate and fair of me to let stand as entirely my own those poems which your criticism improves as much as it has already done in the case of that one poem ["Life among the poets"]? It's right enough for the sake of the poems themselves. But it is otherwise, and will you please tell me if it is?

With lengthy justification she also asked if she might "get any of these poems into Poetry Magazine and other literary publications." While once again she could value publication for its own sake, she believed even the small sum it might bring would make both a real and symbolic difference in her life.

> . . . I feel now that it's important (the way the world makes it so) when the inner props fail, to have the outward ones to hold on to no matter how false they may be. I say that, I'm afraid, with some bitterness which is a feeling I do [not] at all approve of. And there is so much that I have really wanted to do . . . secretly . . . with that dead-locked kind of self-confidence I mentioned before, but didn't and couldn't not so much because of my educational lacks nor my continued money problems . . . but mostly because it's so hard . . . to make words hold their own against all those utilitarian occupations of the world unless one's guilty feeling at being [a] slacker there . . . is mitigated somewhat by knowing other people whose own values condone one's own.

Later the same day, she sent a note correcting a word in one of the poems she had returned and raised a more serious question.

> Maybe I'm making a lot of fuss about a bad poem. But if so, I have no critical sense in regard to my own work, and for me to know *that* (should it be true) has its own importance.[20]

Indeed, at this point, it might have seemed to Williams that she expected him either to sanction her efforts to reestablish her literary career or to advise her to relinquish them. He decided to encourage her.

In June 1942, friendly—if not intimate—collaboration seemed possible to both of them. In a letter dated 12 June, Nardi complains of continuing emotional distress and failing attempts to "collect and piece together all the fragments of my scattered personal identity." Unable to work on her poetry, she asked to see him again, "whether I may, and where and when and how soon.[21] Williams replied (14 June):

> Won't you have supper with me Tuesday at 6:30 in the city? I'll meet you at the corner of 40th St and 6th Ave, there's a good restaurant there on the second floor, if I remember rightly though I cannot remember its name. I'll hang around until 7 o'clock and then go up and take a table. Come when you can—or if you prefer, drop me a card on receipt of this telling me what you can do. I realize your hours may make it impossible for you to get away at the time mentioned.[22]

They did in fact meet this second and final time on 16 June 1942 (coincidentally, "Bloomsday"), and Williams discussed with her the possibility of James Laughlin's publishing a selection of her poems in the *New Directions* anthology that fall, as well as his intention of using her letters in *Paterson*. The very next day Williams returned several poems to Nardi suggesting that she evaluate his changes and send finished copies to him for forwarding to Laughlin. "It was a pleasure to talk with you last evening," he added.[23] That Nardi had been struck by his apparent stability and ease surfaces in her reply (20 June):

> . . . my end of the talk amounted to little more than a rambling inconsequential chatter. This is because conversation brings me up on the surface of my consciousness, whereas it's only from way down in its depths (accessible more easily when one is alone and silent) that I can strike off words more effectively. Moreover, that amazing balance which exists between your private life and your life as a writer, and the calm, sane, well-adjusted and wholesome person that you are, made me particularly self-conscious in regard to my own neurotic, maladjusted, and altogether sickly soul.[24]

Completely—and compulsively—immersed in her own problems, Nardi could not intuit that her feelings of isolation, bouts of depression, and ever-present desire to earn a living by writing Williams understood only too well. His own success, he observes in the *Autobiography*, had been founded on persistence in the face of despair: "I would not 'die for art,' but live for it grimly! and work, work, work. . . ."[25] With hard work and encouragement, couldn't the energy of her neurotic soul find release in writing? It appears to have been this promise—against all the odds of her stultifying existence—that first made Nardi's "case" compelling to him.

A month after their second meeting (13 July 1942), Williams confirmed his plan to use her early letters in *Paterson*.

> My long "Introduction" of which I spoke to you is moving along slowly, the material is so abundant I am having to go slow with its organization. It is in this material I am incorporating your letters.[26]

The notes for *Paterson* at Buffalo include on two separate sheets in Williams' typing; (1) part of Nardi's second letter [undated; Sunday][27] and (2) the entire letter of 12 June in which she asks to see him. The latter is preceded by the word "SHE," indicating either the early identity of Cress with the SHE who appears in the dialogue of Book II or another discarded plan to use the voice of David Lyle as HE and Nardi as SHE.[28] Apart from any context, these two letters give some idea of the character Williams was formulating: an unconventional woman whose physical and emotional suffering grew from her alternately hopeful and despairing temperament ("These intellectual and spiritual comas which sometimes follow acute mental anguish"); an emerging poet who read the little magazines and taught herself French in order to escape "the mental level of grocery clerks or else of the gutter"; a shadow-figure who mirrored his own (and Paterson's) sometimes "deadly inertia of mind and soul." Neither of these letters appears in *Paterson*. Yet the Cress letters of Book II show that Williams' original conception of her did not change. What did change between June 1942 and February 1943—and subsequently in the composition of *Paterson*—was Williams' attitude toward Nardi. In the months following their meeting in New York, as she wrote more impassioned letters about her personal difficulties and sought to rely on his emotional and financial help, Williams' responses grew distant and businesslike, until—on 17 February 1943—he wrote: "This brings our correspondence to a close as far as I am concerned."[29] The letters in Book II, written after this dismissal, strike the reader with more force than the two Williams first planned to use, because the chance of a mutual commitment is gone. Cress exists for Paterson only in fragmented memories.

Before this break occurred, however, the correspondence—increasingly longer letters from Nardi and brief, informational ones from Williams—continued. After their meeting in June, several letters concern Laughlin's less than enthusiastic agreement to publish six of the poems Williams and she had sent him.[30] Nardi was disappointed over Laughlin's coolness and failure to inform her which of the poems he had selected. That summer, too, her search for a job that would take her out of the city began to involve Williams more generally in her life. By mid-summer her request for a $25 loan had led to the confused situation over the money order referred to in Cress's long letter. By the time Williams had sent her $15, intending to forward the rest the next week, Nardi had left New York; she had sent him a card—she later explained—telling him she no longer needed the money. The card had gone astray and when she returned to the city, the money order, as well as a check from Laughlin, were gone.

Later that summer she wrote him from Norwich, New York, where she was stranded after signing on with a New York market as a bean-picker for $6 to $8 a day with room and board. "[A]ll of us (several hundred) found ourselves 200 miles out of N.Y. with no place to sleep, no money for food, and wages amounting to 15 cents an hour under working conditions which are like a chapter out of Tobacco Road."[31] Now washing dishes in a restaurant and sleeping on a cot in the home of a poor family, she asked him to loan her $25 to get back to New York and look for a job. Too busy to write her, Williams had asked his wife to send the money order; she enclosed it in a blank piece of paper. Nardi's next letter (29 September 1942)—twenty-five handwritten pages—is exactly the "avalanche of . . . thoughts" she calls it. Living in Woodstock in a house without running water and again stranded, she feared Williams had deserted her. The letter is in part an harangue over the impossibility of the poet's making even the barest living from writing.[32] Given Williams' constant wish for time to write and the miniscule sum his publication had earned him, Nardi's outburst may have touched him. A week later, before he had completed reading her letter, he wrote to explain Mrs. Williams' involvement with the money order and to inform her of a job opening as a censor of foreign mail at the New York Post Office. He assured her he would write again after hearing from her. "I am very busy as you may well imagine but within my abilities and opportunities I am most anxious to help you," he added (6 October 1942).[33]

One aspect of Nardi's letter Williams must have found difficult to overlook was her analysis of the compounded problems of women who were neither extremely attractive nor young. "Yes, that *is* the sorry scheme of things, that those who are the most beautiful physically should be loved the most. But when it comes to things like jobs, like friendships, to one's life outside of bed, I demand the right not to have to be beautiful, to be positively ugly even, and also to be any age at all, whether 16 or 60, and still be able to hold my own as an intelligent human being." In spite of a tedium in the letter due to wearying digressions, her protest turns insightful when least expected and on surprising topics.

What the "old" require is not some pittance to retire on, but a very different attitude toward old age which will make it possible for working men and women in their 50's and 60's to get jobs according to their intelligence and efficiency, and not according to how successfully they dye their hair. If there weren't another stupid tradition about time . . . old age pensions would be necessary only for those no-longer-young people who are physically handicapped—and not for the physically healthy ones.

In such observations a plea for dignity, for personal or social justice, erupts from the long stream of sadly inconsequential words. Even more to the point, these views stem from an underlying feminism most evident when she reviews the failures of her relationships with men.

My relationship with Harvey Breit was typical of my relationship with any and every man I've ever been fond of. I am completely, irrevocably exiled now from what is "normal" life for a woman, simply because instead of seeking primarily the lover or husband in those men I liked best, I sought primarily the friend, the brother, and the fellow creature, even in the face of my own intense physical desires and of my need for economic security. And no one is going to convince me that my bitter failures in what I sought most and above all else . . . had their roots in the unalterable "sorry scheme" of things—in so-called unchangeable human nature; because if that is so any talk about the "equality of the sexes" is the most idiotic kind of gibberish; and the practice in old China of binding the feet of girl-infants, so that they'd remain tiny and doll-like, should, in that case, never have been discontinued.

Nardi did not answer Williams' brief response to this letter for over a month, not until two days after she had received *New Directions* 7 (19 November 1942).[34] A different tone appears in this letter—one of lassitude. Her problems upon returning to New York had become exacerbated by a concern with age and by overwhelming frustration. In his introduction to her poems, Williams had made her younger: "I am not in my *'early'* thirties, you know; I'm on the *other* side, the late side, now."[35] Her son had run away that fall from the farm where he boarded in order to earn money toward his keep and attend a country school. *Partisan Review* had rejected her poems. Beyond this, although she praised Williams' introduction, it had thrown her into dejection.

As a piece of writing, as your writing, I like it very much; and also it was very kind and generous of you to lend your name to my work which is so deficient according to what I want to do in poetry, and don't, or can't. But it embarrassed me, that preface, because in my private struggles and problems

I prefer to live anonymously, except in some few personal relationships, and because I had asked Laughlin to please just publish the poems in themselves without any comments on me personally.

The conflict she felt between the need for a genuine friendship and the suspicion that her importance to him lay in her emerging role as a literary character was not openly expressed. She was grateful to Williams, but she felt let down. In a postscript she considered the sad effects on her difficult son of having an unusual mother.

I feel a bit guilty at having included that paragraph about my son, because he is a "good boy" in the fashion of nice ordinary boys and nice ordinary people in general. He's inarticulate as most such ordinary people are, and therefore can't find any expression for his rages except that of the streets. And he has a right to his rages because it is really very sad for his sort of person to have a mother who has so little in common with the mothers of his boy friends. He has always felt so inferior among them because of me. . . .

The inhabitants of Paterson would later be described in language sharply reminiscent of Nardi's words.

Two additional letters and a card—beginning "Are you vexed with me, disappointed in me in some way I don't know about?"[36]— arrived in Rutherford before Williams answered her in a curt letter, admonishing her that she should not expect others to be interested in her long accounts nor expect detailed letters in return and, furthermore, that she must get "proper work."[37] He enclosed a money order for $10. A week later (23 December), ill and exhausted from a trying job, she sent a short note thanking him for the money.[38]

Her next letter, the one that may have precipitated Williams' abrupt and unexplained rejection, is the most puzzling Nardi wrote him (19 January 1943).[39] Fearing perhaps that he was about to sever their relationship, she seemed to drop all restraints. The theme is still her "mental solitude" and longing for intellectual exchange; but other details about her life now come forward. She had sent poems that summer not only to *Partisan Review* but also to *Poetry*, hoping to publish without his help. In accepting her poems, Laughlin had informed her "it was entirely your [Williams'] influence which got those others into New Directions." The rejections and consequent uncertainty about her work finally plunged her "into a world comprised of *nothing but sex problems.*"

And the particular jungles and panthers and marshlands which I have to face in my private sex world (when it gets completely cut off from my emotional life) are of such a nature (since I have no recourse to the bridles of conventional

morality) that they can completely destroy me in the course of a single week
. . . should I find myself cooped up with them alone without the escape of other
outlets and concerns and sensibilities on other planes of existence.

The unsafe living she would later refer to in the *Paterson* II letter she
describes here as the result of being poor and of preferring to spend
time with hardened characters rather than would-be Village writers.

There are gains certainly in the way of broader human sympathies in having
been thrust up as intimately as I have been against all kinds of people . . . taxi
cab drivers, longshoremen, and men like that. There was a time a few years
ago when I knew absolutely noone . . . . *except* three semi-underworld characters,
two girls on parole and a man now serving a jail sentence. But those gains
have been cancelled by the great loss to me intellectually . . .

Was she turning into a version of the bizarre Baroness, whom a younger
Williams had fantasized into a forbidden lover? In fact, she was
becoming too real, too great a threat to his control over the situation.

   Once again, she asked him to see her to go over a few poems
and some prose. Not first, however, without talking about love. Was
Nardi in love with Williams or offering him a sexual relationship?
From a certain point of view one could have construed this. Most
women's "major need is the emotional thing," she asserted, "just as
for most men it's connected with worldly success of one kind or
another."

. . . in my own case, no matter how much I might love a man in those ordinary
physical ways of being in love, and no matter how much I might be bound
to him that way . . . without his intellect having an even greater reality for
me, I simply am not contained there.

Love for her, as for most women, she admitted, was indispensable
for happiness; but she could bear unhappiness if her mind was not
thwarted. "It's as if my intellect had been completely lifted out of the
context of my whole life and left suspended in some ghastly void quite
disconnected from all my other experiences. . . ." Scrawled at the
end of the letter is the afterthought: "I'd give up the most wonderful
lover in the world (if such a person figured in my life at the moment)
for those other things I need so badly. And *my* saying that means an
awful lot, because where I fall for anyone in the way of just sex and
desire, I fall pretty hard." Williams' silence did not discourage her
from writing him two more letters (4 February and 14 February, 1943).[40]
In the second, more controlled, she offered two explanations for his
disregard: "where the demands made upon one are for those emotional

things which noone can give at will; and the other, where someone else's life and plight and unhappiness do not ring true somehow and where they lack any great reality for one's self." Too complicated, too egocentric, too demanding—this Muse had outlived her usefulness. Poems were no longer mentioned. Williams could not see her again without admitting he had misjudged her or acceding to her unrelenting pleas for a deep personal commitment from him.[41] He simply withdrew from her reach.

As far as I have been able to determine, three letters Nardi wrote to Williams after his rebuff do not exist in collections. One, dated 22 February [1943], she refers to as her own "last word" in their correspondence, coolly and tersely restating her grievance against him.[42]

The physician and the practical man in you may have found all my neurotic physical ailments and my economic maladjustment decidedly exasperating. (There were indications of that in almost all your notes.) But the writer and poet and psychologist in you could not but know how destructively the repressions of the inner self can take themselves out on the body and on the whole external framework of one's life.

To have been denied the "handful of soil" she sought from him is the more demoralizing to her when she recalls his earlier praise. "Or have you," she asked, "reversed your first high opinion of my intelligence and my creative sensibilities, as to think that there wouldn't have been much there for me to save anyway?" In a postscript she managed to cut away the personal complaints, analyses, and rationalizations to display that insight Williams had earlier acknowledged.

I am not unaware of the great gulf that exists for all of us between those impersonal sympathies offered to a stranger at a safe distance and on paper, and that recoil which we feel at the slightest personal contact with any outsider's naked soul which somehow seems so much more indecent to us, however sincere its need, than the ugliest physical nudity. But I hoped it might be different in this case. . . .

The conditions of Nardi's life may have made quiet withdrawal and transcendence of this experience impossible for her. There remained, too, Williams' praise of her writing, most recently in his review of Anaïs Nin's *Winter of Artifice* for the same volume of *New Directions* in which Nardi's poems had appeared. There was besides his intention of using her letters in what he planned to be his greatest poem. How could he abandon her?

A second missing letter, written sometime after 22 February, can be found in a four-page manuscript at Buffalo, headed—in Williams' writing—*"Interlude"* and signed "La votre / C." (The salutation, "Dear Dr. P," has been crossed out.) From this letter, Williams was to take four sequential sections and arrange them in Parts I and II of Book II (pp. 45, 48, 64, and 75).[43] A second gathering of six sheets contains a revised version of a third letter Nardi sent.[44] In the published text, the first two paragraphs appear in Part III (p. 82); the remainder with certain notable changes became the long letter that ends the book. At some stage in composition Williams intended to use the "Interlude"— with the addition of the first two paragraphs of the third letter— between Books I and II. The material omitted from the "Interlude" letter when it was later interlaced in Parts I and II reveals a less disturbed emotional state than the fragments convey. Nardi had concluded, in effect, that her reason for wanting to see him was simple: "that I like you personally, and indefinably—with the source of that liking located elsewhere than in those regions of one's mind which concern themselves with merely the technical side of writing." He had taken a place in her consciousness "much more as a *person* I should probably like very much, as a *man* whom I should probably like very much, than as merely a good poet and writer of importance." She also wondered if his original image of her had been altered by what others had told him. Their judgments she repudiated, for "outwardly on the surface of our lives we have any number of different selves, and rarely achieve a wholly integrated identity either within ourselves or in the eyes of others, except through love or through our creative work." Finally, she conjectured that he might have been annoyed by her disapproval of his introduction to her poems.

These excisions do not appreciably change the sense of the passages Williams used; the change is rather one of tone. Read sequentially with the omitted paragraphs restored, Nardi's letter communicates a firmer hold on reality. Her depression may be real, her identity fragile, but she is far from hysterical and not a little bold. As she had told him in a prior letter (22 February 1943): "Just because in my daily living . . . I am not tough-skinned and hard enough to keep from bleeding, it does not follow that I am some sentimental blubbering idiot in my thinking. I dare say I am even more ruthless and clean-knifed and unflinching than lots of people whose intellects you particularly respect. . . ."[45] This very tenacity and insistence on being heard make the long letter ending Book II a powerful "attack" Williams himself described as "legitimate."[46]

Williams made a number of changes from the original of this letter (including the two detached paragraphs). In general, he removed some vulgarities, substituted several clichés for more direct phrases, and eliminated references that might identify Nardi. Two examples follow:

1. The first sentence of the published version (82) reads: "and they enable me to tell you a lot of things straight from the shoulder, without my usual tongue tied round-aboutness." Nardi's reads: "and in releasing me from my usual tongue-tied round-aboutness, they enable me to get a hell of a lot off my chest, in the bluntest possible fashion."

2. The second sentence (82) runs in part: "and toss it into one of those big garbage trucks of the Sanitation Department, so long as the people with the top-cream minds and the 'finer' sensibilities use those minds and sensibilities not to make themselves more humane human beings. . . ." Nardi's reads: "and cram them into the toilet-bowl of the nearest water-closet, as long as the people with the good minds and the 'finer' sensibilities use those minds and sensibilities not to make themselves kinder, better, and more decent human things. . . ."

Such changes do not affect meaning, but they reduce the sting of Nardi's protest.

Other changes, however, affect the reader's impression of Cress in important ways. The first paragraph of the long letter, for example, contains the words, "an indication that my thoughts were to be taken seriously." Nardi's actual letter quoted from a Williams letters praising her: "an indication that I possessed an outstandingly 'good mind.' " Williams had valued Nardi's potential more than he permits the reader of *Paterson* to suspect from the Dr. P.-Cress relationship. Another example, from paragraph five, eliminates a comparison that gives more weight to Nardi's point concerning attitude change and the relation of the sexes. The published sentence begins: "The members of any underprivileged class distrust and hate the 'outsider' who is *one of them*, and women therefore—women in general—will never be content with their lot until the light seeps down to them, not from one of their own, but from the eyes of changed male attitudes toward them. . . ." Nardi's letter reads: "The members of any underprivileged class distrust and hate the 'outsider' who's one of them; and so just as the negroes did before the whites went to bat for them, women will remain content with their lot until the light seeps down to them, not from one of their own, but from the eyes of those who are already free and who in their own freedom can understand the wrongs of the wronged better than the latter themselves. . . ." Williams may have disagreed; his syntax is more condensed; but Nardi's point has been oversimplified. To her, only one who *is* free can begin to appreciate struggle of the unconventional person to resist pressure from within the oppressed class to conform.

Several other changes in paragraphs dealing with her requests for financial and job assistance tend to make Cress sound wholly unreasonable. In the paragraph contrasting her side of the railway tracks with his (88), Williams added the words following "Miss Fleming": "nor even the side of those well cared for people like S.T. and S.S. who've spent most of their lives with some Clara or some Jeanne to look after them when they themselves have been flat broke." He also added redundant phrases in the next two sentences of the following paragraph. The published version runs:

> A completely down and out person with months of stripped, bare hardship behind him needs all kinds of things to even get himself in shape for looking for a respectable, important white-collar job. And then he needs ample funds for eating and sleeping and keeping up appearances (especially the latter) while going around for various interviews involved.

Nardi wrote:

> A completely down-and-out person needs ample funds for eating and sleeping and keeping up appearances (especially the latter) while getting around for all the various interviews that are involved in landing "respectable" positions.

Seemingly minor, these additions nevertheless influence Cress's voice: a whine enters where none originally appeared. This is even more evident in other examples.

For instance, Williams added the parenthetical comment (89), "(especially for a woman)"; he also substituted for Nardi's "close friends who'd be glad to put one up at their apartment for a few weeks" the comment, "close friends at whose apartment one is quite welcome to stay for a month or two." In the next paragraph he added the words, "a stranger," and the entire clause, "and it was stupid of me to have minimized the extent of the help I needed when I asked you for that first money-order that got stolen and later for the second twenty-five dollars—stupid because it was misleading." This does explain the postscript reference to a stolen money order, but it does not mention that the original requests were for loans.[47] In another sentence eliminated from the same paragraph, Nardi again emphasizes the psychological importance his advocacy could have had. "And besides, the contributions which the material and psychological make, respectively, to our sense of well-being, are frequently interchangeable, so that the psychological benefits which I would have derived from your help in those plans about the reviews and Yaddo, et cetera, would have minimized my disadvantages in the way of continued financial difficulties." In light of everything else she rehearses here, this may merely beg the issue; but she had made the same point in earlier letters.

By far the most significant change in the letter is Williams' addition of some 220 words (90). Nardi's paragraph ends with the parenthetical remark, "(for reasons I've already referred to)." The additional clauses, the long following paragraph, and a phrase in the next sentence—"not in any of the by-ways and dark underground passages where life so often has to be tested"—are Williams' invention. By further extending it, the long addition makes this section of the letter redundant and self-indulgent. More importantly, by separating Nardi's claim about the "pioneer living" male writers of his social background can avoid from her charge, "You've never had to live," the added paragraph breaks up the interesting continuity of her letter. Too, references to sex appeal and the right set seem out of character with the rest of the letter.

Finally, one omission ostensibly made to protect the letter writer's identity removes some of the force of the first paragraph (86). Nardi had ended this paragraph with the sentence: "And you were able to say 'she might do better if her mind were worse' because that lent itself to a nicely turned phrase in a piece of well-written William Carlos Williams *prose*." The words quoted from his introduction to her poems would certainly have identified her. Eliminating them, however, lessens the impact of the accusation, taken up again at the end of the letter, that Williams had been willing to use her personal life in his writing—after having affected that life—and then to cast her off.

These changes weaken Cress's character, making her vacillation between protest and lament, independence and dependency, more marked. That this characterization is thematically related to the female environment's demand that the poet "Marry us! Marry us! / Or! be dragged down" (83) does not, however, help to clarify to what extent, if at all, Paterson is responsible for Cress's condition. His own remedy for the blockage Cress describes is to "Make a song out of that: concretely" (62). Yet, confronted by the drumming in his own head and the accusation, "You have abandoned me!" Paterson flees from the roar and "the screaming dregs" into the realm of imagination.

Paterson, of course, does not escape Williams' censure. As Bernetta Quinn notes, "One feels sympathy with the recipient of the two letters, together with an awareness that he cannot be completely exonerated from the charge [of dividing art and life], as his own frequent admissions of ineffectuality show."[48] Paterson's culpability extends beyond this charge, however; Cress's attack is aimed as well at his refusal to be the exemplary man, one who because of his recognition of women's difficult plight, should have acted more vigorously on his principles.

Williams was aware, as his various comments on her letter indicate, that Nardi-Cress represented a challenge to him on more than one level. She points out, for example, the insulation his social superiority affords him. In Williams' view Cress herself belongs to a bohemian world outside the boundaries of Rutherford-Paterson, to a New York scene he associates with "perverse confusions."[49] In a frequently quoted letter to Horace Gregory, he remarks about her letter "That it is *not* the same stuff as the poem but comes from below 14th St. is precisely the key."[50] An early scheme for *Paterson* placed her letter near the end of Book IV, where her voice, mingled with accounts of murder and hanging, would have drowned in "a sea of blood."[51] In Book II the letter serves far different purposes. Cress is still an outsider in Paterson's world; but instead of drowning, she pours out her words of righteous indignation until, relenting her anger, she expresses a sad yearning for Paterson's unlikely change of heart. The brunt of her letter Williams spoke of in both humorous and serious terms. To Gregory he wrote, "Here the tail has tried to wag the dog. Does it? (God help me, it may yet, but I hope not!)" From this perspective Cress's attack is spurious: she asks for what can only be a gift, initiates where she should follow, roars when she should be silent. To another correspondent, however, Williams acknowledged a validity in her position.

[The letter] was a reply from the female side to many of my male pretentions. It was a strong reply, a reply which sought to destroy me. If it could destroy me I should be destroyed. It was just that it should have its opportunity to destroy. If I hid the reply it would be a confession of weakness on my part.[52]

Again, the text obscures this "secret." The pretentions rely on a conventional romantic view of woman, on an ideal woman Doc Thurber explains to his wife in Williams' play, *A Dream of Love*, the poet must create in his imagination and then possess in order to complete himself. She appears "in the flesh, warm, agreeable, made of pure consents."[53] The recalcitrant Cress is no such Muse. But it appears Williams had more than this passive ideal of woman in mind. The original Nardi letter refers to two prose pieces by Williams in which he develops an image of Nardi and a theory about women writers in general that her letter does attempt to address.

Of these pieces, the introduction to her poems that so offended
Nardi displays a side of Williams and his writing she was unprepared
for.[54] Why, after convincing James Laughlin to publish a group of her
poems, Williams wrote an introduction that nearly overwhelms them
with dark, romantic innuendoes about her life is difficult to account for
unless one considers two other projects that also engaged him in the
summer of 1942. One was his renewed interest in conceiving a form
for *Paterson* in which Nardi's character had begun to play a central
part. The other was a review of Anaïs Nin's *Winter of Artifice* for the
same issue of *New Directions* in which Nardi's poems were to appear.
Nin herself had suggested Williams for the review. There is little doubt
both she and Nardi anticipated far different results.

183

The impression of Nardi Williams creates in the introduction is
one of a woman who, out of personal defeat and disappointment,
has produced some flawed but promising verse. He romanticizes her
supposedly rebellious, unconventional life and implies that naiveté
and outspokenness have landed her in social exile. The sentences
Nardi may have found provoking contain oblique references to her life
that the poems themselves in no way confirm. "The [woman] who
wanting love, with or without, finds herself embarrassed by her own
courtesy breaking her brain on the hard stone of necessity." Was
Williams informing Nardi how he perceived her? "She uses the language
for a purpose, the purpose is to make poems which in themselves
tell what her whole body is screaming to make clear but nothing comes
of it." If, as he observes, there are only a handful of exceptional lines
in the "rubble" of these poems, is the woman's life—or his interpretation
of it—more interesting than the poems?

In all likelihood Williams was projecting into his description of
Nardi tensions he knew had existed in his own character over many
years. In a letter to Evelyn Scott, written in May 1920 when he was close
to Nardi's age, he describes a frustration clearly at the root of the
younger Dr. Paterson's despair.[55]

> I cannot make use of others except to draw from them an abstract energy.
> I cannot give them anything but the sense of an unearthly beauty that kills
> their hope of me. I die for the hope of me that those who say they love me
> give. This style should be sufficiently surprising to you to warrant a few
> moments more attention. What do I want except quite conventionally to drown
> myself in those I love. But were I to do so I would overpower them and myself.
> My desire is inordinate, childish, insupportable. No one could tolerate me
> for a moment if I behaved with all the stops open. Can no one understand that
> I am a king? That I am a baby who is always right?

At the end of this "sort of love letter," he expresses what I think he believes Cress was unable to say. "But the worst thought of all is that I have said nothing or that saying perhaps in part what I mean it is only again an evasion. Why do I keep up my pretenses? Why do I not say I love you? Who else could I write to as I have written tonight?"

The reason in his case was, it appears, the hard stone of necessity, a stern check on his desire. "Bitterly I still insist that I at least will remain aloof, consumed as I am with fear. Fear is my guiding star. I would rather be fastened by fear than run loose in the world." Cress's voice pursues Paterson when the "amnesic crowd" hears only one voice: "Pleasure!" Might this baffling, reckless siren have lured him into drowning? In his discussion of the *Autobiography*, Herbert Leibowitz identifies the conflict between love and fear as fundamental to an understanding of the poet.

> In Williams' life and art, the desire for intimacy and a need for distance fought long, exhausting skirmishes. This major rhythm . . . governs the repertoire of voices at his command. . . . Intimacy means to him contact, empathy, touch, sexual abandon, the temptation of infidelity and the dread of being carried away and losing his identity; distance means perspective, detachment, the correction of error, the husband, a kind of cosmopolitan knowingness and the ignominy of safety.[56]

Paterson finds it increasingly difficult to repress Cress's voice, not only because his feelings toward her claims run the gamut from superiority to guilt, but also because she reminds him of his own longing and despair and exemplifies all too vividly the consequences of the lost battle.[57]

The letter to Scott further underscores Williams' efforts to control his own inordinate desire by disembodying the object of his love.

> My theme is you. I am trying to discover you inside myself. I am striving to feel you moving in me. It makes me laugh quietly to read such stuff as the Little Review once printed of letters written by some man to some woman or vice versa, I wasn't interested enough to notice. And all these disillusioned sonnets of whoever it may be. As far as that miserable sort of thing is concerned isn't it enough to know that the end was there when the beginning began and that all disillusioned writing is stupid writing revealing an infantile brain. I have done it too but only out of despair to gain a hearing in any other way. It is the transient surface of love that obsesses everyone. If I love I finish as I begin. It is an act that neither wants nor requires reciprocal action on another's part. It is a thing that may occur from time to time but never the same way and the composition, permanent and unique, can neither be destroyed nor repeated.

Harboring and nurturing such a love in imagination becomes an act of self-love; and, eventually, from this disembodied intimacy emerges the poem. The image of a screaming body entering the language of Nardi's poems seems another of Williams' projections of his own experience. Indeed, what consumed his interest in writing the introduction, as in the review of *Winter of Artifice,* was the creative process, defined in terms of what he believed were the contrasting modes of men and women writers. He took the occasion of the Nin review to propound a theory about how the woman writer could develop "an authentic female approach to the arts."[58] As her long letter attests, Nardi took note of the lesson.

In the review Williams contends that "an opportunity to approach the arts from a female viewpoint has been badly neglected by women." To escape a self-conscious "artiness" and "astringency," he advises women to locate major themes that will obviate in their work "a certain pseudopsychologic profundity of style well known among women." What would such a theme be? "In a woman, something that links up her womanhood with abilities as a writer will allow her to draw abundantly upon that for her material." The writing of one woman, aside from Nin, provides an example: "A young poet, Marcia Nardi, succeeds in it more seriously and unaffectedly than any woman writer I can recall at the moment."

That Williams felt uneasy about such theorizing he concedes several times. "Am I right," he asks, "in presuming that Anais Nin cares a fig about [the necessity for male and female writers to develop separate modes] or even agrees with me in my main premise?" Her answer was to be an unqualified "no":

Williams Carlos Williams invents an antagonism between men and women which I never considered, which only exists in his own mind, revealed by his high-pitched, strained, a-sexual voice.
He is describing his own personal vision of woman, not mine.[59]

For Williams that vision with respect to the woman writer involved "a secret having to do profoundly with her sex" and extended by biological analogy to a polar difference between male and female creativity.

The male scatters his element recklessly as if there were to be no end of it. . . . That profusion you do not find in the female but the equal infinity of the single cell. This at her best she harbors, warms and implants that it may proliferate. Curie in her sphere was the perfect example of that principle. Naturally some men write like women and some women like men, proving the point; two phases with a reciprocal relationship.

He attributed the confidence and vigor in Nin's fiction to her assurance as a *woman* artist, "consciously, basically and . . . tenderly! without rancour!" She was a woman, in words Cress was to throw back at him, "sailing free in her own element." She did not imitate men and her style, when most direct, showed restraint: no "straining after effects," no "touch of neurosis *in the writing.*"

For the woman writer, the problem as Williams defined it was "not to succumb to . . . that maelstrom of hidden embitterment which engulfs" so many. "I feel [their] struggle and find myself deeply moved by it. It's the writing itself which effects this sense of doomed love striving for emergence against great odds." Intentional or not, the lesson must have seemed to Nardi aimed at her.

> It is woman trying to emerge into a desired world, a woman trying to lift herself from a minor key of tenderness and affection to a major love in which all her potentials will find employment, qualities she senses but cannot bring into play. The age and times are against her.

Nin's writing, he continues, succeeds for she "begins to show the change in a positive attitude toward her opportunities and not a defeatist, reactionary one." Cress's reply accuses Paterson of being too sheltered and egoistic to understand the compromises exacted from a woman in her position trying to follow such pontifical advice.

> I didn't need the *publication* of my poetry with your name lent to it, in order to go on writing poetry, half as much as I needed your friendship in other ways (the very ways you ignored) in order to write it. I couldn't for that reason, have brought the kind of responsiveness and appreciation that you expected of me (not with any real honesty) to the kind of help from you which I needed so much less than the kind you withheld. (88)

His "literary man's ego" and pride, she finally concludes, required a deference from her that her own pride refused to grant.

That another poet of Nardi's generation found fault with Williams' inclusion of her letters in *Paterson* on literary and personal grounds may only be a sign of the sharpness with which certain readers respond to them. But Elizabeth Bishop's observations are difficult to dismiss. Having re-read Books I and II and then taken up Robert Lowell's review, she wrote to Lowell that she was not in absolute agreement with him, not over what he had said but what he had failed to say.

> . . . but really when I re-read it all (the poem) I still felt he shouldn't have used the letters from that woman—to me it seems mean, & they're much too overpowering emotionally for the rest of it so that the whole poem suffers. . . .

reality thwarts these dreams [of the voluptuous night]. It is embodied in the powerful, irrefutable complaint of the woman's letters challenging the male poet's whole way of life and thought." See their "William Carlos Williams' *Paterson*," *Sagetrieb* 1, no.1 (Spring 1982), 18.

4. Roger Seamon, "The Bottle in the Fire: Resistance as Creation in William Carlos Williams' *Paterson*," *Twentieth Century Literature* 11 (1965), 16–24; reprinted in *Studies in Paterson*, p. 38.

5. The first phrase is from Robert Lowell's review, "*Paterson II*," *Nation*, June 19, 1948, pp. 692–94; reprinted in *Profiles of William Carlos Williams*, p. 75. The second, from James Guimond, *The Art of William Carlos Williams* (Urbana, Ill.: University of Illinois Press, 1968), p. 186.

6. Joel Conarroe, *William Carlos Williams' Paterson* (Philadelphia: University of Pennsylvania Press, 1970), pp. 102, 103.

7. Mike Weaver, *William Carlos Williams: The American Background* (Cambridge: Cambridge University Press, 1971), p. 133.

8. Seamon, "The Bottle in the Fire," p. 40.

9. Michael André Bernstein, *The Tale of the Tribe: Ezra Pound and the Modern Verse Epic* (Princeton: Princeton University Press, 1980), p. 221.

10. Letter to Helen Russell (22 October 1949) in *The Selected Letters of William Carlos Williams*, ed. John C. Thirlwall (New York: McDowell, Obalensky, 1957), p. 274.

11. William Carlos Williams, *The Autobiography* (New York: Random House, 1951), p. 343.

12. Marcia Nardi roundly denies that she regarded Williams as a mentor in the sense of teacher, for she did not in 1942 consider herself a novice poet or protégée. By "mentor," I mean here "a wise, loyal adviser"; by "patron," "an advocate or supporter." Personal details about Miss Nardi are from an interview with her in Cambridge, Massachusetts, 6 June 1981, and from subsequent letters and telephone conversations.

13. Williams' letters to Nardi in the Williams Collection of the HRC include nine single-page typed letters dated from April 10, 1942, to February 13, 1943. The second set includes twenty-two letters, several of them much longer, and two cards. Nardi's letters to Williams are divided between YALC and Buffalo and may be seen only with Miss Nardi's permission.

14. Paul Mariani places the date as Palm Sunday, 29 March 1942, in *William Carlos Williams: A New World Naked* (New York: McGraw-Hill Book Company, 1981), p. 461. Details about Nardi's personal life and interpretations of her letters here, it may be noted, sometimes differ from those Mariani offers.

15. With Miss Nardi's assistance I have located the following from among her publications in these early years: three sonnets, two entitled "Sonnet" and the other, "Skeptic," *Measure*, no. 43 (September 1924), 4–5; "Sonnets I and II," *New York Herald Tribune Book Review (NYHTBR)* 5:2, November 9, 1924; "They Thought, Of Course" and "Most Certainly" (sonnets), *NYHTBR*, 4:2, March 29, 1925; "Reverie," *NYHTBR*, 5:1, July 25, 1926; a review of H.D., *Heliodora*, in *New Republic (NR)*, January 28, 1925, p. 266; a review, "Five Women Poets," in *NR*, August 15, 1928, pp. 180–81.

16. YALC.

17. HRC.

18. HRC.

19. YALC.

20. YALC.

21. YALC.

22. HRC.

23. WCW to MN (17 June 1942), HRC.

24. Buffalo.

25. *Autobiography*, p. 192.

26. HRC.

27. YALC.

28. For the association of Cress with "SHE," see early notes for *Paterson* (Buffalo), as well as Benjamin Sankey, *A Companion to William Carlos Williams's Paterson* (Berkeley: University of California Press, 1971), pp. 74–75. In his study of Williams, Mike Weaver discusses Lyle's influence on the poet's conception of Faitoute (pp. 122–27) and observes that Williams at one point considered sharing the authorship of the poem with Lyle and Nardi. Evidence may be found in the early notes in YALC where a rough title page in Williams' handwriting reads: "PATERSON or Any/Every Place. By W.C.W. D.J.L. M.N." A line is drawn through the initials. Above them appears "Wm Car Wms" and below, "with the assista [sic] of D.J.L. and M.N."

29. HRC.

30. In fact, seventeen of her poems were finally published.

31. [n.d.], General Delivery, Norwich, New York, YALC.

32. Buffalo.

33. HRC.

34. Buffalo.

35. As previously mentioned, Nardi was thirty-eight in 1942. Interestingly, the speaker in Williams' poem "The Flower" (1930) observes: "A flower, at its heart (the stamens, pistil, / etc.) is a naked woman, about 38, just / out of bed, worth looking at both for / her body and her mind and what she has seen / and done. She it was put me straight / about the city. . . ." In *The Collected Earlier Poems of Williams Carlos Williams* (New York: New Directions, 1951), p. 327.

36. Letters: 2 December [1942] and 8 December [1942]; card postmarked 11 December 1942; Buffalo.

37. WCW to MN (16 December 1942), HRC. Paul Mariani asserts that Nardi's response to this letter was "her own very long letter which Williams read with dismay, until he saw that it was just what he would need for *Paterson*," and places the probable date of her letter in late December 1942. He also indicates that Nardi ceased writing to Williams after his letter telling her the correspondence was at an end (17 February 1943): "Nardi took the hint and did such a good job of disappearing that when Williams went looking for her in '45 to get permission to quote her letter in the first part of *Paterson*, he could no longer locate 'the bitch,' " *A New World Naked*, pp. 474–75. One letter Miss Nardi retains a copy of is dated 22 February [1943] and from internal evidence in this letter and her copy of the long Cress letter, it appears that the latter was written sometime after 22 February. Of the letters in collections, her final one in this early set is dated 14 February [1943]; YALC. See discussion, pp. 176–78.

38. Buffalo.

39. Buffalo.

40. YALC.

41. Of their literary counterparts, Dr. Paterson and Cress, Rosenthal and Gall remark: "Short of devoting his life to her, there would be no way the poet could begin to solve her problems. Still, and rightly, he is tormented by her assumption that, having shown some real interest and given some real help, he bears a certain responsibility toward her whether or not he can act on it . . .," "William Carlos Williams' *Paterson*," p. 22. Whether Williams believed a continuing relationship with Nardi would have meant devoting his life to her is debatable. In a letter he wrote his lawyer, James Murray

(22 September 1950), in which he enclosed a letter from Nardi written on 19 September 1950, Williams implies that he believed she had wanted them to become lovers: "The woman and I remain friends, as you see, though I early foresaw what was happening and cut our correspondence as of that early date off short. She has never quite forgiven me. . . . I wish I could do more for her without getting myself emotionally involved which I refuse to do." Quoted by Mariani, *A New World Naked*, p. 587. Nardi unqualifiedly denies any such intention: "He re-created me for his own purposes" (telephone conversation, 6 December 1981).

42. Miss Nardi permitted me to reproduce two letters she had retained copies of: one, 22 February [1943]; the other, the long letter that ends Book II. The latter, undated and headed "21 Grove Street, New York City," does not contain a signature nor does it include the postscripts that follow "La votre / C" in the published form.

43. Page references in parentheses are to the New Directions 1963 edition.

44. See *The Manuscripts and Letters of William Carlos Williams in the Poetry Collection of the Lockwood Memorial Library, State University of New York at Buffalo: A Descriptive Catalogue*, comp. Neil Baldwin and Steven L. Meyers (Boston: G.K. Hall & Company, 1978), entries "E5," p. 209, and "E19," pp. 217–18.

45. Author's copy.

46. Letter from WCW to Robert D. Pepper, 21 August 1951, quoted in Mike Weaver, *William Carlos Williams: The American Background*, pp. 208–9.

47. In an undated postcard written probably in late November 1942, Nardi informed Williams excitedly that she had found a job connected with books paying $15 a week and reiterated her earlier intention: "just as soon as I possibly can, I shall pay you back the money you loaned me." YALC.

48. Sister M. Bernetta Quinn, "On *Paterson*, Book One," *The Metamorphic Tradition in Modern Poetry* (New Brunswick, N.J.: Rutgers University Press, 1955), pp. 89–106; reprinted in *William Carlos Williams: A Collection of Critical Essays*, ed. J. Hillis Miller (Englewood Cliffs, N.J.: Prentice-Hall, Inc., 1966), p. 119.

49. Williams' description of Book IV from the dust jacket of *Paterson*, Book III (Norfolk, Conn.: New Directions, 1949).

50. Tuesday [1948], *Selected Letters*, pp. 265–66.

51. See Sankey, *A Companion*, pp. 170 and 194–95, for specific references to notes in YALC and Buffalo for Book IV.

52. WCW to Robert D. Pepper; see Note 46.

53. William Carlos Williams, *A Dream of Love*, in *Many Loves and Other Plays* (New York: New Directions Publishing Company, 1961), p. 200. Written between April and November 1945, when *Paterson*, Book I was still in manuscript, the play's subject indicates that Williams was as concerned at this time with justifying marital infidelity as he was with affirming the "first wife." There is an underlying suggestion in Book I, supported by the arrangement of key passages in the manuscript in the Williams Collection at the University of Virginia, that Cress had turned Paterson's thoughts to the *Geographic* picture, to the "uppointed breasts" of the chief's latest wife, "charged with / pressures unrelieved," and to those lightnings that "stab at the mystery of a man / from both ends" of the phallic log she and the first wife straddle (pp. 13–14).

54. *New Directions 7* (Norfolk, Conn.: New Directions, 1942), pp. 413–14.

55. Unpublished letter from WCW to Evelyn Scott ("Dearest Else"), dated 17 May 1920, in the Evelyn Scott Collection, HRC.

56. Herbert Leibowitz, " 'You Can't Beat Innocence': *The Autobiography of William Carlos Williams*," *American Poetry Review* 10 (March/April, 1981), 36. Leibowitz also observes of Williams' sometime distrust of women's power: "To possess woman is to

be possessed by her, and that, despite the intoxicating scent of danger, brings the threat of self-extinction" (p. 41).

57. Cf. Paul Zweig's discussion of the self-love of the Gnostic heroes in the *Poimandres* through whom an insight into the nature of pride is projected: "that its self-delighting purity implies as well a painful loneliness. This mythical division into purity and guilt dramatizes the hidden complexity of self-love. It is the technique of storytellers who make the opposite sides of a dilemma come alive in the characters of the hero and the villain. Hero and villain belong to one another, and therefore must choose a common ground on which to meet. Yet one acts out his fate and is wrong; the other, for deeds not unlike those of his enemy, is glorified." See *The Heresy of Self-Love: A Study of Subversive Individualism* (Princeton: Princeton University Press, 1980), p. 13.

58. "Men . . . Have No Tenderness," *New Directions 7*, pp. 429–36.

59. Anaïs Nin, *Diary, 1939–1944* (New York: Allan Swallow Press, 1969), p. 205. That Williams was uneasy about his theorizing on this point is clear from the review itself and from a letter he wrote to James Laughlin about his difficulties in composing it: "I'm having a hell of a time with the Anais Nin thing. I've rewritten it four times and am going into the fifth. It requires as much discretion as insight" (17 June 1942). Quoted by Mariani, *A New World Naked*, p. 819.

60. Mariani observes: "his sharp diagnostician's eye saw that Nardi's letter would serve to recapitulate nearly all the major themes with which his autobiographical poem had been concerned: the woman as victim, complaining, accusing, crying out in pain; the divorce between the two sexes and the danger that the woman would turn to other women for solace; the woman as the energy and the flower of a man's life; the poem itself as a confession of inadequacy; the socioeconomic ills that had created so many of the tensions between men and women, making of the man a false nurturer and forcing the woman into an unnatural dependency on the man." (*A New World Naked*, pp. 474–75). He also asserts that in Nardi's long letter Williams "found . . . the exact monstrous female voice to complement his own monstrous hydrocephalic self" (pp. 462–63). While these thematic concerns have been noted before, this restatement ignores the parallel isolation and loneliness of Cress and Paterson; furthermore, the view that they are "monstrous" is far from convincing.

61. Elizabeth Bishop to Robert Lowell, 30 June [1948], the Houghton Library, Harvard University. Used by permission. My thanks to Emily Wallace and Bonnie Costello for pointing out this letter.

62. Rachel Blau DuPlessis, "Family, Sexes, Psyche: An Essay on H.D. and the Muse of the Woman Writer," *Montemora* 6 (1979), 145.

63. YALC.

64. WCW to James Laughlin, 30 March 1949. New Directions Archive, Norfolk, Connecticut. Used by permission.

65. Geoffrey Chaucer, *Troilus and Criseyde*, Book IV, 1, 799–805, in *The Works of Geoffrey Chaucer*, 2nd ed., ed. F. N. Robinson (Boston: Houghton Mifflin Company, 1957), p. 449. It is Troilus, however, to whom Chaucer gives numerous complaints in the convention of the courtly lover pleading for the attention of a reluctant mistress and assailing his fate. He first uses the signature "Le vostre T." But Williams' irony seems pointed at a comparison with Criseyde's apology for her *short* final letter: "I dar nat . . . wel lettres make, / Ne nevere yet ne koude I wel endite. / Ek gret effect men write in place lite; / Th'entente is al, and nat the lettres space" (1, 1627–30, p. 477). Chaucer's genuine sympathy with Criseyde bears further comparison with Williams' regard for Cress's viewpoint.

66. Quoted by Sankey from an early manuscript version of Book II at Buffalo, *A*

Companion, p. 75. It is difficult to avoid the impression from the first few letters in the second set that Williams' later friendliness and patronage in Nardi's behalf was at least in part motivated by concern that she might have sued him for using the letters. Yet a letter of 22 September 1950 indicates the long distance he had come: "I do not reply out of politeness, as you put it, but out of a very deep respect for your extraordinary abilities and your tragic situation, tragic in that you cannot escape it." He continued: "As artists we do our best work when we are most moved, not when we are unhappiest, tho' it comes sometimes to that. We need close friends, surely, to whom to 'confess' at times with a sure feeling that we shall be given unfailing sympathy and unquestioning support in our emotional agonies. I am that sort of friend to you. But the battle itself we must undergo entirely alone." HRC.

Part Four

Poets in Their Letters

9. Gists and Piths: From the Letters of Pound and Williams

James Laughlin

These "gists and piths," as Pound would have called them, have been culled from the some 1500 letters of Pound and the over 1000 letters of Williams which I reread recently in preparing their correspondence for publication. I was fortunate in knowing both poets from the mid-thirties until the time of their deaths; over the decades I published about twenty-five books for Pound and nineteen for Williams, all but one still in print on the New Directions list.

The letters of the two men were very different. Those of Williams had logical continuity. Those of Pound were sporadic, like a machine gun going off in all directions. I'd be told to do six or more things in a single letter: find out if So-and-so would republish the complete works of Martin Van Buren, see if Senator So-and-so could be persuaded to become interested in Social Credit, and so on. One of the most delightful things Pound might do, if feeling good, would be to compose little poems for my benefit, written right into the middle of a letter.

As an undergraduate I left Harvard (where there were no poets at the blackboard) for Italy, there to be tutored at Pound's "Ezuversity" at Rapallo. A great and glorious experience. As well as reading all the books Pound loaned me, I was trying very hard to write. But the results were awful—copies of Pound without his virtues. Ezra would take his pencil and slash away, with "No, no, that won't do! You don't need that word. That is slop!" Finally, after the term was over in this tuition-free university, where all you had to do was pay for your own meals while you sat with him at lunch and dinner, he got me aside and said, "No, Jas, it's hopeless. You're never gonna make a writer. No matter how hard you try, you'll never make it. I want you to go back to Amurrica and do something useful."

"Waal, Boss, what's useful?"

He thought a moment and suggested, "Waaal, you might assassinate Henry Seidel Canby." (For the young, I should explain that Canby was the editor of the *Saturday Review* who wrote a famous essay proving that there was no character development in Joyce's *Ulysses*.)

But we agreed I wasn't smart enough to get away with it. For a second choice he suggested, "Go back and be a publisher. Go back to Haavud to finish up your studies. If you're a good boy, your parents will give you some money and you can bring out books. I'll write to my friends and get them to provide you with manuscripts."

And that's how it happened. I went back to Haavud.

The first pamphlets were printed by the *Harvard Advocate* printer in Vermont. Then I found a printer in Harvard Square, and so it went. Ezra made me a publisher. In the interim, while gearing up to be a publisher, I acted as his literary agent, placing some of his political articles—chiefly about Social Credit, about what was wrong with the American government; or giving his interpretations of American history—with such magazines as the *Harvard Advocate*, the *North American Review*, the Yale magazine the *Harkness Hoot*, *Dynamic America*, and Gorham Munson's Social Credit magazine, *New Democracy*. None of these places paid much, if they paid at all. But I would usually send him a modest check—ten or fifteen dollars—after something had been accepted. I was still on an allowance from my family, who were waiting to see if I was going to be a good boy or not. One reply came from Ezra: "Don't take your chewing gum and candy money to pay me. That no. The aged shd not sponge on the next generation." Another time, when I sent him a little check, he tore it in half, sent half back to me, and wrote, "Grato a Jaz himself for edichoorial soiviziz. Ez."

When in 1938 I published William's *Life Along the Passaic River* (a book of short stories about the poor people Williams doctored around Paterson and Rutherford), I sent Pound a copy. He wrote:

> BUTT as few people EVER does anything ov the faintest goddam use or in'erest lemme SAY THAT PASSAIC RIVER is in most parts as good as W. H. Hudson at his BEST / so the rest of yr: mispent life iz fergiven yuh . . . SOME BUKK / but as fer Bill bein local / a place wiff some civilization is

just as LOCAL as the Passaic TRiver / but Bill iz Bill and thaZZATT. (Rapallo, 4/15/38)

Then, when I sent him William's novel *White Mule*, he wrote, "I dare say *White Mule* ought to get the Nobel Prize if the Swedes ever heard of it. I spose it is as good as Varga or Verga or however they spell it." (Rapallo, 11/15/38)

Considerably later, when we reissued Pound's *Guide to Kulchur* in 1970, he did a little introduction to the new edition:

Guide to Kulchur: a mousing round for a word, for a shape, for an order, for a meaning, and last of all for a philosophy. The turn came with Bunting's lines:

> *"Man is not an end product,*
> *Maggot asserts."*

The struggle was, and still might be, to preserve some of the values that make life worth living
  And they are still mousing round for a significance in the chaos.

When we first brought out this book, in 1938, we were timid about using the spelling KULCHUR and settled for CULTURE. Emboldened as time went by, and with Ezra now more famous, we reissued it with its present title.

I was majoring in Latin and Italian at Harvard and thought I'd make a hit with one of my professors, the great E. K. Rand (who didn't like Ezra) by doing an essay on Pound's *Homage to Sextus Propertius*, in which I would point out that Pound had his Latin a bit mixed up. He had done things like translating "Minas Cimbrorum" ("threat of invasion by the Cimbrians") as "a scandal in Welsh mines." This prompted Ezra to be fairly coherent on the subject. He wrote,

The Homage is on a list of mine somewhere as a persona [which means he was writing under the guise or mask of another person]. D / n suppose S propertius hadn'd died / or had RipvanWinkled. and come to and wrote a poem / In yanqui. I NEVER said the Homage was a translation. Some of it coincides / as if I rewrote a poem I had done twenty years ago / The Hardy [Thomas Hardy] prob / Hit it when he said it wd / have helped the boob reader if I had called it "S.P. soliloquizes." "boob" / is not textual. Mr. Hardy's langwidg waz choicer. Continuin' / My contribution to classical scholarship if any / wd. consist in blasting the idea that Propertius wd. have been an editor of the New Republic / or that he was a moon-headed decorator / smaragdos chrysolithosve, As thesis it wd be that he had a bean / plus a bit of humor and irony which the desiccated do not see . . . Perhaps 'nowhere seeking to make or to avoid translation' wd. answer query. (1935)

One day, to jump now to the middle fifties, when I was down in Washington visiting Ezra at St. Elizabeths Hospital, I got him to talk about the structure of the *Cantos.* When one went down there, it was usually very hard to keep him on the track because he was what they used to call "distracted." His mind would jump sideways, from subject to subject, but on this day he was very calm as he dictated notes on the *Cantos.*

A. Dominated by the emotions.
B. Constructive effort—Chinese Emperors and Adams, putting order into things.
C. The domination of benevolence. Theme in Canto 90. Cf. the thrones of Dante's "Paradiso."

There will be 100 or 120 cantos, but it looks like 112. First 50 cantos are a detective story. Looking around to see what is wrong.
Cantares—the Tale of the Tribe. To give the truth of history. Where Dante mentions a name, EP tries to give the gist of what the man was doing.

Then he talked about the Frescoes of del Cossa in the Palazzo Schifanoia (the name means "chase away care") in Ferrara, which E.P. saw after World War I:

Schifanoia frescoes in three levels.
Top. Allegories of the virtues. (Cf Petrarch's "Trionfi") study in values
Middle. Signs of the Zodiac. Turning of the stars. Cosmology.
Bottom. Particulars of life in the time of Borso d'Este.
The contemporary.

a) What is there—permanent—the sea
b) What is recurrent—the voyages
c) What is trivial—the casual—Vasco's troops weary, stupid parts.

That was the closest I ever came to having him summarize what he really intended in the architecture of the *Cantos.* As the poem lengthened over the years, I think he changed his mind considerably as to its general objective.

Pound dearly loved T. S. Eliot. So did I. Eliot and I worked together, doing Pound's books jointly for about fifteen years. Ezra often became disturbed over the length of time it took Eliot to get out a book—he was even slower than New Directions is nowadays. And yet Pound approved of the results:

The old Eliotic serpent has done a damn clever job in selectin the Perlite [*Polite Essays*]. I didn't suspect it until yesterday when the prooves come. Seems much easier readin than M.I.N. [*Make It New,* Yale] and not too damned OBsequious after all.

and again:

Eliot's low saurian vitality—when the rock was broken, out hopped Marse Toad live an chipper after 3000 or whatever years inclaustration. When Joyce and Wyndham L. have long since gaga'd or exploded, ole Possum will be totin round deh golf links and giving bright nickels to the lads of 1987.

Delays on this side of the Atlantic also provoked outbursts in the correspondence. I used to go skiing in Utah, I must confess, for about a third of the year when I was publishing the early New Directions books. Mail was sent to me there, which I would answer with the help of a dictaphone. But things did slow up.

Are you doing ANYTHING? Of course if you spend ¾s of your time slidin' down ice cream cones on a tin tea tray. If you can't be bothered with detail, why t'hell don't you get Stan Nott over from London who could run it. (1947)

Youse guys seem to think Ez made of brass with steel springs and no attrition / god damn DElays, fer years and years beginnin to git the ole man down. (1950)

Perhaps out of such irritations came the little poem he wrote for me:

> *Here lies our noble Lord the Jas*
> *Whose word no man relies on,*
> *He never breathed an unkind word,*
> *His promises are piz'n.*

Many of us will recognize its source in Rochester's Impromptu on Charles II:

> *God bless our good and gracious King,*
> *Whose promise none relies on;*
> *Who never said a foolish thing,*
> *Nor ever did a wise one.*

I was in pretty good company on that one. As I was in a letter that associated me, though in no disparaging way, with Yeats, who had come down to visit Pound in Rapallo:

The aged Yeats left yester / I had several seereyus reflexshuns re doing a formal document requesting you to chloriform me before I get to THAT state. However must be a trial to be Irish in Oireland. (6/12/34)

One of the letters presents us with the kind of riddle we sometimes find in the *Cantos:*

> Jas.
>
> Can't merember everything during yr / flits
> HAVE you remembered to send Mrs.Dutch Holland (Regina)
> the Confucius STONE Classics?
> fer to show her yu can do something else except
> split yer britches??
> Yu got'r edderkate 'em at the top. (1953)

The explanation is somewhat personal. Skiing one day at St. Anton, in Austria, I went out on a tour with the Queen of Holland, her consort, and the consort's girl friend. At one point I fell down and split my pants. Well, bless me, if Queen Juliana didn't have, in her little sitzpack that skiers wear, a needle and thread. With the greatest of motherly care, averting her eyes, Her Majesty sewed me up so that I could get down the mountain without disgrace. I wrote this tale to Ezra, as something to divert him. His reaction shows how his mind worked. He immediately said to himself, "Now I've got a contact with the big people in Holland." A chance to convert Holland to Confucianism if I sent her his *Ta Hio.* I sent her the book, received a polite thank you from a secretary, but have noted no change in the Dutch national ethos.

And, here, if you'll forgive me, is a somewhat naughty little poem to T. S. Eliot, addressed to me as "Dilectus mihi filius and bro / (ther) in Xt If you can figger out them relashunships."

> The Rt/Rev/bidding him corajo.
>
> *Come now old vulchuh, rise up from thy nest*
> *Stretch forth thy wing on Chimborazzo's height,*
> *Strip off thy BVDs and undervest,*
> *Display thy WHANGUS in its antient might!*
>
> *The old scabs is a droppin' orf the world its score*
> *And men wd. smell they cornCOB poipe wanct more. (1934)*

Pound hated all the books I published, except those of Bill Williams and his own. There were constantly, in every letter, suggestions to publish Martin Van Buren or Alexander Del Mar or some economist who lived God knows where. He wrote about the New Directions list:

possibly a politik move on Jas's part / gt / deal of sewage to float a few boats. Possibly useful / nasty way to educate the public / 4% food, 96% poison. (1955)

He had read the work of someone named "Henrietta" and wrote:

Most of it considerably better than the trype you print in yr. Lewd Directions Annual Crapcan . . . As to Jas's damlitantism / why the hell don't he recognize LIVE mind as distinct from dead and stop dabbling. If he wants to READ books, let him ask WHAT. That might save him loading his pub / list with rubbish. (1950)

Sometimes his concern for my publishing practices led him to more general reflections on the commercial aspects of literature:

I can't make out whether you have given up thought altogether in favor of bookselling. Mebbe it is better for bookselling but I doubt if it is in the long run advisable. After all you should go on existing a long time over 30 . . . and it is an error to build your life on too small a base . . . For Xt's sake meditate on something I once told you. Nothing written for pay is worth anything: ONLY what has been written AGAINST the market. There is NOTHING so inebriating as earning money. Big cheque and you think you have DONE something, and two years later there is nothing wol bloody to show for it. (11/13/40)

The death of all the old estabd / american pubing / houses wd / be a sign of God's favor to humanity. There are no known acts on the part of these firms that ever favoured living writers or literature. (1949)

I had become very upset about Ezra's anti-Semitism, because, although I had been raised with 100% anti-Semitism in Pittsburgh, I had gotten away from those ideas as I became more sophisticated at Harvard. I would argue with Ezra about anti-Semitism, and he would say such things as, "How can you expect a man whose name is Ezra to be anti-Semitic?" Then, when we were about to publish the fourth (I think) volume of *Cantos*, I got it into my noggin that I would put a stipulation into the contract that there would be no anti-Semitic material in the volume. This raised the roof! He wrote back saying:

Again in Cantos all institutions are judged on their merits / idem religions / no one can be boosted or exempted on grounds of being a lutheran or a manichaean. nor can all philosophy be degraded to status of propaganda merely because the author has ONE philosophy and not another. Is the Divina Commedia propaganda or NOT? From 72 on we will enter the empyrean, philosophy, Geo Santayana etc. The pubr / can NOT expect to control the religion and philosophy of his authors / certain evil habits of language etc / must be weighed / and probably will be found wanting

I shall not accept the specific word anti-semitic . . .there will have to be a general formula covering Menonites, mohamedans, lutherans, calvinists. I wdn't swear to not being anti-Calvinist / but that don't mean I shd / weigh protestants in one balance and anglo / cats in another. ALL ideas coming from the near east are probably shit / if they turn out to be typhus in the laboratory, so is it. So is Taoism, so is probably ALL chinese philos; and religion except Kung / I am not yet sure (2/24/40)

204   There are of course political references in the letters, some so violent that Pound himself might not want them repeated here. In 1960 he wrote:

> Violent language DEPlorable, and not intended for publication even when written privately. Also intended in some cases to be taken unseriously.

But some political references throw an interesting light on his conception of the world of politics. In 1959 he wrote:

> You might note that the last message EP got into print in America was the suggestion that we give Guam to the Japs but insist on getting 300 sound films of Noh plays in exchange.

He actually suggested this formula when he called on politicians in Washington in 1939, but no one took him seriously. At another time he expressed a wish for a Georgian grammar so that he could write Stalin about Confucius. He also had plans for rebuilding the Temple of Jerusalem, plans which he said he had sent to the authorities in Israel.

So much for my beloved Ezra, who was a second father to me. After 1961 he found himself unable to concentrate. For four years there were no letters at all, and only two during the last eleven years of his life.

Williams was very different. It was hard at times to understand how he and Pound, who were such opposites, remained good friends, especially with Pound forever riding him about how he ought to come over to Europe to live because New Jersey was no place for literature. Williams did make three European visits, one of which, lasting almost a year, is described in his novel *A Voyage to Pagany,* in which he goes around Europe and meets four different girls. An astute critic has pointed out that they represent the four main characteristics of his wife, Floss. Hurrah for literary criticism!

I won't say much about Williams because one can find the essential data in Volume 5, Number 2 of the *William Carlos Williams Newsletter.* But I would like to offer a few of his letters, to give an idea of the more placid relationship one had with Williams. He could get excited, but

only rarely. Often he would write an impassioned recommendation
for some hopeless young poet who had sent him some of his work, or
perhaps left it on the kitchen stoop. "You must look at this—even
publish it," he would say, but then concede, at the end of the letter,
"as you see fit." Here is his famous "Dear God" letter, the only letter
I've ever received in my capacity as one of the hundred million Hindu
gods. It was written after I had told Williams I had raised the money
to publish *White Mule*, the first novel in his Stecher trilogy. It begins:

Dear God:
 You mention, casually, that you are willing to publish my White Mule,
that you will pay for it and that we shall then share, if any, the profits! My
God! It must be that you are so tall that separate clouds circle around that head
giving thoughts of other metal than those the under sides of which we are
in the habit of seeing. [10/27/36]

I've always treasured that letter, because it seems so typical of Bill
and the enthusiasm with which he responded to anything good that
happened. I wrote a postscript for the book, which began, "Reader,
you have read a pure book. One book in thousands is pure . . . " and
so on for nearly a page, after which I went on to attack all the
publishers—except myself:

It is time, I think, to damn the book publishers as hard as you can damn them.
They have made literature a business. They have made the writing of books
the production of cheap goods. They have made a book a thing no more valuable
than an automobile tire. They have sold the honor of language for money.
They have made writing, which was an art, a business.

So by that time there must have been something of Ezra in me also.
 A number of later letters refer to *White Mule*, in such terms as
these:

It's a splendid book, excellently presented, but it still seems strange to me. I
think you have realized it better than I could do in the slow process of writing
it, to the accompaniment of discouragement, inevitable in view of the small
likelihood of any immediate appreciation. You have put a critical estimate upon
it which has made it yours, somewhat to my amazement. This is the rare
collaboration between writer and publisher, which is almost unheard of today.
I feel it keenly. You've done a fine piece of work, of criticism, in focusing
the book at the mind as it should be focused. [5/31/37]

 Letters like this, which Williams would write at the drop of a hat,
were especially encouraging to a young publisher. He almost never

found fault, unless it seemed I had done something particularly dreadful.

Though Williams had reservations about the roles he thought Pound assumed and felt that he had sometimes "mortally offended the darling Ezra," he had a deep and sincere admiration for the poetry itself, as such letters as these reveal:

It's easy to forget, in our dislike for some of the parts Ezra plays, and for which there is no excuse, that virtue can still be a mark of greatness.

It is hard to appraise, for the honors earned. It is even possible that Pound himself is self deceived and performs his miracles unconsciously while he frowns over some asininity he proposes and leans upon so heavily. His language represents his last naiveté, the childishness of complete sincerity discovered in the child and the true poet alike. All that is necessary to feel Pound's excellence in this use of language, is to read the work of others, from whom I particularly and prominently exclude e.e. cummings. In the use of language, Pound and Cummings are, beyond doubt, the two most distinguished American poets of today. It is the bringing over of the language of the day to the serious purposes of the poet, that is the difficult thing. Both of these men have evolved that ability to a high degree. Two faulty alternatives are escaped in the achievement of this distinction: there are plenty, who use the language well, fully as well as Pound, but for the trivial purposes either in journalism, fiction, or even verse. I mean the usual stroking of the meter without penetration, where anything of momentous significance is instinctively avoided, there are, on the other hand, poets of considerable seriousness, who simply do not know what language is and unconsciously load their compositions with the minute anachronisms, as many as dead hairs on a mangy dog. These, by virtue of all academic teaching, simply make their work no good. They would, and need to go through, the crises both Pound and Cummings experienced in ridding themselves of all collegiate taint. Not very nice to the "beaneries," as he used to call them. It is impossible to praise Pound's lines. The terms for such praise are lacking. There ain't none. You've got to read the line and feel first, then grasp through experience in its full significance, how the language makes the verse live. It lives. Even such uncompromising cataloguing as his Chinese kings, princes and other rulers, do live and become affecting under his treatment. It is the language and the language only, that makes this true. [9/25/40]

It all revealed itself to me yesterday when I was reading his new Cantos, "Chinese Numbers" I calls it. He doesn't know a damn thing about China, the Chinese, or the language. That's what makes him an expert. He knows nothing about music, being tone deaf. That's what makes him a musician. He's a misplaced romantic. That's what makes him a historical realist. And he's batty in the head. That's what makes him a philosopher. But, in spite of it all, he's a good poet. I had to acknowledge it as I read along in that Chinese abacus frame of his enumerating verse. It had charm, it had sweep, it had even childish innocence written all over it. He thinks he's being terribly profound, frowningly serious, and all he's doing is building blocks, and it's lovely. He hasn't the least idea of where he hits true and where he falls flat.

He wants to be praised for one thing, and he contradicts himself upon the same count in the next paragraph. He's got to be loved, to be praised, as one loves a mongoloid idiot; for his sweet character. [9/24/40]

Williams' remarks about Pound's friend Eliot took quite a different tone:

I'm glad you like his verse, but I'm warning you, the only reason it doesn't smell is that it's synthetic. Maybe I'm wrong, but I distrust that bastard more than any writer I know in the word today. He can write, granted, but it's like walking into a church to me. I can't do it without a bad feeling at the pit of my stomach. Nothing has been learned there since the simplicities were prevented from becoming multiform by arrested growth. Bird's-eye foods, suddenly frozen at fifty degrees below zero, under pressure, at perfect maturity, immediately after being picked from the cane. It's pathological with me perhaps, I hope not, but I am infuriated by such things. I am infuriated because the arrest has taken place, just at the point of risk, just at the point where the magnificence might possibly have happened, just when the danger threatened, just when the tradition might just have led to the difficult, new things. But the God damn liars prefer popes, prefer order, prefer freezing, prefer, if you use the image, "the sterilization of the Christ they profess." And the result is canned to make literature; with all the flavor, with all the pomp, while the real thing rots under their noses and they duck to the other side of the street. I despise and detest them. They are moles on a pig's belly instead of tits. Christ, how I hate their guts, and the more so because Eliot, like his monumental wooden throne on wheels that he carries around with him to worship, Eliot takes the place of the realizable actual, which is that much held back from realization precisely, of existence. [3/26/39]

What upset Bill so much was the arrival of *The Waste Land* at the moment when he was beginning to get going on a really American kind of verse and an American idiom. He was thrown into a deep depression by the success of *The Waste Land;* Eliot was a writer he really disliked. No wonder that Eliot, after seeing a few letters of this kind, came in turn to dislike Williams.

When Book III of *Paterson* was published, Williams, in response to my request, described so clearly his intentions in the first four books (he later wrote a fifth) that we printed his letter on the back of the jacket.

Paterson is a man (since I am a man) who dives from cliffs and the edges of waterfalls, to his death—finally. But for all that he is a woman (since I am not a woman) who *is* the cliff and the waterfall. She spreads protecting fingers about him as he plummets to his conclusions to keep the winds from blowing him out of his path. But he escapes, in the end, as I have said.

As he dies the rocks fission gradually into wild flowers the better to voice their sorrow, a language that would have liberated them both from their distresses had they but known it in time to prevent catastrophe.

The brunt of the four books of *Paterson* (of which this is the third, "The Library") is a search for the redeeming language by which a man's premature death, like the death of Mrs. Cummings in Book I, and the woman's (the man's) failure to hold him (her) might have been prevented.

Book IV will show the perverse confusions that come of a failure to untangle the language and make it our own as both man and woman are carried helplessly toward the sea (of blood) which, by their failure of speech, await them. The poet alone in this world holds the key to their final rescue. [9/28/49]

208

I conclude with a letter almost too painful to read. The end of Bill's life was tragic; he had three strokes. He recovered from the first two, but after the second he could barely speak, barely move around the house, and was quite unable to type. I suffered for him during the visits I made to Rutherford. He'd try to talk, struggling for the words that often would not come. If Floss or I couldn't help him, he'd quiet down and try another tack.

But Williams, one of the most courageous men I've ever known, was determined to write again. Though his wife was upstairs, he would make himself go to his desk and, with two fingers, painfully type out a letter to her. This he did every morning for months; some of these letters survive in the archives. Perhaps they said only: "Dear Floss, Isn't it a lovely morning?" Many mistakes at first but fewer and fewer as he persisted. He recovered his ability to type well enough to work on *Pictures from Brueghel* and *Many Loves,* his volume of plays, though I had to help him with the stage directions.

By the time *Pictures from Brueghel* was in the press his condition had seriously deteriorated. Every day he would write me to ask how the book was coming along; his hope was that he would live to see its appearance. Usually Floss, who was given the letters to mail, would tear them up. She did however send this one along, the last letter I received from him. I am never able to read it without tears.

WILLIAM CARLOS WILLIAMS
9 RIDGE ROAD
RUTHERFORD, N.J.

Dear Jim: (31)
    I finally got your letter enclosing
your letter enclocussing your letter which was so
ompportant foe me, thannkuok ynonvery much. In time

this fainful bsiness will will soonfeul will soon
be onert. Tnany anany goodness. If S lossiee eii
wyyonor wy sinfsignature.

I hope I hope I make it.
[Bill]

209

10. Ezra Pound and William Carlos Williams Collections at the University of Pennsylvania

Neda M. Westlake, with contributions by Francis James Dallett

The two poets met at Pennsylvania in the academic year 1902–03 when Pound was eighteen, a sophomore in the College, and Williams was twenty, beginning his medical training. Their long friendship is frequently referred to in the correspondence listed below.

Pound's letters to faculty members are largely concerned with his reaction to conservative criticism of his work, his proposal for creative fellowships, and comments on his professors. To May Sinclair, he writes in appreciation of her own work and of her reaction to his poems. He reveals, in a letter to Henry B. Parkes, that he had practically composed one of T. S. Eliot's poems. In letters to James T. Farrell, Ford Madox Ford, and Van Wyck Brooks, he mentions their writing, the contributions of Hemingway and Williams to the *Transatlantic Review,* and nominates other poets for membership in the National Institute of Arts and Letters. The letters to Mary Moore are the record of a brief and exuberant engagement that resulted in a friendship that continued through the years of Pound's stay in St. Elizabeths Hospital and his return to Italy.

Williams expresses his appreciation of Waldo Frank's comments on *In The American Grain.* To John C. Miller, he writes of his pleasure at attending a Pennsylvania Phi Beta Kappa meeting where he was reminded of his student days at the University. His letters to E. Sculley Bradley offer poems and a brief biography which Bradley published in a University publication. He thanks Bradley for his comments on *Paterson II* and mentions work in progress, as well as offering copies of his books for Bradley's disposition.

The Carl Gatter collection, emphasizing Pound, also includes some photographs and other material on Williams.

The listings from the University Archives supply details of the academic careers of the two friends, as well as clippings of articles by and about Pound and Williams, photographs, and obituaries.

The original letters by Pound and Williams, apart from those donated by University personnel, have come to the University Library as part of the collections of Burton Rascoe, Waldo Frank, Theodore Dreiser, May Sinclair, Van Wyck Brooks, James T. Farrell, and by gifts from other individuals to whom the letters were addressed. The recipients are identified at the heading of each category.

Correspondence from Pound and Williams is arranged under the names of the recipients, in the order listed below, followed by manuscript materials, memorabilia, and archival holdings:

Pound

     I. Felix Schelling
    II. Mary Moore
   III. May Sinclair
   IV. Harold Hersey
    V. Ford Madox Ford
   VI. Horace Liveright
  VII. Lewis George Sterner
 VIII. James T. Farrell
   IX. Henry Bamford Parkes
    X. Arnold Gingrich
   XI. Herman V. Ames
  XII. Roy F. Nichols
 XIII. C. Seymour Thompson
 XIV. University of Pennsylvania Press
  XV. Van Wyck Brooks
 XVI. Robert E. Spiller
XVII. Ronald Bayes
XVIII. Manuscripts, typescripts, and broadcasts
 XIX. The Carl Gatter Collection
  XX. Materials in the Archives of the University of Pennsylvania

Williams
I. Burton Rascoe
II. Waldo Frank
III. E. Sculley Bradley
IV. John C. Miller
V. Typescripts
VI. Materials in the Archives of the University of Pennsylvania

212

Rare Book Collection

EZRA POUND

I

Eight letters, 1907–1938, to Felix Emmanuel Schelling (1858–1945),
Professor of English at the University of Pennsylvania.

1. T.l.s. Ezra Pound, Wyncote, Pennsylvania, 15 January [1907] 1 p.
"I have already begun work on 'Il Candelaio' [by Giordano Bruno]
which is eminently germain to my other Romance work and in
which I have considerable interest."

2. T.l.s. Ezra Pound, London, 1 July 1915 2 pp. with envelope.
"Gaudier-Brzeska has been killed at Neuville St Vaast, and we
have lost the best of the young sculptors and the most promising.
The arts will incur no worse loss from the war than this is. One
is rather obsessed with it."

3. T.l.s. Ezra Pound [London] 17 November 1916 2 pp.
"I keep on writing on the subject of fellowships for creation as a
substitute for, or an addition to, fellowships for research." Pound
suggests as possible candidates Carl Sandburg, Edgar Lee Masters,
and Padraic Colum.

4. T.l.s. Ezra Pound, Paris, 11 May 1921 1 p.
" 'Corny' will be interested to know that the Irish Times is now
trying to bribe someone to write a nice ladylike book about Erin,
without 'brogue *or* psychoanalusis.' " Pound refers to Professor
Cornelius Weygandt (1871–1957), who wrote on Irish literature.

5. T.l.s. Ezra Pound, Paris, 8 July 1922 11 pp.
In this long letter, Pound responds in detail to Dr. Schelling's
"Originality and Creative Gift of Ezra Pound Produce

New Volume of Iconoclastic Poetry," a review of Pound's
Poems, 1918–21 (New York: Boni & Liveright, 1921), in the
Philadelphia *Public Ledger*, 13 May 1922, 13. 1–2. Dr. Schelling
concluded his review by saying, "What I like least in Mr. Pound
is this itch to wound respectability, sentiment and decency at
times. . . . When this sort of thing is buoyed up with wit, it is
forgivable; it is not always so buoyed." Pound replies, "My
main objection is to your phrase about being buoyed by wit. If
the poets don't make certain horrors appear horrible who will?
. . . Humanity is malleable mud, and the arts set the moulds
it is later cast into."

213

6. T.l.s. Ezra Pound, Rapallo, Italy, 11 November 1933 3 pp. with
   envelope.
   In a letter, Dr. Schelling had apparently termed Pound
   "embittered" and "expatriated." Pound replies, "As for my being
   embittered, it won't wash, everybody who comes near me,
   marvels at my good nature. . . . As for 'expatriated' . . . you know
   damn well the country wouldn't feed me. The simple economic
   fact, that IF I had returned to American I shd/ have starved. . . ."

7. T.l.s. E. Pound, Rapallo, Italy, 21 November 1933 1 p.
   As a postscript to his complaint about the University's inviting
   Shane Leslie to lecture, Pound adds, "Nic Butler president of
   the 'academy' & no one resigned when THAT was elected!"
   Nicholas Murray Butler (1862–1947), was president of the American
   Academy of Arts and Letters from 1928 to 1941.

8. T.l.s. Ezra Pound, Rapallo, Italy, 30 May [1938] 1 p.
   Elected to the Institute of American Arts and Letters in 1938,
   Pound suggests that "The Institute COULD with a little gumption
   at least stimulate the reprint of American classics, flagrant
   omissions from present imprint being the letters of Adams and
   Jefferson...."

II

Seventy-six letters, 1907–1959, to "Mary Moore of Trenton" to whom
Personae (1909) was dedicated. Pound met Mary Moore in the summer
of 1907. The romance continued while Pound was teaching at Wabash
College in Crawfordsville, Indiana, and the affair ended shortly before
his departure from Crawfordsville in 1908. They remained friends

and when Mary Moore visited London in 1912, Pound and his wife entertained her. The correspondence continued intermittently through the years of Pound's stay in St. Elizabeths Hospital in Washington, D.C.

Few of the letters are dated and fewer envelopes are included. Dating has been assigned by references in the text or by association with other letters, making debatable the precise order of listing. To facilitate identification, the first lines are quoted.

The first eight letters are from Wyncote or Philadelphia, Pennsylvania, to Miss Moore in Trenton, New Jersey, in the summer of 1907.

1. A.l.s. EP [Wyncote, summer, 1907?] 2 pp.
   "Maridhu I am sorry? But when the very high gods. . . ."

2. A.l. unsigned [Wyncote, summer, 1907?] 1 p.
   "Dear Santa Teresa: Forgive us our stupidities. . . ."

3. Autograph postcard unsigned [Philadelphia, summer 1907?]
   "Please litte furry cloud. . . ."

4. A.l.s. EP [Wyncote, summer 1907?] 6 pp.
   "Maridhu:—Of course I didn't say all I had to say in my hurry-scratch this morning...."

5. A.l.s. E. Pound [Wyncote, summer 1907] 2 pp. in pencil
   "My dear Miss Moore. Have just borrowed enough ink from the ticket agent for address."

6. A.l.s. EP [Philadelphia] 11 July [1907] 3 pp.
   "Delectable Rabbit: The enclosed which I return to you is definite?"

7. A.l.s. E [Wyncote] 1 September [1907] 2 pp.
   "Dear Your Ladyship. That show party will have to be on Wednesday. . . ."

8. A.n.s. EP [Philadelphia, summer 1907] 1 p. in pencil
   "Calling Tuesday A.M. on one meow-ful kitten. . . ."

The thirty-three following letters were sent to Miss Moore from

Crawfordsville, Indiana, where Pound taught French, Spanish, and Italian at Wabash College until his dismissal in January 1908.

9. A.l. unsigned, en route from Buffalo to Crawfordsville, early September 1907. 6 pp. in pencil.
"Stopped in middle of corn field. 1½ or 2 hrs. late or at least we were when I began. This makes about 28 to 30 hrs. straight going."

215

10. A.l. unsigned, Crawfordsville, Crawford Hotel [early September 1907] 8 pp.
"Your ladyship: Please it is some time since I have been allowed to curl up in that navigable nest. . . ."

11. A.l.s. E. P., Crawfordsville, Crawford Hotel [early September 1907] 8 pp.
"I have just eaten a hotel dinner, which is a much more immoral thing to do than to get drunk." Pound describes the attractive room he has found.

12. A.l. unsigned [Crawfordsville, early September 1907] 7 pp.
"Maridhu. Last note said I had just been immoral & eaten of the hotel flesh pots."

13. A.l.s. E, Milligan Place [Crawfordsville, 18 September 1907] 7 pp. with envelope.
"Grey Eyes: hmm! I wonder if thee will see this place as I see it." He goes on to say that he is not afraid that she will be disappointed "when I bring you here."

14. A.l.s. E, Milligan Place [Crawfordsville, September 1907?] 7 pp.
"Delightful person: Having dispatched three missives to theeward this day. . . ." He is glad to hear that Mary is concerned about their relationship, marriage being a rather important step in one's career.

15. A.l.s. EP [Crawfordsville, late September 1907?] 8 pp.
"Of a Truth o Beloved. . . ." He tells her that she should be there hemming his new green table cover.

16. A.l. unsigned [Crawfordsville, October 1907?] 3 pp.

"Maridhu. I this evening went into a book shop . . . and found one Peter Pan by Rackham. . . ." Pound describes Mary's "namesake," a cultivated lady with Miss Moore's initials. "We are the only two people here who think London & Paris are nearer the hole the earth goes round. . . ."

17. A.l.s. E. P. [Crawfordsville, October, 1907?] 6 pp.
"Chere Cigale: And in what manner shall I write to you. persiflage—my raiment & my metier, is not a thing kept polished here." Pound complains about the provinciality of Indiana.

18. A.l. unsigned, Milligan Place [Crawfordsville, October 1907?] 4 pp.
"Quite dear person with grey eyes." Pound discusses his classes and says it is ridiculous to expect him to look over 61 papers four times a week.

19. A.l. unsigned [Crawfordsville, October 1907?] 4 pp.
"It is very much fun playing here I am like a sleepy tabby-cat." He mentions his landlady, Mrs. Kummel.

20. A.l.s. Ezra [Crawfordsville, October 1907?] 2 pp.
"Beloved Your Grace: It is most justly observed that I do nothing but eat & write to you."

21. A.l. unsigned, Milligan Place [Crawfordsville, October 1907?] 2 pp. in pencil
"Dear Miss Mary Moore: I a quite impersonal person am toasting myself 'en face de' a pile of red flamey cannel coals." Pound asks Mary to send him some cigarettes, illegal in Indiana.

22. A.l.s. EP [Crawfordsville, October, 1907?] 3 pp.
"You are Maridhu—veree nice rabbit-kitten to send me real cigarettes."

23. A.l. unsigned [Crawfordsville, October 1907?] 5 pp. in pencil.
"Saturday before breakfast. Woof. I have read your letter once...."

24. A.l. unsigned [Crawfordsville, October 1907] 2 pp.
"Maridhu. I have even now sent thee a note dull & dolorous past all need." The letter is daubed with red and green oil paint.

25. A.l. unsigned [Crawfordsville, October 1907?] 4 pp.
"Maridhu: You are as bad as goin' down town. I always forget
something." Later in the letter, he says it would take all of five
years to get caught up with all the things they wanted to do
together.

26. A.l. unsigned [Crawfordsville, October 1907?] 3 pp.
"Maridhu: dear That does not quite fit Del alma mi Maria." He
tells Mary that she is going abroad with him the next summer.

27. A.l.s. Ezra, Milligan Place [Crawfordsville, October 1907?] 4
pp.
"Maridhu del Alma: Now ariseth the question of a ring." Until
they can find a suitable one, he sends one which Katharine
Heyman had given to him.

28. A.n. unsigned [Crawfordsville, 2 October 1907] 1 p. with
envelope. A fragment referring to "Sacrifice at the Prato," by
Maurice Hewlett.

29. T.l. unsigned [Crawfordsville, 7 October 1907] 5 pp. with
envelope.
"Yes Dear, thank you for that about the family, but you err one
branch I can trace no further than the battles of Crecy and
Poictiers." He says that Oscar [MacPherson] may marry her.

30. T.l. unsigned [Crawfordsville, October 1907] 1 p.
"Oh Sister Teresa. Ave et tibi gaudia plena salve et gratia."

31. A.l. unsigned [Crawfordsville, October 1907?] 3 pp.
"Maridhu: This day Saturn's day and after late arising. . . ."

32. A.l. unsigned [Crawfordsville, November 1907?] 4 pp. in pencil.
"Maridhu:—There is a learned Herr Doktor . . . wobbling thru a
synopexflanasis of the Niebelungerlied in the chapel & I have
discourteously escaped."

33. A.l. unsigned [Milligan Place, Crawfordsville, November 1907?]
2 pp.
"The little 'yous' approve highly of the 'me to you.' "

34. A.l.s. E.P. [Crawfordsville, November 1907?] 2 pp. in pencil

"Maridhu:—I wonder   wonder—where weakness commences"

35. A.l. EP [Crawfordsville, November 1907?] 4 pp.
   "Cher Cigale: Let us kiss & make up."

36. A.l.s. E [Crawfordsville, November 1907?] 3 pp.
   "Maridhu:—To the very nice butterfly you in front of the fire
   place."

37. A.l.s. E. [Crawfordsville, November 1907?] 3 pp. in pencil.
   "Hail most beloved absurdity: I have just met the town artist."
   Pound refers to Fred Nelson Vance.

38. A.l.s. E [Crawfordsville, November 1907?] 2 pp. in pencil.
   "M S M: 'For thy love's sake' Don't think thy love (for any thing
   but thine own furry self) is strong enough to pay postage on
   even one pome?"

39. A.l.s. E [Crawfordsville, December 1907?] 5 pp.
   "Dear Funny Little Rabbit. I do not love you at all except as I
   love all beautiful things that run around in the sunlight & are
   happy." Mary had told him of her engagement to Oscar
   MacPherson, and Pound concludes that since they are not
   bothered about marriage, their acquaintance can be lovely and
   amusing.

40. A.l.s. E [Crawfordsville, December 1907?] 3 pp. in pencil.
   "Maridhu. There is in certain masculine minds an inherent
   dullness. . . ." He asks how many people beside Oscar is she
   intermittently betrothed to.

41. A.l.s. E [Crawfordsville, 23 December 1907] 3 pp. with envelope.
   "Maridhu del alma: Last night because Vance hath the nerve
   illimited to use his canvasses as Christmas gifts. . . ."

42. A.l. unsigned [Crawfordsville, January 1908?] 3 pp.
   "I think perhaps that toward Oscar's fiancée I have been perhaps
   indiscreet."

The following twenty-seven letters, 1908–1938, from Pound to
Mary Moore cover the years of his stay in London and in Rapallo, Italy,
from his letter from Philadelphia announcing his departure for Europe

after leaving Wabash College to his last letter to her from Italy in 1938.

43. A.l.s. E. P., Philadelphia [February 1908] 2 pp.
    Pound announces his departure for "sunny Italia" on the following March 17th.

44. A.l.s. E. P., on board the Cunard "Slavonia" en route to Gibraltar [March 1908] 3 pp.
    Pound says he is going to kiss her goodbye again.

45. A.l.s. E. P., Gibraltar [March 1908] 7 pp. with envelope.
    Pound writes to Mary first on landing in Gibraltar, asking her to befriend two of his former acquaintances from upper New York State.

46. A.l.s. E. P., Gibraltar [April 1908] 3 pp.
    "Greeting in the name of the great imperial rabbit of rabbits."

47. A.l.s. EP, Venice [April 1908] 2 pp.
    "I am about to be published here in Venice." Pound suggests that she might help by trying to have the book reviewed in America. *A Lume Spento,* Pound's first book, was published in Venice in June 1908.

48. A. postcard s. EP, Venice, 25 April 1908.

49. A.l.s. E, Venice [1909?] 4 pp.
    Pound asks Mary to entertain a pupil of Katherine Heyman.

50. A.l. unsigned [Venice, May 1908?] 6 pp.
    Pound describes his enjoyment: "Venice is Italy's cosmopolis."

51. A.l.s. E. P., Venice, 16 June 1908 5 pp.
    Pound sends a manuscript of "somebody's music to a M. Maeterlinck song."

52. A.l. unsigned, Venice [1908] 2 pp.
    "3 nights ago Mr. D'Annunzio & I were present at a veree gee-lorious presentation of his play 'La Nave.' " Gabriel D'Annunzio's play was published in Milan in 1908.

53. A.l.s. E P. [London, September, 1908] 2 pp.

Pound has just arrived in London and gives his address as 8 Duchess St., Portland Place—"Deah old Lunnon."

54. A.l. unsigned [London, September 1908] 2 pp.
"I have the pleasure to inform you that Mr. Ezra Pound of San Trovaso, Venezia is now in London where the king lives."

55. A.l.s. E P [London, October 1908] 4 pp. with typescript.
Pound describes his quarters in Kensington.

56. A.l. unsigned [London, November 1908?] 5 pp.
Pound comments on some reviews of *A Lume Spento.*

57. A.l.s. E [London] 24 December 1908 5 pp.
"Mary Moore, whom I love more than according to certain opinions I should."

58. A.l. unsigned [London] 31 December 1908 4 pp.
Pound writes that he hopes his next book can be printed on parchment in Florence. He is referring to his third volume, *Personae,* published in London, 1909, and dedicated to Mary Moore.

59. A.l.s. E [London, February 1909?] 4 pp.
"London is fun and I am supposed to meet Mr. Yeats on Friday."

60. A.l.s. E [London] 23 March 1909 3 pp.
Pound speaks of one of Katherine Heyman's concerts in London.

61. A.l.s. E P [London, February 1909] 6 pp.
Pound speaks of meeting Laurence Binyon, Ernest Rhys, and May Sinclair and attending the Poets' Club dinner, where Bernard Shaw's speech "was really the only endurable one."

62. A.l.s. E [London, 1909?] 7 pp.
In the letter, Pound sends a poem for her, "made to sing & not to talk."

63. A.l.s. E [London, 24 December 1909] 5 pp.
Pound has many comments on William Butler Yeats and George Bernard Shaw.

64. A.l.s. E. P. [London] 1 January 1910 2 pp.
A new year's greeting "even tho it is against my habit to stand with the majority."

65. A.l.s. E. P., Lago di Garda, Italy [April 1910] 6 pp. with envelope.
Pound writes that he is coming to the States in August.

66. A.l.s. E, Venice, 12 May 1913 4 pp.   *221*
"I've been horrifying the godly by my poems in 'Poetry' for April." "Contemporania," a collection of 12 poems, appeared in *Poetry* 2, no. 1 (April 1913), 1–2.

67. T.l.s. E. P., London, 27 December 1918 1 p.
On the letterhead of *The Little Review,* he asks if she is "coming over when dear Woodrow goes back."

68. T.l.s. E, Rapallo, Italy, 5 March [1933] 2 pp.
Pound writes that his wife Dorothy will thank her for the flowers when they arrive.

69. T.l.s. Ezra, Rapallo, Italy, 17 January [1938] 1 p.
"My own daughter has just made her literary debut in Japan." His daughter Mary, at the age of 12, wrote an article, "The Beauty of the Tirol," which Pound translated from the Italian into English and sent it to Japan, where it appeared in 1938 in a Japanese magazine for girls called "Girls' Circle."

The following seven letters, 1950–1959, were sent to Mary Moore Cross by Pound from St. Elizabeths Hospital, Washington, D.C., and from Rapallo, Italy.

70. A.l.s. EP., St. Elizabeths Hospital, Washington, D.C. [1950?] 1 p.
A brief note on the chief American characteristic.

71. A.l.s. E., St. Elizabeths Hospital, Washington, D.C., 20 March [1955?] 2 pp.
Pound tells Mrs. Cross how to apply for a visitor's permit.

72. T.l. unsigned [St. Elizabeths Hospital] 11 August 1955 1 p.
Pound supplies addresses of English friends.

73. T.l. unsigned [St. Elizabeths Hospital] Washington, D.C. 2

October [1956?] 2 pp.
Comments about Mrs. Cross's husband.

74. A.l.s. E, St. Elizabeths Hospital, Washington, D.C. [1957?]
   2 pp.
   Comments on mutual friends.

75. T.l.s. E P [St. Elizabeths Hospital, Washington, D.C.] 7 September
   1957 1 p.
   A note directed to a mutual friend for Mrs. Cross' benefit.

76. T.l.s. E, Rapallo, Italy [1959] 1 p. with envelope.
   Again, comments on mutual friends.

The following nine folders contain mss./typescripts of poems or
prose that Pound sent to Mary Moore by separate mailing or enclosed
with letters that have long since been divorced from the enclosures. Title
and dates are given where possible.

77. Typescript, "Malgrin," 3 pp.

78. Typescript, "Defiance," 1 p.
   signed Ezra Pound, Wyncote.

79. Typescript, "Ballad of the Gibbet," 1 p.

80. Typescript, "La Regina Avrillouse," 1 p.
   signed Ezra Pound, Wyncote.

81. Typescript, "Baltasare Levy: Zionist," 2 pp.

82. Typescript, "Capilupus sends Greetings to Grotus," 5 pp. with
   "Paris, 06" in Pound's hand on p. 5.

83. Three typescript fragments beginning: "Now it befell that there
   went a company of travelors from Joppa," "I lay on my back
   and stretched," and "In the beginning Kito was born out of
   sunlight and cactus milk."

84. Typescript, "Verbum Hominium," 1 p.

85. Typescript, "Vilonaud For This Yule," 1 p.

86. Folder with five fragments of unmatched pages belonging to correspondence.

III

Twelve letters, 1909–1920, to May Sinclair (1865?–1946), from London and Paris. Many of the letters can be only tentatively dated by addresses or contents. The letters mention social engagements, mutual friends, comments about Pound's work, and his appreciation of Miss Sinclair's writing.

1. A.l.s. "O.B.L.P." [London, 1909?] 2 pp.
   "You state that your flowering soul delights itself sipping ambrosial 'rickys' and guzzling the magical 'bass' on the Terraces of heaven."

2. A.l.s. Ezra Pound [London, 1909?] 2 pp.
   Pound refers to his "Sestina: Altaforte" which was published in London in the *English Review* 2, no. 3 (June 1909), 419–20, as "blood-curdling."

3. A.l.s. Ezra Pound [London, 1909?] 2 pp.
   "But the sestina is not in the least beautiful; but gore-bedabbled or the head of Coligny or Marlowe's houses in Tamberlaine."

4. A.l.s. E. P. [London, 13 April 1909] 2 pp. with envelope.
   An invitation to meet his friend, Katherine Heyman, in England on a visit.

5. A.l.s. Ezra Pound [Paris, 1911?] 3 pp.
   Pound says that he wishes he could divorce Miss Sinclair from London.

6. A.l.s. Ezra Pound [Paris, 1911] 9 pp. with envelope.
   Pound praises Miss Sinclair's latest book [probably *Divine Fire*, London, Eveleigh Nash, 1911]: "I want to talk over nearly every line I've read so far."

7. A.l.s. E. P. [London, 1911?] 6 pp.
   Pound admires Miss Sinclair's literary industry: "A novel would send me mad thru seven woods & over the four seas. . . ."

8. A.l.s. E. P. [London, 22 September 1911] 2 pp. with envelope.

Pound confirms an engagement for the following Monday.

9. A.l.s. Ezra [London, 29 September 1911] 6 pp. with envelope.
Pound suggests that Miss Sinclair might like to meet his
American friend, Hilda Doolittle, who "is—in her lucid
intervals—rather charming."

10. A.l.s. E. P. [London, 31 December 1912] 2 pp. with envelope.
Pound thanks her for "sinful luxuries."

11 . T.l.s. E, London, 19 [March] 1920 7 pp.
Pound discusses at length Miss Sinclair's criticism of "Homage
to Sextus Propertius," which appeared in *Poetry* and *New Age*
from March to August 1919. "I don't think I have consciously
paid *any* attention to grammar anywhere in the 'Homage'.
Rendering is purely ideographic, i.e. whole thing rendered into
Chinese and then into English." In this letter, Pound refers
to letter no. 12: "I enclose a letter I did *not* send in reply to Hale.
Please keep and return to me."

12. T.l. unsigned [London, 1920?] to the editor of the *Chicago Tribune*
5 pp. Pound addressed the editor of the *Chicago Tribune*
concerning Professor William Hale's attack on "Homage to Sextus
Propertius" in *Poetry* and in the *Chicago Tribune* on the ground
that the poem was an inaccurate translation. Pound denied that
he had attempted a translation. "At no time had I attempted
more than a portrait, or a presentation of a certain spirit."

IV

Two letters to Harold Hersey, assistant to the secretary of the executive
committee of the Authors' League of America, 1916, concerning the
banning of Theodore Dreiser's *The "Genius".* Hersey sent the letters
on to Dreiser.

1. T.l.s. E. Pound, London [September 1916] 1 p.
"I hasten to return signed Dreiser protest. Will have it printed
in the Egoist as soon as possible. Am glad the "Authors
League" has been *at last* arroused to do *something....*"

2. T.l.s. Ezra Pound, London, 24 October 1916 2 pp.
"I made the note brief and as strong as I could in the few minutes

I had to do it. I thought the more contempt one could get per sq. inch, the better for your purposes."
Pound's protest against the banning of Dreiser's *The "Genius"* appeared in the *Egoist* 3, no. 10 (October 1916), 159.

V

Two letters, 1924, to Ford Madox Ford, then editor of *The Transatlantic*   225
Review, January 1924–January 1925.

1. A.l.s. E P, Florence, Italy, 31 March 1924 3 pp.
   "Impossible to collect any more music matter before Apr- 5th. But there was that nod of Atheling—which I thought was calculated to fill the 1st four musical supplements. for the rest consult Antheil." Pound refers to "Notes For Performers. Foreword by E.P." and "Notes for Performers by William Atheling [Ezra Pound], with marginalia emitted by George Antheil," pp. 100–115, and "Sonata 3" by George Antheil, pp. 106–8, *The Transatlantic Review* 1, no. 2 (February 1924).

2. A.l.s. E., Assisi, Italy, 7 May [1924] 2 pp.
   Pound comments on the April and May issues of *The Transatlantic Review*. "April number good. Especially Hem. & Djuna." ["Indian Camp" by Ernest Hemingway, pp. 230–34 and "Aller Et Retour" by Djuna Barnes, pp. 159–67, *Transatlantic Review*, 1, no. 4 (April 1924)].
   Pound continues, "Pore ole Bill Carlos trundling erlong—quite good on Mac's stories" ["Robert McAlmon's Prose" by William Carlos Williams, *The Transatlantic Review*, 1, no. 5 (May–June 1924) 361–64].

VI

Seven letters, 1929–1930, to Horace Liveright (1886–1933) of Boni & Liveright, New York, publishers of Pound from 1921 to 1926.

1. T.l.s. E. P., Rapallo, Italy, 23 March 1928 1 p.
   Pound suggests Louis Zukofsky as a translator of German books.

2. T.l.s. E. P., Rapallo, Italy, 9 January 1929 2 pp.
   Pound praises a manuscript by "ole Joe," recommended to him by Edward J. O'Brien; in the carbon of his reply, Liveright says

the praise is enough to make them eager to see it and the house is writing to O'Brien "about Ole Joe, not that I have any idea who he is or what it's all about."

3. T.l.s. E. P., Rapallo, Italy, 24 March 1929 3 pp.
   Pound proposes a small translation factory with himself doing the finishing editorial touches.

4. A.l.s. E. Pound, Rapallo, Italy, 12 May [1929?] 2 pp.
   Pound sent a copy of Maurice de Vlaminck's *Tournant Dangereux* (Paris, 1929), suggesting an English translation. In his reply, Liveright wrote that he would "gamble that it will not sell 1000 copies."

5. T.l.s. E, Rapallo, Italy, 6 September [1929] 1 p.
   Pound recommends *Un Terrorista* by Umberto Notari (Milan, 1910).

6. T.l.s. E. P., Rapallo, Italy, 12 September 1929 1 p.
   "I note by 'royalty statement' that the second edtn. of Personae is wandering on. Do you think the time has come to bring out some Cantos." Liveright responded that the time had not come to bring out the *Cantos* in an American edition. *Personae: The Collected Poems of Ezra Pound* was first published by Boni & Liveright in 1926. Twenty-seven Cantos had been variously published in London and Paris by 1929. The first American edition, *A Draft of XXX Cantos*, was published by Farrar & Rinehart in 1933.

7. T.l.s. E. P., Rapallo, Italy, 5 August 1930 1 p.
   "Werrerbout that 'Collected Prose'? Are you still in the running?" In the margin of the letter, Liveright has penciled a large question mark.

VII

One letter to Lewis George Sterner.

T.l.s. E. Pound, Rapallo, Italy, 8 November 1930 1 p.
   Pound writes that Elkin Mathews does not have the American

copyright of his work. "The usual anthology fee is 25 dollars. payable through Liveright Inc."

VIII

Thirteen cards and letters, 1931–1935, to James T. Farrell (1904–1979). The correspondence is concerned chiefly with literary matters. The dating in many cases is tentatively assigned by reference to the texts.

1. Autograph postcard signed E. Pound, Paris, 6 May 1931, addressed to Farrell at the Hotel Acadamie.
   Pound gives instructions on the transport of manuscript.

2. T.l.s. E. P., Rapallo, Italy, 3 February [1932] 2 pp.
   "Started yr/ romance last evening. and got to galley 35.," probably referring to *Young Lonigan. . . .*, 1932.

3. A.l.s. E. P. [Rapallo, Italy], 30 May 1932 2 pp.
   A note enclosing the fifth sheet of a letter Pound had sent to Farrell two days earlier.

4. T.l.s. E. P., Rapallo, Italy, 27 October [1932] 2 pp.
   "Am having your artcl/ on Mead translated for next issue of IL MARE." Pound refers to Farrell's "La filosofia del presente, di G. H. Mead." *Il Mare, Supplemente Letterario* 1 (12 November 1932), 3.

5. T.l.s. E. P., Rapallo, Italy, on the letterhead of Il Mare [January 1933] 1 p.
   "Have rather rashly stated in this years Almanacco Letterario . . . that there is a new phase of criticism in the U.S.A., mentioning you as an exponent." Pound refers to his ". . . Il libro americano: status rerum." *Almanaco Letterario [Bompiani]*, Milan (1933), 264–67.

6. T.l. unsigned, Rapallo, Italy, 5 April [1933?] 2 pp.
   "My wife enjoyed McGinty. I enjoyed parts of it." Pound refers to Farrell's *Gas-House McGinty* (New York: Vanguard, 1933).

7. A.l. unsigned [Rapallo, Italy, 1933?] 2 pp.
   Pound evaluates Farrell's stories to be included in *Calico Shoes and Other Stories* (New York: Vanguard, 1934).

8. T.l.s. E.P., Rapallo, Italy [January, 1934] 2 pp.
   "Thanks for yr Xmas greeting. also thanks for the damn good story in Dynamo." Farrell's story, "The Buddies," was published in *Dynamo* 1 (January 1934), 18–22.

9. T.l.s. E. P., Rapallo, Italy, 23 February 1934 3 pp.
   Pound discusses his economic theories and says " 'scoop' seems to border on the sensational." Farrell's story, "Scoop," was published in the *Daily Worker*, 30 January 1934, p. 5.

10. T.l.s. E.P., Rapallo, Italy, 16 February [1934] 2 pp.
    Pound refers to Farrell's story, "Jewboy," *New Review* 1 (August–September–October, 1931), 21–26, and "Scarecrow," titled "Children of the Twilight," *New Masses* 11 (29 May 1934), 13–16.

11. Note signed E.P., Rapallo, Italy, [n.d.] on printed column titled "Volitionist economics." 1 p.

12. T.l.s. E.P., Rapallo, Italy, 1 May [1935] 1 p.
    "I think you did right to finish off Studs." Pound refers to *Judgment Day* (New York: Vanguard, 1935), the last in the Studs Lonigan trilogy.

13. One-line signed E.P., Rapallo, Italy, [n.d.] 1 p.
    "Sorry. Try Lowenfels anonymous."

IX

Five letters, 1932–1933, to Henry Bamford Parkes, historian and literary critic.

1. T.l.s. E. Pound, Rapallo, Italy, 12 May [1932] 1 p.
   "Could you persuade yourself to give us a very brief (one or two paes) of typescript artice on the weakness of English criticism. . . ."

2. T.l.s. E. P., Rapallo, Italy, 16 December [1932] 2 pp.
   "Good writing as such can't escape being useful/ whereas bias'd and doctinaire writing is always shit on all plates, conducing to typhoid."

3. T.l.s. E. P., Rapallo, Italy, on letterhead of Il Mare [January 1933]

1 p.
Another copy of letter no. 5 to James T. Farrell, January 1933.

4. T.l.s. E. P., Rapallo, Italy, 2 January 1933 3 pp.
"Haow the blitherin KRRRRist you can influence another chap's
subject matter, unless you actually write his goddam poem
FOR him . . . I don't quite know.
"Only case where I tried it was a success. I led Eliot up to her
wot posterity now knows as 'Grishkin' with the firm inutito
that a poem wd. result, & intention that it should
"But that is an UNIQUE experiment in my annals."
The reference is to "Grishkin" in Eliot's poem, "Whispers of
Immortality," one of "Four Poems," *Little Review* 5 (September
1918), later included in *Poems By T. S. Eliot*, Richmond, Hogarth
Press, 1919.

5. T.l.s. E. P., Rapallo, Italy, 29 January 1933 2 pp.
"T.S.E. influence deplorable//as religion//the attempt to stop
Amygism O. K., and did more or less. at least dirverted the soft.
"W/C/W/ OFTEN distressin. . . . but about the best thing left
in U.S.A."

X

Seven notes and letters, 1934, to Arnold Gingrich (1903–1976), editor
of *Esquire* from the first issue in 1933 to 1945. *Esquire* published eight
articles by Pound between August 1934 and January 1936.

1. T.l.s. E.P., Rapallo, Italy, 2 August [1934] 2 pp.
"Marconi's yacht is visible from breakfast table." Pound suggests
that he might try an article on Marconi, about the same length
of text as his "Gaudier [-Brzeska]: A Postcript," which had
appeared in *Esquire* 2, no. 3 (August 1934), 73–74.

2. T.l.s. E.P., Rapallo, Italy, 5 August [1934] 2 pp.
"AND more an more people (little by little etc.) are bein' made
to recognize that I see just as straight in matters outside art and
letters, as I DID 20 years ago when I was pickin' winners inside
the gawden of the muses."

3. T.l.s. E.P., Rapallo, Italy [10 August 1934] 2 pp.
"Ef yew an me iz a goin to be friends, you got to be patient.
THE material in this essay is DAMN important. If I haven't yet

229

got it into form you can use, I propose to stick at it, until I DO."
Pound refers to his "Reflexshuns on Iggurunce: Being a
Seminar Session with Ole Ez to Which Only the Very Brightest
Readers Are Invited" which appeared in *Esquire* 3, no. 1 (January
1935), 55, 133.

4. T.l.s. E.P., Rapallo, Italy [28 August 1934] 3 pp.
"Hem [Ernest Hemingway] may shoot lions; but he don't play
round with 'em in the domestic cage."

5. Typed postcard, signed, Rapallo, Italy, 26 October 1934.
Pound refers to an unpublished photograph of Brancusi's work
which he has just received and will forward it to Gingrich if
he intends to publish an article. [Cf. item 5, Manuscripts,
following.]

6. T.l.s. E. P., Rapallo, Italy [30 October 1934] with envelope 2 pp.
Pound suggests that Gingrich try to get articles from other
writers: "Also wot about Kumrad E. E. Kumminkz?? 'EIMI' more
alive, and I think damn sight bettern later Joyce or Gertie az ever
cd/ be."

7. T.l.s. E.P., Rapallo, Italy, 19 June [1935] with envelope 3 pp.
Responding to some comment from Gingrich: "All I want to get
into ur/ head is that I do not propose to be a liability/ and you
do NOT have to write to me as if I were the late Mr Galsworthy.
. . ."

XI

One letter to Dr. Herman V. Ames (1865– 1935), Professor of History,
University of Pennsylvania

T.l.s. Ezra Pound, Rapallo, Italy, 18 February 1935 1 p.
Pound asks for information about American finance during the Civil
War and Cleveland's administration. "Trouble with cantankerous
cusses like myself is that you get 'em interested in a subject, and
they go on, crop up 40 years later and still want to know MORE about
it."

XII

Three letters, 1935, to Dr. Roy F. Nichols (1896–1973), Professor of
History at the University of Pennsylvania.

1. T.l.s. Ezra Pound, Rapallo, Italy, 8 April 1935 2 pp.
   On 27 March 1935, Dr. Nichols replied to Pound's letter to Dr.
   Herman Ames, 18 February 1935, announcing Dr. Ames' death
   and answering some of Pound's questions. Pound responds, "I
   am very sorry to hear of Dr. Ames death, and there is an added
   drop of regret that he shdn't have had the minor entertainment
   of knowing that his patience and indulgences of 30 years ago
   hadn't been wholy wasted on one of his most cantankerous
   pupils."

2. T.l.s. E. P., Rapallo, Italy, 25 May 1935 3 pp.
   Pound thanks Dr. Nichols for sending book information in a
   letter of 14 May 1935. Pound continues, "The Hist. Dep/ can take
   the LEAD (prob/ by 20 or 40 years over all other U.S. univs.
   IF you orient it on MONEY as key to history."

3. T.l.s. Ezra P, Rapallo, Italy, 18 June 1935 3 pp.
   Dr. Nichols had sent Pound a current syllabus of American
   history at Pennsylvania. Pound thanks Dr. Nichols, but lists
   names of writers not included in the bibliography, such as Ferrero,
   Frobenius, and Fenollosa. "What about the Wharton School?
   are they still expelling Scott Nearing or is anything really being
   done there to STUDY economics IN ACTION. . . ."

XIII

One letter to C. Seymour Thompson, Librarian, University of
Pennsylvania.

T.l.s. E Pound, Rapallo, Italy, 16 May [1935] 1 p.
Requesting the loan of a book on economics, and asking if the
University would be interested in his bibliography of economists:
". . . perhaps such work has relation to LIBRARY, the Library, with
the lead mottos in the glass work (I suppose they are still there?)"
Pound refers to the old University Library, known presently as the
Furness Building, with the mottos still intact.

XIV

Two letters to the University of Pennsylvania Press and to Phelps Soule,
Director of the Press.

1. T.l.s. Ezra Pound, Rapallo, Italy, 26 November 1936 2 pp.

Addressing the University of Pennsylvania Press, Pound mentions the memorial volume for Dr. Herman V. Ames and deplores the publication of a title by Art Salter [Sir James Arthur Salter, *World Trade and its Future,* Philadelphia, University of Pennsylvania Press, 1936].

2. T.l.s. Ezra Pound, Rapallo, Italy, 19 December 1936 3 pp.
Addressing Phelps Soule, Pound complains about the publications by the Press. "Another Penn man whom the campus frumps ignore is Doc. Williams. To the shame of Weygand and co/ Bill/sprouted with a degree in medicine / untainted by the 'arts' courses."

XV

Four letters, 1938–1958, to Van Wyck Brooks (1886–1963), largely concerned with the National Institute of Arts and Letters to which Pound had been elected in 1938.

1. T.l.s. Ezra Pound, Rapallo, Italy, 16 April [1938] 3 pp. with envelope.
Pound discusses the policies of the National Institute of Arts and Letters.

2. T.l.s. E. P., Rapallo, Italy, 4 June [1938] 3 pp. with envelope.
Pound nominates W. C. Williams, e. e. cummings, W. E. Woodward, and Marianne Moore to membership in the Institute and says that more communication among members is needed.

3. T.l.s. Ezra Pound, St. Elizabeths Hospital, Washington, D.C., 10 December [1946?] 1 p.
Pound's friend, Harry Meacham, has told him that he is in Brooks's debt. "I don't know that I am expected to know it. But thanks anyhow."

4. T.l.s. Ezra Pound [St. Elizabeths Hospital, Washington, D.C.] 13 January 1958 3 pp.
An article by Brooks in the *New York Times* stirs Pound to comment on economics, education, and the treatment of Italy.

XVI

Two letters, 1946, to Dr. Robert E. Spiller, Professor of English, University of Pennsylvania.

1. A.l.s. E Pound, St. Elizabeths Hospital, Washington, D.C., [28 April 1946] 1 p. with envelope.
   Pound comments on two professors at Pennsylvania: "Sorry to hear of dear Shellings death—interested to know what & particularly WHEN. Cl. Child is the man with real love of letters & true flair." Felix Emmanuel Schelling (1858–1945) and Clarence Griffing Child (1864–1948) were both Professors of English at the University. 233

2. A.l.s. E Pound, St. Elizabeths Hospital, Washington, D.C., 22 November 1946 1 p. with envelope.
   Pound suggests that Dr. Spiller trace a former graduate school colleague, Harry Smith, interested in philosophy and logic. Pound probably refers to Henry Bradford Smith (1882–   ), who received his doctoral degree at Pennsylvania in 1909.

XVII

One letter to Ronald Bayes.

Form letter, with typed marginalia, signed EP, St. Elizabeths Hospital, Washington, D.C. [December 1957] 1 p.
The form letter urges support for *EDGE*, edited by Noel Stock in Australia. The marginalia states that Bayes' proposed visit to Pound is "O. K. with me. get permit from Supt. St. Elizabeths."

XVIII

Manuscripts, typescripts, broadcasts.

1. "On First Editions," typescript, ribbon copy with ms. corrections, signed [Rapallo, Italy, 1933] 2 pp.
   "Obviously a disgrace to our pretended civilization that it can not produce books which are, AS MATERIAL OBJECTS, paper, printing etc. equal to those produced several centuries ago."

2. "A Prophecy of England's Downfall." Ms. unsigned, undated. 6 pp.
   A review of a reprint edited by Arthur Bennet of *Eighteen Hundred and Eleven*, a poem by Anna Laetitia Barbauld, first published in 1812, a despondent view of England's future.
   "All this girding at the manner of the eighteen century narrative, which is indeed her manner, does not so much affect Mrs.

Barbauld for she was, poor dear, only a lyrist, a prophet and a satirist—of the pseudo Juvenalian vein."

3. "Reflexshuns on Iggurunce." Typescript, ribbon copy with ms. corrections, unsigned, [1935] 8 pp.
The essay by the above title was published in *Esquire* 3, no. 1 (January 1935), 55, 138. In this piece, Pound comments on reactions to the publication.

4. "Brancusi and Human Sculpture." Typescript, ribbon copy with ms. corrections, signed, undated. 8 pp.
Article with photographs on Constantin Brancusi, apparently submitted to *Esquire*. The text is not the same a Pound's "Brancusi," *Little Review* 8, no. 1 (Autumn 1921), 3–7.

5. Broadcast over Rome Radio, 23 April 1942. Typescript supplied by British Information Services 2 pp.
Urging the elimination of the Roosevelt administration, "The alternative is annihilation for the youth of America and the end of everything decent the U.S. ever stood for."

6. Broadcast over Rome Radio, 5 May 1942. Carbon typescript. 4 pp.
An anti-Semitic speech in which the transcriber had a number of errors and lacunae in recording Pound's speech.

XIX

THE CARL GATTER COLLECTION OF EZRA POUND

Mr. Gatter has lived many years in the Pound home at 166 Fernbrook Avenue in Wyncote, Pennsylvania, where Pound spent his early years. Mr. Gatter wrote to Pound about the residence, and a correspondence developed between them. When Pound was returning to Italy after his release from St. Elizabeths Hospital in 1958, Pound spent the night of June 27th with the Gatters and renewed his childhood memories of the Philadelphia suburb. Mr. Gatter collected photographs of that visit and then researched the area for material on Pound, from his childhood to his 1958 visit, including copies of letters, school and college records, and photographs of Pound and his friends and family. The collection of twenty-one binders of material was presented to the University in 1976. A summary inventory follows.

Book 1   Friends and Associates: F. Ankenbrand to T. Hare.

Book 2   Friends and Associates: E. Heacock to M. Lovell.

Book 3   Friends and Associates: M. Moore to A. Polk.

Book 4   Friends and Associates: C. Reed to W. C. Williams.

Book 5   Negatives for photographs and original picture owned by Homer Pound.

Book 6   Newspaper and magazine articles, , 1903 –1958.

Book 7   Newspaper and magazine articles, 1959 –1975.

Book 8   "Wyncote Revisited, June 27, 28 , 1958,"
"Wyncote Visit, June 15, 1969,"
Manuscript: "Ezra Pound in Wyncote."

Book 9   Pound material reproduced from *Jenkinstown Times, Times-Chronicle.*

Book 10   Pound material copied from *Hatboro Public Spirit, Jenkintown Times, Times-Chronicle.*

Book 11   Reproductions of letters to M. Doolittle, F. Ridpath, C. W. Gatter, E. K. Gatter.

Book 12   Reproductions of letters to C. W. Gatter, E. K. Gatter.

Book 13   Correspondence sent to E. K. Gatter and C. W. Gatter concerning Pound.

Book 14   Grace Presbyterian Church; Calvary Presbyterian Church; First Italian Presbyterian Church; Eastburn, Mariners Bethel.

Book 15   "Miss Eliot's Dames School." Chelten Hills School, Wyncote Public School.

Book 16   Cheltenham Military Academy; Cheltenham High School.

Book 17   University of Pennsylvania, Part 1: 1901–1903.

Book 18   University of Pennsylvania, Part 2: 1905–1907; Hamilton College, 1903–1905.

Book 19   Pound family residences: 208 S. 43rd St., Phila.; 417 Walnut, Jenkintown; 166 Fernbrook Ave., Wyncote, etc.

Book 20   Homer L. Pound, Isabel Pound, S. Angevine Pound, Thaddeus C. Pound, Florence Foote, Frances A. Weston.

Book 21   U.S. Mint; Early Publications; Early Wyncote; Wanamaker fire.

University Archives

XX

236

EZRA POUND

MANUSCRIPT

University of Pennsylvania Department of Philosophy (The Graduate School), "Record Book," bound, 10 pp. Booklet issued on 3 October 1905, date of admission of "Mr. Ezra Weston Pound" as a regular student; records, 9 January 1906, acceptance as candidate for degree of A.M., and 29 September 1906, acceptance as candidate for degree of Ph.D. and appointment as Fellow 1906–7. Lists, by year and term, courses by name, hours, credits, course instructors (who sign), and remarks, simply a stamp indicating that grade was recorded. (Alumni Record folder)

Undergraduate Matriculation card, 4 June 1901. Gives date of birth; where prepared; father's name, address, and occupation; and record of academic standing until withdrawal, 8 June 1903. (UPB 1.45#4C)

Undergraduate Course grade card, 1901–2, 1902–3. (UPB 1.45 #4C)

"Alumni Catalogue" Information Circular, 4 pp., compiler's facts corrected and supplemented by Pound in mss., n. d. but 1910. Pound has pasted Elkin Mathews' printed flyer advertising *Exultations* on p. 4. (Alumni Record folder)

Newsclippings about Pound's poetry, 1912 and 1913, mounted with sarcastic comments in mss. by Professor Cornelius Weygandt. (Alumni Record folder)

Xerox copies of two University letters of 1972, one regarding Pound's proposed membership in Board of Libraries; the other regarding condolences to be sent at his death. (Alumni Record folder)

Correspondence with four researchers working on Ezra Pound, 1960–78. (Alumni Record folder)

PRINTED

The Record of the Class of 1902. Yearbook, listing Pound as Freshman on p. 73. (He may be in Freshman Class photograph on p. 70.)

The Record of the Class of 1903. Yearbook, listing Pound as Sophomore on p. 66. (He may be in Sophomore Class photograph on p. 64.)

"Penn Graduate Honored by England as a Poet," *Old Penn Weekly Review*, 4 December 1909, p. 154.

"The Poetry of Ezra Pound," *Old Penn Weekly Review*, 11 December 1909, p. 170.

Wallace Rice, "Mr. Ezra Pound and 'Poetry', *The Dial*, 1 May 1913. (Clipped article, Alumni Record folder)

Cover, *The Independent*, vol.116 no. 3952, 27 February 1926, illustrating portrait of Pound by Wyndham Lewis (clipping in Alumni Record folder)

"Ezra Pound Crowned," and "Mr. Pound on Prizes," *The Literary Digest*, 14 January 1928, pp. 22–23, 26. (Clipped article in Alumni Record folder)

Douglass MacPherson, "Ezra Pound of Wyncote," *Arts in Philadelphia*, May 1940, pp. 10, 28.

Emily Mitchell Wallace, "Penn's Poet Friends," *The Pennsylvania Gazette* 71, no. 4 (February 1973), pp. 33–36.

Collection of miscellaneous clippings from University publications, Philadelphia and New York newspapers of 1909, 1913–14, 1922, 1928, 1933, 1939, 1943–49, 1957–59, 1965, 1968, 1975. Chiefly critiques, reviews, profiles, and publicity on political views. (Alumni Record folder)

Collection of obituaries of Pound from newspapers across the United States (1972), and of other subsequent newsclippings. (Alumni Record folder)

General Alumni Catalogue of the University of Pennsylvania 1917 (Philadelphia, 1917), p. 462. Capsule biography.

Ibid. 1922 (Philadelphia, 1922), p. 401. Capsule biography.

PHOTOCOPY

Transcript of "Record Sheet" of courses in Department of Philosophy (Graduate School), 3 October 1905–9 June 1906. Personal information (name; address; name, occupation, and address of father; maiden name of mother; precollegiate and collegiate education and knowledge of languages) is in mss. of Pound. (Alumni Record folder; original is in Graduate Faculty office)

Photostats of letters of Pound, 26 November 1936 and 19 December 1936, to Phelps Soule, Director of the University of Pennsylvania Press, and a copy of Soule's reply to first letter. (Archives General Collection; the originals of the two Pound letters are in the University's Rare Book Collection.)

Rare Book Collection

WILLIAM CARLOS WILLIAMS

I

One letter to Burton Rascoe (1892–1957) critic and journalist.

T.l.s. W. C. Williams, Rutherford, New Jersey, 1 May 1919 1 p.
"I have read Lesemann's stuff . . . the best lines are very good and reveal the quality of the whole but there is still 50% at least of haphazard work in the long poem if not in the others. . . ."

II

Four letters, 1919–1925, to Waldo Frank (1898–1967).

1. A.l.s. W. C. Williams, Rutherford, New Jersey, 5 June 1919 2 pp.
"I gather that my poems appealed to your intelligent appreciation."

2. A.l.s. Williams, Rutherford, New Jersey, 20 June 1919 4 pp.
"I am returning your MSS. to you not because I do not like the poems but because I could not use them—and because I am through with *Others*—for the present. . . ."

3. T.l.s. Williams, Rutherford, New Jersey, 3 July [1925?] 1 p.
"You did read the book [probably *In The American Grain*, New York, Albert & Charles Boni, 1925] and you did enjoy it to the point of enthusiasm, that will be enough for me to remember."

4. T.l.s. Williams, Rutherford, New Jersey, 11 July [1925?] 1 p.

"You are the first who has valued the Columbus chapter [*In The American Grain*] or in fact paid any attention to the design in the book at all."

III

Sixteen letters, 1939–1959, to E. Sculley Bradley, Professor of English, University of Pennsylvania.   *239*

1. T.n.s. W. C. Williams, Rutherford, New Jersey, 26 February 1939 1 p.
   "I was a Med when Ezra Pound was carrying on his wild early imaginative career there." Williams refers to the period 1902–1906, when he and Pound were students at Pennsylvania.

2. T.l.s. W. C. Williams, Rutherford, New Jersey, 20 November 1939 1 p. with envelope.
   "I have been working on the second volume of White Mule." [*In The Money,* Norfolk, Connecticut, New Directions 1940].

3. A.n.s. W. C. Williams [Rutherford, New Jersey, 29 October 1940] on verso of publisher's announcement of *In The Money.*

4. T.l.s. W. C. W., Rutherford, New Jersey, 27 April 1945 2 pp.
   "I go on practicing medicine and writing as a sort of corrective to my medical psychoses." Williams offers some poems to Dr. Bradley for inclusion in *The General Magazine and Historical Chronicle.*

5. T.l.s. Williams, Rutherford, New Jersey, 14 May 1945 1 p.
   Offering three poems which Dr. Bradley published in *The General Magazine and Historical Chronicle* 47, no. 4 (Summer 1945), with the signed typescripts of the poems "The Statue," "April 6," and "The Dish of Fruit," with Bradley's instructions to the printer.

6. T.n.s. W. C. Williams, Rutherford, New Jersey, 27 July 1945 1 p.
   Thanking Bradley for the publication of the previously mentioned poems.

7. A. postcard s. W. C. Williams, Rutherford, New Jersey, 2 May 1947

Responding to a request, "My practice & Paterson II are making it impossible for me to do anything else—at all!"

8. A.l.s. W. C. Williams, Atlantic City, New Jersey, 8 April 1948
4 pp.
Submitting "Something for a Biography," published in *The General Magazine and Historical Chronicle* 50, no. 4 (Summer 1948), with the signed typescript of four pages bearing Bradley's instructions to the printer.

9. T.l.s. W. C. Williams, Rutherford, New Jersey, 16 April 1948
1 p.
"Thanks for what you sent Laughlin concerning Paterson II, it is well said and enough." James Laughlin is the publisher of *New Directions*, which published *Paterson II* in 1948.

10. T.l.s. Williams, Rutherford, New Jersey, 8 May 1948 1 p.
"Do I remember rightly that you wanted two poems for the Gazette?" Enclosed are signed typescripts of "Notes to Music: Brahms 1st Piano Concerto," and "The Pause," published in *The General Magazine and Historical Chronicle* 50, no. 4 (Summer 1948).

11. T.l.s. Williams, Rutherford, New Jersey, 31 May 1948 1 p.
Mentioning the Loines Memorial Award and submitting a new brief biographical sketch which bears Bradley's editorial emendations.

12. T.l.s. W. C. Williams, Rutherford, New Jersey, 23 January 1951
1 p.
Asking when his biographical sketch had been published (*The General Magazine and Historical Chronicle* 50, no. 4 [Summer 1948]).

13. T.l.s. W. C. Williams, Rutherford, New Jersey, 2 November 1951
1 p.
Declining to talk to a group of graduate students.

14. T.l.s. W. C. Williams, Rutherford, New Jersey 3 January 1952
1 p. with envelope.
Williams comments on a statement which Bradley had made,

adding "Jane Heap's face was heavy jawed. She was short and stocky. She *did* look like an Esquimo."

15. T.l.s. Bill, Rutherford, New Jersey, 8 April 1957, addressed to Edward F. Corson 1 p.
This letter was sent on to Bradley by Dr. Corson who had asked about Williams' manuscripts. Williams says, "Three years ago Yale tied me up, with a grant, so that I will have no manuscripts to dispose of for the rest of my life. But I feel that anything else I can do for Sculley Bradley in completing his list of new books by me, dispose of them as he will, I will eagerly take on. . . ."

16. T.l.s. William Carlos Williams, Rutherford, New Jersey, 16 November 1959 1 p.
Williams asks Bradley's advice about his grandson's application for entrance to Pennsylvania.

17. T.l.s. Rutherford, New Jersey, 25 November 1959 1 p.
"I'm getting along in years piled on top of which are several disabilities which have combined at times to make me rather forgetful. I have been able at the same time to publish several books which I want you and the U. of P. to have. You'll be getting them before Xmas. I hope you'll like them."

ADDITIONAL WILLIAMS MATERIAL IN DR. BRADLEY'S COLLECTION

Eight letters and cards, April 1951–April 1965, from Florence Williams to Dr. Bradley concerning Dr. Williams' health, reviews of Dr. Williams' books by Bradley, the memorial service for Williams, and the gift to Pennsylvania of the collection of first editions of Williams' books inscribed to Florence Williams.

Twenty letters and documents, April 1948 to April 1965, concerning Dr. Williams, principally Bradley's carbon copies of letters to Dr. and Mrs. Williams and to students interested in Dr. Williams' writing. There is also the citation which Dr. Bradley read presenting Williams for the Litt.D. degree at Pennsylvania in 1952, and Dr. Bradley's address at the dedication of the Williams Collection in 1965.

IV

Three letters, 1951–1952, to John C. Miller, president of the Delta Chapter of Phi Beta Kappa, were given to Dr. Robert E. Spiller, who passed them on to the Library for the Williams Collection.

1. T.l.s. W. C. Williams, Rutherford, New Jersey, 17 November
   1951 1 p.
   "Thank you for your invitation to speak before the Delta Chapter
   of U. of Pennsylvania Phi Beta Kappa. . . . This will be first
   time that my Alma Mater has officially asked me to speak before
   any of its groups. . . ."

2. T.l.s. W. C. Williams [Rutherford, New Jersey] 5 January 1952
   1 p.
   Confirming the arrangements for Williams' engagement in
   Philadelphia on January 11, 1952.

3. T.l.s. Williams, Rutherford, New Jersey, 12 January 1952 1 p.
   "My only regret following last night's meeting is that I cannot
   remember the names of all of those I met and of whom I have
   so much that is pleasant to recall. I can't get over meeting and
   talking with my old favorite Dr. Spiller's son, it was like being
   in the old boy's very presence to see that figure sitting opposite
   me at the table. The whole past became alive again."

V

TYPESCRIPTS

"A Parisian Cafe Klotch"
Typescript of farce, William Carlos Williams, producer, with Edgar
Williams and Florence Williams in the cast. With playbill. 14 pp.

"Note: Ezra Pound"
Typescript, corrected and signed, of an article about his memories
and evaluation of Ezra Pound, directed to Charles Norman, from
Rutherford, New Jersey, 2 November 1945. 5 leaves.

University Archives

WILLIAM CARLOS WILLIAMS

VI

MANUSCRIPT

List of Students Enrolled in Department of Dentistry, 1901–1929;
list for "Session 1902–03," typescript, signed by State Examiner;

"Entrance Credentials, Session 1902–03." (UPC 4.60 #1)

Medical Matriculation Book, 1895–1911; entries for 15 October 1903; 26 September 1904; 26 September 1905. (UPC 2.7 #20)

Printed questionnaire, "The War Record of Pennsylvania University 1914" completed in mss. by Williams, 27 June 1919. (Alumni Record folder)

Printed biographical questionnaire of Office of Recorder, completed in mss. and typescript by Williams, 19 September 1936. (Alumni Record folder)

Typed letter signed by Williams, Rutherford, New Jersey, 31 March 1948, to Fred H. Stapleford of the University, covering sending of biographical "stuff"; mentions Loines Prize, Professor Sculley Bradley ("my best rooter"), and recent photo sent *Daily Pennsylvanian;* off to Atlantic City to make "comeback" from attack of angina. (Alumni Record folder)

Correspondence with two researchers working on Williams, 1976, 1981. (Alumni Record folder)

PRINTED

University publications (undergraduate career)
Catalogue of the University of Pennsylvania 1902–03 (Philadelphia, 1902), p. 512; ibid. *1903–04* (Philadelphia, 1903), p. 526; ibid., *1904–05* (Philadelphia, 1904), p. 603; ibid. *1905–06* (Philadelphia, 1905), p. 618. Name, home address, and dormitory location.

The Record of the Class of Nineteen Hundred and Five [College year book]; Williams in group photo of cast of Mask & Wig "Mr. Hamlet of Denmark," p. 157; in group photo of Varsity Fencing Team, p. 219.

The 'Scope 1904 [Medical School year book]; Williams listed as member of Stillé Medical Society, p. 44, but not in group photo on p. 45.

Ibid. *1905;* Williams listed as member of Stillé Medical Society, p. 64, and in group photo, p. 65.

Ibid. *1906;* Williams biography with portrait on p. 76; described in article on Mask & Wig, p. 154, and photo, in costume, as "Polonius," p. 155; described as expert fencer in article on Athletics, p. 144, and photo, in fencing uniform, p. 150; named as member of Stillé Medical Society and in group photo of the Society, n. p.

University publications (literary career)
William Carlos Williams, "Three Poems," *General Magazine and*

Historical Chronicle 48, no. 4 (Summer, 1945), pp. 220–21.

William Carlos Williams, "Shakespeare Famous Because He Knew Life Through His Own Living," *Daily Pennsylvanian*, 16 January 1948, pp. 1 and 8; his picture (head) on p. 8.

Donald Woodward, reviewer, "*William Carlos Williams*, by Vivienne Koch," *General Magazine and Historical Chronicle* 52, no. 4 (Summer, 1950), pp. 253–54.

William Carlos Williams, "Picasso Breaks Faces, *General Magazine and Historical Chronicle* 53, no.1 (Autumn 1950), pp. 40–41.

Sculley Bradley, reviewer, "Two Volumes by William Carlos Williams, '06 M.," *General Magazine and Historical Chronicle* 53, no. 2 (Winter 1951), pp. 127–28.

Sculley Bradley, "William Carlos Williams Poet-Physician," *Medical Affairs* 2, no. 4 (Spring 1962), pp. 2–3, 34–35.

Emily Mitchell Wallace, "Penn's Poet Friends," *Pennsylvania Gazette* 71, no. 4 (February 1973), pp. 33–36.

Biographical
Collection of miscellaneous clippings from University publications and Chicago, Oklahoma, Passaic, Hackensack, New York, Jackson (Tennessee), Huntington (West Virginia), Baton Rouge, and Bloomington (Indiana) newspapers of 1926–27, 1948, 1951, 1952, 1954, 1957, 1958, 1960–61. Chiefly critiques, reviews, profiles, and articles concerning his poetry readings and exhibition of his books and his lectures at the University. (Alumni Record folder)

Collection of obituaries from newspapers across the country, 1963, and of other subsequent news clippings. (Alumni Record folder)

Correspondence regarding reproduction by the University of photograph used in *New York Times* news story on Loines Award (1948), and gift by Random House of advance copy of *Autobiography* (1951). (Alumni Record folder)

Press Releases: of Carson-Ruff Associates regarding the Loines Award (1948); of the University of Pennsylvania Library on Williams' talk in the Rare Book Room, 25 February 1948; and of the University News Bureau on Williams' honorary Doctor of Letters degree, 18 June 1952 (including text of degree citation) and the Bureau's release on the Williams exhibition in the University Library, opening 30 April 1965. (Alumni Record folder)

General Alumni Catalogue of The University of Pennsylvania 1917
(Philadelphia, 1917), p. 836. Capsule biography.

Ibid. *1922* (Philadelphia, 1922) p. 639. Capsule biography.

PHOTOGRAPH

Original profile photograph, 4 × 5 matte, of Williams in surgical
gown, looking through microscope, in physician's office. Inscribed
on reverse in his hand "Dr. W. C. Williams   9 Ridge Road
Rutherford N. J." (Alumni Record folder)

PHOTOCOPY

Department of Medicine "Blank for Registration, Sess. '03–'04."
Detailed questionnaire completed by Williams on 15 October 1903.
(The original, in UPC 2.7 #30, has disappeared. A photocopy of
the original is in Williams' Alumni Record folder.)

Contributors

HUGH KENNER, Mellon Professor of Humanities at The Johns Hopkins University, is the author of many critical works, including *The Pound Era, A Homemade World, A Colder Eye*, and studies of T. S. Eliot, James Joyce, and Wyndham Lewis.

EMILY MITCHELL WALLACE is president of the William Carlos Williams Society and a former member of the English Department at the University of Pennsylvania. She teaches at the Curtis Institute of Music. She is editor of the letters of Williams and Pound to one another, to be published by New Directions in 1985. In researching the essay in this volume she found that Virginia Judith Craig, under whom she studied argumentation, rhetoric, and modern poetry at Southwest Missouri State College, received a Ph.D. in Classical Languages at the same University of Pennsylvania Commencement in 1906 at which degrees were awarded to Pound and Williams.

RONALD BUSH, a graduate of the University of Pennsylvania, teaches literature at the California Institute of Technology. He is the author of *The Genesis of Ezra Pound's Cantos* (1976) and *T. S. Eliot: A Study in Character and Style* (1983).

MICHAEL F. HARPER discovered the poetry of Ezra Pound while working as a journalist in his native England. He came to the University of Pennsylvania as a Thouron Fellow in 1967 to study at the source, taking his B.A. and Ph.D. there. Since 1973 he has taught at the University of California at Berkeley and at Scripps College. His essay in this volume is excerpted from a forthcoming book, *Truth and Calliope: The Poetry of Ezra Pound*.

WENDY STALLARD FLORY took her degrees from Birkbeck College, University of London and the University of Texas. She is an Assistant Professor of English at Pennsylvania. Her first book was *Ezra Pound and the Cantos: A Record of Struggle* (1980); she is completing *The American Ezra Pound* on a fellowship from the National Endowment for the Humanities.

DENISE LEVERTOV has published over a dozen books of verse, most recently *Collected Earlier Poems 1940–1960*. A collection of her essays and reviews, *Candles in Babylon*, appeared in 1981.

PAUL CHRISTENSEN is Associate Professor of English at Texas A. & M. University. He is the author of *Charles Olson: Call Him Ishmael* (1979), written as his dissertation at Pennsylvania, and of a forthcoming study of literature and the modern city, *Urban Wordscapes*. Two books of poems, *Gulfsongs* and *Sings of the Whelming*, appeared in 1983.

THEODORA R. GRAHAM is editor of *The William Carlos Williams Review*. She did her graduate work on Williams with Joel Conarroe at the University of Pennsylvania, and is writing a book on Williams' work. She teaches at the Middletown campus of the Pennsylvania State University.

JAMES LAUGHLIN, poet and publisher, is the founder of New Directions Publishing Corporation and for over forty years was Pound's and Williams' publisher and friend.

NEDA M. WESTLAKE is Curator of American manuscripts of the Van Pelt Library, University of Pennsylvania, and general editor of the University of Pennsylvania Press edition of the works of Theodore Dreiser.

FRANCIS JAMES DALLETT, University Archivist, received his A.M. from the University in 1955. He is the compiler of *Guide to the Archives of the University of Pennsylvania from 1740 to 1820* and was a contributing author to *Gladly Learn and Gladly Teach*, by Martin Meyerson and Dilys Pegler Winegrad.

DANIEL HOFFMAN is Poet in Residence and Felix E. Schelling Professor of English Literature at the University of Pennsylvania, where he directs the Writing Program. He is the author, most recently, of the poem *Brotherly Love*. He edited and wrote the chapters on poetry in the *Harvard Guide to Contemporary American Writing* and is the author of *Poe Poe Poe Poe Poe Poe*. In 1973–74 he served as the Consultant in Poetry to the Library of Congress.

247